SHIRTMAKING

SHIRTMAKING

DEVELOPING
SKILLS FOR
FINE
SEWING

DAVID PAGE COFFIN

The Taunton Press

COVER PHOTO: SUSAN KAHN

First printing: January 1993
Printed in the United States of America

A THREADS Book

THREADS® is a trademark of The Taunton Press, Inc.,
registered in the U.S. Patent and Trademark Office.

The Taunton Press, 63 South Main Street, Box 5506,
Newtown, CT 06470-5506

Library of Congress Cataloging-in-Publication Data

Coffin, David Page.
    Shirtmaking : developing skills for fine sewing /
David Page Coffin.
        p.   cm.
    "A Threads book"—T.p. verso.
    Includes bibliographic references and index.
    ISBN 1-56158-015-5
    1. Shirts, Men's.   I. Title.
TT612.C64   1992   92-27291
646.4'3502—dc20   CIP

Acknowledgments

I'd like to thank my editor, Chris Timmons, for making the countless hours we spent poring over the details of this book a delight instead of a chore; book designer and layout artist Jodie Delohery and photographer Susan Kahn for their wonderful work and for knowing how to make me feel that my opinions were actually helpful; copy editors Peter Chapman and Ruth Dobsevage for their eagle eyes and clear heads; Deborah Cannarella, Mark Feirer and John Kelsey for sticking in there until the book project became a reality; Dennis Colban at Charvet in Paris, and New York shirtmakers Adriana and Avery Lucas for the fascinating hours of shirt talk I enjoyed with them; all my dear friends and family for believing me whenever I had to say, "Sorry! I've got to work on my book"; and finally my wife, Ellen, for her incredible support and encouragement. Love to you all.

Dedicated to amateurs everywhere

Contents

Introduction

I wrote this book because no one else had. Fifteen years ago when I decided I wanted to make top-quality dress shirts, I was surprised to find no information on shirtmaking beyond basic pattern instructions. So I began to comb libraries, magazines and bookstores for answers. From what I've found over the years, and from what I've had to improvise, I've evolved the techniques presented in this book. It would perhaps be more accurate to say that from the "hints" I found I've evolved the present techniques, since in no case was I able to use information from other sources without somehow modifying or adding to it to achieve what I was after—namely, a simple,

efficient way to make a shirt at home as good as the best shirts available, which I could ill afford.

Throughout my early days of shirtmaking, I felt certain that once I could make my own shirts, they would be better than the best I could buy because I could refine and experiment endlessly. But, first, the question was how to make even a serviceable shirt, one that needed no apologies, that would not look homemade. Nobody seemed to have gathered and written down all the information on shirtmaking in one place; in fact, lots of it seems not to have been written down at all. To those whose "hints" paved the way, I am supremely grateful (I've listed some of them in the Bibliography on pp. 168-169).

As a self-taught sewer who started sewing as an adult, I've always found sewing instructions in general frustrating. Those that come with patterns remind me of the instructions for model airplanes from my youth, the ones that would sum up some impossible-sounding task with a few terse words, like "cover wings with tissue paper, dampen and stretch to fit." More than once I've found in some long-sought book what appeared to be a solution to precisely the sewing problem I faced. But in the end I was unable to interpret the author's minimal instructions, or I found that they raised more questions than they answered. This may explain why, in my own written directions, I've chosen to err on the side of too much explanation rather than too little. So I hope any experienced sewers reading these pages will forgive my choice to speak, in my own instructions, as if to beginning sewers. They're the ones I have the greatest sympathy for.

The basic problem I had with pattern instructions was that they seemed totally generic: Shirts were made essentially the same way as dresses, as if the person writing the directions had never examined a shirt. I was after the real thing, not just a shirtlike replica. That's why I don't even discuss sewing techniques or shirt construction in this book until we've thoroughly examined the real thing. That's also why you'll see some ready-to-wear shirts in this sewing book—if you want to make something well, you need to know what the standards are.

My basic theory has been to discuss sewing skills in detail (suggesting periods of practice on fabric scraps for any new techniques) before assembling these skills into shirtmaking procedures, by which time you should be

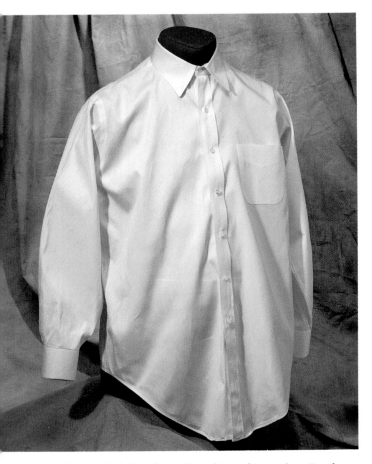

The standard: The classic dress shirt —this one from Brooks Brothers —in the author's size is displayed on a torso form molded to his exact shape. It's well made, but not a good fit.

comfortable with them. I've tried throughout to duplicate as much as possible the skills and techniques of professional shirtmakers, who develop incredible precision doing the same things day in and day out on specialized machines—skills that we're trying to duplicate perhaps once or twice a month (or year!) when we get the time. Gathering a few shirtmaking tools (which you can use for many of your other sewing projects) and being patient enough to practice at least a little will get you launched and make a world of difference.

Once you're even a little confident with your ability to make shirts, I hope you'll want to make more. In the final chapter you'll find a catalog of variations on the classic dress shirt, all of which can be approached with the basic skills and patterns you'll have used to make your first dress shirt, whether it was for a woman or a man.

Why make your own shirts?

This may seem a foolish question in a book devoted to the subject, but let me outline why I make my own shirts, so that my own biases and opinions are out front from the start. I'm writing for anyone who's interested in shirtmaking, but my own involvement is that of an amateur: I'm on a challenging and satisfying quest for the best and most personal in shirts—or whatever I'm making—regardless of the time or reasonable expense. I make shirts for the sheer pleasure of the process, rather than as a time-saving or money-saving necessity. For instance, I have no interest in serging machines since, to me, they substitute an ugly seam done in a trice for a beautiful one that takes a little longer. Sergers may be great for many things, but, as far as I'm concerned, they spell cheap work in shirtmaking.

Even with my attitude, there's no question that you can save money making shirts, provided you don't charge for your own time and you compare oranges to oranges. By this I mean that if you're spending $35 on extraordinary material to make one shirt, don't compare this shirt with one made of ordinary fabric you could buy downtown for $35. Your $35 shirt—once you've learned to make it to your own satisfaction and so that it really fits—couldn't be had for three times that price. This is true of all home sewing, as I am sure you know. But you may not know just what the world charges for custom shirts these days,

probably not made as well as you're going to make them. Ready-made (not custom-fitted) shirts from Turnbull & Asser, shirtmakers to Prince Charles, are currently sold for well over $100. True custom-made shirts like the one we're going to make (using a pattern unique to your body and detailed precisely as you wish) are extremely rare and, where they can be found, can cost as much as $300 each (minimum order four, please). So the reasons to make your own shirts besides savings are superb fit and total freedom of choice in style, detail and fabric—but chiefly for your own personal pleasure.

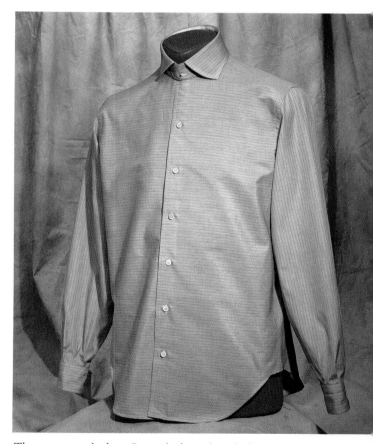

The custom-made shirt: Cut to fit the author's body precisely, this custom version of the classic dress shirt incorporates most of the details of the ready-to-wear standard. It also features a detachable collar and front cut on the cross-grain.

PART ONE
SHIRTS EXAMINED

THE MATERIALS OF FINE SHIRTS

hoosing appropriate fabrics for sewing projects — fabrics that flow when you want drape and that aren't too stiff when all you want is character — vies with fitting as the most challenging skill in garmentmaking. Fortunately for the maker of dress shirts, the issue of fabric has been decided well in advance. You need not experiment to be sure that all your sewing techniques will work on a particular material and that your garment will look as it should. You need only locate the shirting fabrics in your fabric store and then select the classic fabric of choice in any weight you like. That fabric is cotton.

COTTON SHIRTING FABRICS

If you've never handled a fine shirting cotton, you may not realize how truly extraordinary cotton fabric can be. The best fabrics are made from three varieties of cotton fiber, listed in order of increasing desirability: pima cotton, from the southwestern United States; Egyptian cotton; and Sea Island cotton, which is produced on the chain of islands of the same name off the coast of Georgia, South Carolina and Florida. The individual fibers (called staples) in each of these plants are much longer than those in less distinguished cottons, which allows them to be spun into finer, smoother yarns. After spinning, the yarns for shirting are usually plied together into 2-ply threads and numbered by size from 20 to 30 up to 180 to 200, with the higher numbers

being finer threads. A typical fine shirting fabric might, for example, be designated as a "2x2 120," meaning that both warp and weft are 2-ply 120 thread. A "60-singles" fabric is woven from 1-ply 60 thread. Shirting fabric made of these fine yarns must be imported because American cotton mills were not designed to work with ultrafine threads. Switzerland, England, Italy and Japan seem to weave the best cotton these days.

Fine shirting cotton is generally characterized by a subtle and beautiful gloss, or sheen, which rivals silk and, in my opinion, exceeds it by understatement. There are good-quality and expensive cottons without sheen, of course, but, if present, this luster is a reliable indicator of quality. Another clue can be found by examining the fuzziness of the fabric. The next time you're looking at cotton fabrics, hold the folded edge of a few of them up to the light and look

The most basic dress-shirt fabric is cotton poplin broadcloth, a plain-weave variation whose lengthwise (warp) threads are packed more densely than the crosswise (weft) threads. In the plaid swatch, you can clearly see the effect of this weave, which obscures the weft threads and makes the crosswise stripes less distinct than the lengthwise ones.

closely at the fold. The less fuzz you see, the smoother and longer-stapled the yarns are. (Don't be fooled by a crisp, wash-away finish on an obviously coarse fabric like denim.) Good shirting cotton marvelously combines softness and crispness, which is just what's called for in a dress shirt.

Dress shirting fabric that's patterned is never printed; the patterning is always woven in. These fabrics are referred to as "yarn-dyed" because the threads are colored before weaving.

Solid-color woven effects, like satin stripes, small diamonds, zigzags, twill, herringbones, and so on, are achieved by changing the arrangement of the weaving threads. On all-white shirts, these effects are known as "white-on-white" and are occasionally combined with colored stripes for complex effects.

The names of classic shirting fabrics all refer to different weave effects, some of which are obvious and some subtle. Among the most common shirtings is *poplin broadcloth*, a tightly woven, subtle variation on a plain-weave fabric (see the photo on the facing page). Poplin broadcloth is characterized by a very high thread count — in the range of 100 to 200 threads per inch — which produces a thin, but relatively opaque fabric with a crisp, hard finish. Also characteristic of the fabric is its fine horizontal ribbing, produced by the lengthwise warp threads being packed more densely than the crossing weft threads. This ribbing is scarcely noticeable but makes any on-grain stripes very clear and appear solid color, and it also adds a little shine to the fabric. If the cotton fiber itself has any shine, it will enhance the shine of the ribbing and produce a very dressy effect. Poplin broadcloth comes in solid colors, stripes, plaids and checks.

Lawn is a less densely woven, summer-weight broadcloth. The famous Tana Lawn from Liberty of London is a fine-quality cotton usually available in a few patterns suitable for dress shirts.

Voile in its finest form is an exquisite summer-weight broadcloth that is much less densely woven than lawn and consequently almost transparent. Voile yarns are more tightly spun than regular yarns, making them stiffer and smoother. They can be combined with other weaves to produce novelty fabrics, like those in the top photo at right.

Novelty fabrics combine two or more weaves or different thread weights to produce interesting pattern effects. In these swatches, wide voile stripes alternate with differently colored or shiny satin-weave stripes.

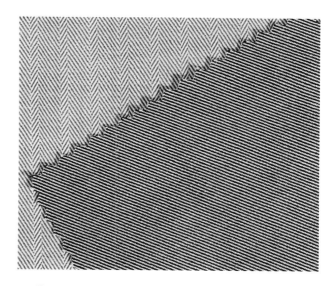

Twill weaves are popular alternative weaves for shirting fabric. When woven in a single color, these weaves create only texture. When the warp and weft threads are different colors, as they are in these samples, a subtle pattern is produced.

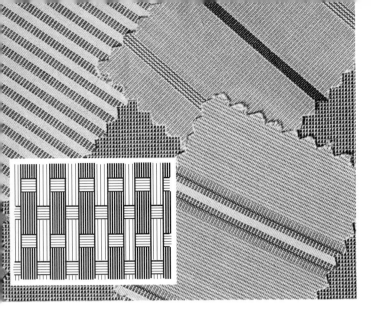

End-on-end, also called end-and-end, is a common, multicolored variation of a poplin-broadcloth weave. Used most often as an overall texture (background swatch), this weave is sometimes used in stripes, either as a background for plain stripes (pale blue swatch) or in the stripes themselves (pink and grey swatches).

Oxford cloth is a basketweave (warp and weft threads cross each other in pairs) that's often woven in two colors like chambray. The background fabric is a rare three-color oxford.

Batiste fabrics are woven in a plain weave like voile but are made of less tightly spun yarns. Batiste is softer than voile and more often used for blouses and fine undergarments, though you could, of course, use it for a fine shirt if you find a batiste you like.

The best batiste and voile come from Switzerland and are very expensive. These fabrics are seldom seen in the U.S. in menswear since transparency is not considered very "macho," but they are nonetheless the ultimate in hot-weather comfort.

End-on-end is a multicolored variation of a poplin-broadcloth weave. This fabric is worked with two colors to produce a tiny graph-paper effect in the fabric, with the grid lines usually worked in white and the spaces in color, as shown in the photo at top left. From a distance, the fabric looks solid color but, close up, it has a marvelous visual texture. End-on-end weave can be incorporated into striped patterns as well.

Chambray (shown here in various weights from heavy to nearly transparent) is a plain weave whose warp and weft are different colors, one of which is usually white.

Chambray also looks solid color but is a plain weave worked with two colors of yarns, usually a white warp and a colored weft. Chambray fabrics are woven in all weights; the heavier variety worked in blue is the basic material of work shirts (see the bottom photo on the facing page).

Oxford cloth is also usually a two-color weave, using a white warp with a colored weft, but it can, of course, be worked in all white. I've occasionally seen beautiful three-color oxford cloths, and it's often woven in stripes and tattersalls. The difference between oxford and chambray is that, in contrast to chambray's plain weave, oxford cloth is woven in a basketweave, that is, the warp and weft threads cross each other in pairs, which produces the fabric's characteristic soft bulkiness. When worked in a finer weave, oxford cloth is called pinpoint oxford, which makes it a dressier fabric. Oxford cloth is commonly associated with button-down collars and so is quite distinctive when used for a shirt with a plain collar.

OTHER SHIRTING FABRICS

Although I know some folks will be tempted by polyester and poly/cotton blends, these fabrics have only one, rather dubious advantage over 100% cotton shirting: they tempt one to avoid ironing. In fact, these fabrics resist ironing, which constitutes a defect for the shirtmaker, since a beautiful shirt demands to be skillfully ironed. Ironing, mind you, does not simply remove wrinkles. It builds shape, gives final form to details like the collar, cuffs and plackets, and provides the crowning finish to a beautiful material. Polyester and poly-blend fabrics can be beautifully designed and patterned, but they cannot aspire to the wonderful texture and qualities of fine cotton, which are enhanced by ironing. It's also annoying to sew on fabric that will not take a crease well; details that need to be pressed into shape will fight back.

The chief argument against polyester and poly/cotton blends, however, is that they can be uncomfortable to wear. On any but the coolest days,

a polyester or poly-blend shirt soon begins to feel like the plastic it is. By contrast, cotton is king when it comes to absorbent breathability.

Nonetheless, you can make shirts from lots of fabrics besides cotton, as you'll see in Chapter 9. I've used silk, linen and many kinds of wool as well as blends of these natural fibers. You can make shirts out of any fabric, as long as you know how to handle it. But the keys to making shirts successfully and enjoyably from any fabric the way I'll describe in this book are twofold: You need to be able to create a crisp, knife-like crease in the fabric with your iron (and be able to press it out); and you need to be able to pull firmly on the fabric on the straight grain without damaging it. Silk, for example, often requires stitching under a little tension, pulling on it both in front and in back of the needle, to avoid puckering—at least on my machine.

The only things you'll need to know about a fabric in order to follow the directions in this book are that it feels like a fabric you would enjoy wearing as a shirt, that you're willing to experiment to discover how to handle it, and whether you'll need to wash or dry-clean it. Whenever I'm working with a fabric I'm unfamiliar with, I always start off by reading about it in Claire Shaeffer's excellent book *Fabric Sewing Guide* (see the Bibliography on pp. 168-169), and by buying enough extra (¼ yd. will do) to test sewing and ironing.

SELECTING AND PREPARING SHIRTING FABRIC

Although it may be obvious, I think it's worth pointing out that for your first efforts at shirtmaking opaque materials are better than sheer ones because they don't require that every seam and seam allowance be flawlessly even. Because these elements will show through the right side of a shirt made of thin material, I suggest getting a little practice before working with a voile or fine white poplin broadcloth.

Interfacing

The best-quality all-cotton shirts always use woven, sewn-in cotton interfacing rather than a fusible interfacing for the collar and cuffs (and the front buttonhole section, if it is interfaced). I use and recommend plain bleached muslin (not permapress muslin), sometimes double thick, for interfacing. It's cheap, easy to work with and traditional. Nonetheless, any plain white, soft cotton will do. Oxford cloth, for example, would be a good, but expensive choice. Shirtmakers have a wide variety of all-cotton interfacing to choose from, all specially woven for collars or cuffs, or for different degrees of stiffness and levels of quality (see the Sources of Supply on pp. 164-167 for sources of interfacing, and pp. 106-109 for information on making collars). I collect soft white fabrics in different weights to use as interfacings, but for dress shirts I nearly always use bleached muslin because I like a soft collar that can be stiffened with starch if desired.

Until recently I wasn't interested in the "professional" shirt interfacings I had seen because they seemed mostly to be loosely woven, muslin-type fabrics stiffened with some kind of permanent chemical finish — not something I thought I wanted in a shirt. A little while ago, however, I discovered a source for the all-cotton collar and cuff interfacings sold to professional custom shirtmakers, and they're wonderful (see the entry for American Sember Trading Corp. under "Shirting fabrics" in the Sources of Supply on pp. 164-167).

All the characteristics of these last interfacings come from the density of the weave rather than an after-the-fact finish. They're all tightly woven, very smooth-textured and not so much stiff as substantial. Some of the cotton canvases I've collected in fabric stores are similar, but they're so textured I would not want to use them under a fine, thin shirting. I've tried all three of the collar fabrics and the one cuff fabric American Sember offers, using the techniques in this book, and find them all superior for use with classic shirtings, differing only in their thickness.

For wool shirts, I've successfully used tailor's hymo for collars, cut on the bias for a smooth fold at the top. For lightweight silk shirts, I even stoop to a fusible. The Fabric Carr (see Sources of Supply, pp. 164-167) sells an ultralight all-cotton interfacing called Silk-weight that's perfect cut on the bias for simple, one-piece collars like those on the silk shirts I made for Chapter 9. I fuse the interfacing, cut just slightly smaller than the collar, to one side only, then draw the precise stitching line on the interfacing with a regular pencil or a water-soluble marker. So far, I've had no bubbling, but these shirts are never machine-washed or machine-dried, which makes a big difference.

If you're unsure of the content of a certain fabric, whether for use as shirting or interfacing, you can always burn a small scrap to test it. All-cotton fibers turn to soft ash when burned. If there are any polyester fibers in the blend, they'll burn to hard, melted pellets amidst the ash — they're plastic, after all.

Washing and drying fabric

I suggest always machine-washing cotton fabric and interfacing and drying them in a hot dryer before beginning to sew. Then after you've made the shirt up, be careful to take it out of the dryer before it gets baked completely dry — or better yet, line-dry it since dryers very gradually turn clothing into lint. The theory behind this is to give the fabric the worst treatment it will get at the outset and thereby maximize the shrinkage before you begin sewing. I think it's unnecessary to prewash the fabric and interfacing twice, but it can't hurt, although it does of course delay a little longer getting started on your shirt.

Ironing and storing fabric

You must, of course, also iron the fabric to get it smooth before beginning to work with it, and you should take some care with this step. I iron — not press — to refinish the cotton, revive any gloss and restretch it back somewhat to the tension it held on the loom and during the finishing process. Generally what you want to accomplish in ironing yardage is to stretch it gently and evenly lengthwise and avoid distorting it widthwise. Thus, you need to iron with the straight, lengthwise grain of the fabric — that is, parallel to the selvage — rather than side to side, across the grain.

The reason for ironing rather than pressing fabric is so that you'll be able to sew on fabric that's stretched the way it will be when ironed as a completed garment. If, instead, you carefully pressed the fabric to avoid stretching it — that is, just laid the iron down on the fabric, applying only downward pressure — the body and sleeves of the final garment would be much more elastic than the seamed areas, which would make it very difficult to avoid wrinkles at the seamlines when ironing the garment.

This is also the time to pay attention to grain to ensure that the threads are straight and square to each other and that any woven patterns are not distorted. I align the selvages of the fabric parallel to the ironing board, spray the fabric with water and iron until it's dry, sliding the iron back and forth with the grain. I hold the iron in my right hand, while pulling the fabric straight and flat with my left.

Crinkled selvages may tempt you to iron across the grain, but this is a mistake because you're bound to stretch the more elastic cross-grain, or weft, threads unevenly. Stroke each section lengthwise with the iron only to stretch the whole piece of cloth evenly so that its woven patterns will match and it will react uniformly to sewing and later ironing. The stretching should be moderate, not to the extent of removing all the fabric's lengthwise elasticity — but stretch it you must. This is true ironing because you're moving the iron while it rests on the fabric, which inevitably moves the threads. The downward pressure varies with the weight of the fabric and the weave: lighter fabric needs lighter pressure.

If the weave is open, loose or textured, or if the fabric is very lightweight, you'll need to iron more delicately, or perhaps even press, with no sideways movement. But if the fabric needs that much restraint in ironing, it will be a challenge to iron in shirt form, so think twice before making it up. I've come to trust my iron's high-heat setting for cotton, but I do adjust it lower for very thin fabric.

I've always loved the ritual sensuality of ironing a length of gorgeous yardage back into shape after its first washing. And I enjoy it even more now that I've made myself a rectangular ironing surface — ironing boards are such an irritating shape! For a description of my ironing setup, see pp. 13-14.

FOLDING IRONED YARDAGE FOR STORAGE

After initial ironing, fold yardage parallel to selvages.

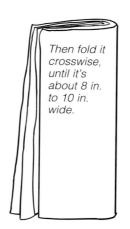

Then fold it crosswise, until it's about 8 in. to 10 in. wide.

Don't catch folds in hanger.

Store fabric flat, or hang it from a pants or skirt hanger.

Since the yardage will be stored at least briefly before I start cutting into it, I fold it in half lengthwise (the way yardage usually comes on the bolt) as I complete ironing each length, smoothing it carefully so no wrinkles get stored away with it. Then I fold it crosswise until it's about 8 in. or 10 in. wide (see the drawing above and the first photo following the Introduction), again avoiding wrinkles. Thus folded, the fabric can be hung from one end on a pants hanger or stacked on a shelf for many months, needing only a little touchup with an iron when it's time to make it up into a shirt. (See pp. 88-89 for a discussion of construction ironing and p. 119 for information on ironing the completed shirt.)

CHAPTER TWO

THE SHIRTMAKER'S TOOLS

The tools you'll need to make shirts are mostly those required for any kind of sewing. I love tools and tend to collect them, but here I've made an effort to distinguish between tools that are essential to great results and a few helpful options.

The key to using tools to the fullest is to spend some time getting comfortable with how they work and exploring the effects they can help you achieve. Good tools don't replace skills, but they do make it easier to acquire them. As you gain skills with your hands and develop your standards of workmanship, you'll find that these "tools" are the most important of all and that they'll help you improve the quality of the work you do.

ESSENTIAL TOOLS
FOR SHIRTMAKING

STRAIGHT-STITCH SEWING MACHINE with interchangeable feet and preferably with a free arm. You'll need interchangeable feet (see below) to do the felling and hemming stitches required for shirts; a free arm is also handy for making the flat-felled sleeve seams, although you can do without it. There are no zigzag stitches required in a shirt, except for the buttonholes. If your sewing machine does not zigzag, you'll need a buttonhole attachment.

FELLING FOOT AND ROLLED-HEM FOOT (both ⅛ in. or 4mm). You should be able to find these inexpensive tools at your local sewing-machine dealer or have the dealer order them for you. If you can't, I've included a reliable mail-order source in the Sources of Supply on pp. 164-167. For a detailed discussion of how to use these feet, see pp. 91-94.

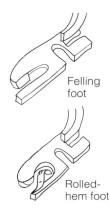

Felling foot

Rolled-hem foot

COTTON EMBROIDERY THREAD. If you've ever tried repairing a ready-made shirt, you'll know how difficult it is to blend into the topstitching or edgestitching with ordinary, U.S. size 50 thread. This thread looks like rope compared to what manufacturers use on fine shirts.

Sewing your shirts with a beautiful, mercerized cotton thread of the right size will produce astonishingly professional-looking results. I use 100% cotton machine-embroidery thread for all the construction of dress shirts and shirts of similar weight. DMC Broder Machine size 50 (equivalent to U.S. size 80), Madeira Tanne size 50 and Mettler Article 240 60/2 are good examples. These are all 2-ply threads, similar to the yarns in dress shirting

(see pp. 4-7), so they're a little weaker than typical, 3-ply cotton sewing thread, but strong enough. I've been wearing shirts sewn with these threads for years.

Cotton embroidery threads come in lots of colors and all make great buttonholes since they're designed to satin-stitch beautifully. For heavier materials, there's nothing wrong with 3-ply thread, but for a custom-made dress shirt use 2-ply. Since most dress shirts still use white thread, mail order makes sense if you can't find 2-ply thread locally — try sewing-machine dealers — but the sources listed on p. 166 will also match colors for you if you send a swatch of your fabric.

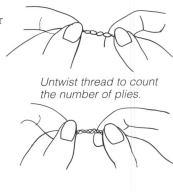

Untwist thread to count the number of plies.

SIZE 60/8, 65/9 OR 70/10 MACHINE NEEDLES are appropriate with good shirting fabric and the cotton embroidery thread I've recommended. Use "sharp needles" if you can find them (Singer Red Band or Schmetz 70/10 HJ), which are the best needles for woven fabric. Or use an all-purpose universal needle, whose point is slightly rounded and designed for both woven and knitted fabrics. Do not, however, use a ballpoint needle, which is designed just for knitted fabrics. Instead of piercing the threads of the fabric, the rounded nose of a ballpoint needle is deflected by the threads into the space between them, which prevents you from stitching an arrow-straight line.

GOOD FABRIC SHEARS for cutting out patterns. Choose whatever brand

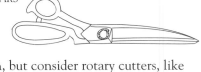

you're happy with, but consider rotary cutters, like the Olfa cutter and others described on pp. 15-17.

SHORT, HEAVY-BLADED SCISSORS, preferably knife-edged, for clipping and trimming seam allowances, which can get pretty thick. Choose scissors with 2-in. or 3-in. blades that will cut 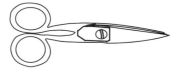 through heavy layers right to the tip. Gingher's 5-in. Tailor's Points (#G5C) are my favorites.

TAPE MEASURE AND RULER. There are various kinds of tapes and rulers, and I suggest you use measuring devices you're comfortable with. I particularly like transparent rulers, especially as a guide for my rotary cutter. You may also want a dressmaker's curve of some sort, especially if you need to do a lot of sleeve adjustment.

LONG, GLASS-HEADED PINS. I use silk-weight pins (0.50mm diameter) so that the holes they make in the fabric are tiny. Glass heads make handling pins much easier, so go ahead and indulge yourself.

WASHABLE, BASTING GLUE STICK. I use this tool a lot, as you'll see in the discussion of shirt construction in Chapter 7. The trick to not making a mess with a glue stick is to twist it only barely beyond the case, so you can spread a thin dot. Don't twist it out like lipstick.

WATER-SOLUBLE MARKERS. I use water-soluble markers (available at art-supply stores) for marking specific points like pattern notations, buttonholes, and so on. The marks tend to reappear when the fabric is ironed, so mark lightly and as small as possible, though the marks will wash out completely in the first washing or thorough wetting. Use whatever marker you like that will make a clearly visible, completely removable mark that is fine enough to be accurate. Chalk also works well if you keep it sharp.

You can also make very serviceable marks on smooth fabrics with a hard object like a smooth-edged tracing wheel, a fingernail or a Japanese tool called a *hera* (shown in the drawing at right). With your fabric on a hard surface, press firmly with the marker, which will make a shiny, visible indentation. This is a great way to mark against a ruler or template.

IRON, IRONING BOARD AND SPRAY BOTTLE. You don't necessarily need a steam iron. In fact, I use a lightweight, smooth-soled, nonsteam iron — a Sunbeam Ironmaster that's probably older than I am and which I treasure. I spray the fabric with water to create very controllable steam. Steam irons do perfectly well, mind you, but the holes leave marks when you're pressing and catch on collar points when you're ironing. Although some people are fond of detachable, Teflon-coated sole plates for their irons to prevent scorching, I'm not satisfied with the ironing results I get with them on cotton. The fabric needs a little polishing from the iron's metal sole. Avoid scorching instead by lifting the iron often so that heat doesn't build up. And for best results, cover your ironing board with cotton drill. Don't use aluminum- or Teflon-coated ironing-board covers. They bounce the heat back into your fabric, so you're more likely to scorch it.

I like to iron yardage after its first washing on a larger surface than a regular ironing board. I use a ¾-in. piece of plywood that's 33 in. wide by 55 in. long, which I've covered with several layers of wool blanket and over which I've tightly stretched well-washed cotton drill. To iron on this surface at a comfortable height, I prop half of the board on my ironing board and support the other half with books stacked on my sewing table. I attached a loop of string to the ceiling right above the board with a nail, and I string the iron cord through it to keep it from dragging across the fabric.

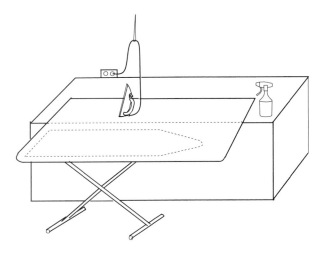

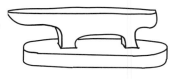

POINT PRESSER for turning collar and cuff seams. This tool is essential for opening seams fully.

POINT PRESSER for turning collar and cuff seams. This tool is essential for opening seams fully.

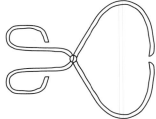

POINT TURNER. A point turner that looks like a pair of ice tongs, called "Mrs. Designer Multipurpose Point and Tube Turner" (available from Nancy's Notions, see the Sources of Supply on pp. 164-167) is by far the best tool of its kind available. It will grab the fragile points of collars and cuffs firmly and safely. We'll discuss point turning more fully on pp. 105-106.

Making this setup may seem like a lot of trouble to go to, but I'll usually wash and iron a few pieces of fabric at a time, and it's much more pleasant to be set up for maximum efficiency. In addition, this padded surface is a perfect place to make patterns from existing shirts (for a discussion of this process, see pp. 37-39).

Clean & Glide iron cleaner, a standard sewing notion, works fine to clean your iron. This cleaner is noxious, so make sure you do the cleaning outdoors. You can also use a razor-blade scraper to scrape buildup off the flat parts of the sole, but be careful not to scratch it.

SPRAY STARCH. I've had good results with Texize Spray 'n Starch, but I much prefer to buy liquid starch (like Linit, listed in the Sources of Supply on pp. 164-167), dilute it and put it into a standard spray bottle. That way I can control the dilution for different degrees of stiffness. I keep two batches: a very light one (one part starch to three or four parts water) for the shirt body and a heavier one (one part starch to two parts—or less—water) for the collar. If you want a really stiff collar, try this suggestion from George Bolton, a devotee of vintage costume: Dilute the liquid half-and-half with water, then dip the collar in the liquid and let it dry. Repeat the process, and finally spray the collar with a heavy dilution of starch when you're ironing it.

FOR PATTERN PREPARATION AND SEWING PRACTICE

WOVEN COTTON/POLYESTER GINGHAM. You'll need about 2½ yd. to 3 yd. of gingham per shirt to be fitted. Gingham is better than muslin for fitting because the woven pattern makes the grainlines very easy to see.

SCRAP, ALL-COTTON BROADCLOTH, about 1 yd. To practice seams and collar construction, cut six to ten pieces of the cloth on the lengthwise grain, 2 in. to 3 in. wide by 12 in. to 15 in. long. For sleeve practice, cut two pieces of cloth 11 in. by 17 in.

BLEACHED MUSLIN, about 1 yd., for interfacing (see p. 8).

A DARK, PERMANENT MARKER for marking the gingham pattern.

HEAVY PAPER   for making the final pattern for the shirt body and for making your own collar and cuff patterns. Patternmakers use a heavy manila paper called oaktag, which many art-supply stores carry in 24-in. by 36-in. sheets. A good alternative is poster board, which is sold in large sheets at art stores and can be used for the body and sleeve patterns. The poster board sold in smaller sheets in drug and grocery stores is fine for details like cuffs, collars and plackets. The cardboard that usually comes with folded shirts from the laundry also is good, especially if it's white so that you can see what you've drawn on it. This cardboard makes good templates, which you'll find are useful for making pattern details (see Chapter 6).

DRESSMAKER'S CURVE AND TAILOR'S SQUARE   for truing up patterns you've copied or are perfecting. It's very reassuring to know that your armscye (the garment's armhole) has some standard curves in it, and that duplicated curves are identical. The square could be replaced by a straightedge, but it's often handy to be able to make a right angle from a center line when, for example, you're

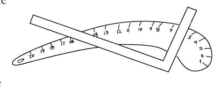

checking the position of the side seams.

The curve is used by holding it against a sketched or traced line, moving the curve until you find a section of it that seems to match the line, and then guiding your pencil along that section to redraw a smooth line. You then move the curve up the sketched or traced line, matching it to the line, section by section, until you've smoothed out the entire line. Redrawing the line with the curve not only smooths it out but also permits you to note the section used, flip the curve over and exactly duplicate the shape on the other side of the pattern.

DESIRABLE, BUT OPTIONAL TOOLS

ROTARY CUTTER   (Olfa, Salem, Dritz or other brands). Of all the new products introduced to home sewers in the past decade or so, the rotary cutter gets my vote as the most revolutionary. Most of these products—like the walking foot, the free-arm sewing machine and the serger—are simply domestic versions of tools long standard in the garment industry. The rotary cutter is no exception.

Commercial garments are, of course, not cut with scissors. Manufacturers use die-cutting machines that stamp through numerous layers of fabric, with one press of a button, to cut out identical sleeve plackets and collar bands, for example. For larger pattern pieces, they use motorized saws with razor-sharp knife blades instead of saw teeth. These saws either move up and down like a bandsaw or are rotary, working like pizza cutters. Quite apart from the sheer number of identical garment pieces that can be cut at once, these cutting tools are far superior to scissors because their cuts are uniform and they distort the fabric very little. The nonmotorized rotary cutter shares these virtues and has in fact become a standard tool among small manufacturers.

The rotary cutter is a true blessing for the home sewer because it can reduce pattern-cutting time by as much as 80% and at least double the accuracy of scissor cutting, particularly when there's more than one layer of fabric. The cutter is a radical improvement on scissors when you're grading seams, which is always an awkward job. Cutting straight lines is as easy as drawing a line with a ruler, and there's nothing better for cutting smooth curves.

Adjustable cutting guide

The one drawback of the cutter is that it's only half of what you need to cut out your pattern. The companion tool required is a cutting surface that will not dull the blades, and this can be expensive. While the cutters cost about $10 to $12 and new blades about $5 at the time this book went to press, most cutting mats big enough to cut a shirt front (at least 24 in. by 36 in.) can cost as much as $40. And even if you buy one this size, you'll wish it were much bigger every time you cut out a long garment. These mats (made by Olfa, Dritz, Salem and some art-supply companies) are usually called "self-healing," meaning that the cuts made in the surface by the blade are invisible, unless the mat is bent to spread them open. If you're willing to put up with visible, hairline scoring of your cutting surface, you can get a cutting mat large enough to cover your whole worktable without spending a lot of money. I feel I even get a cleaner cut on these harder, "nonhealing" surfaces.

Nonhealing (or "score-able") mats come in sizes up to 4 ft. by 8 ft. and can be easily rolled for shipping and cut to the exact size of your table. A 4-ft. by 8-ft. sheet costs about $60, but a 32-in. by 60-in. sheet (big enough for cutting pants out of 60-in. wide fabric) is only about $40. I leave my mat covering the table at all times, so that I can cut out details and trim right next to the sewing machine, just sliding the machine away to use the whole surface. I think it's the only way to go. In fact, since I bought a rotary cutter, I haven't once used my expensive shears for cutting out a pattern.

Here are a few tips for using a rotary cutter. Since the cutting blade is basically a razor blade in the round, it will easily slice through anything, including your fingers. But because the cutter is very well designed for safety, it's not difficult to avoid cutting yourself. The main concern is miscutting your fabric. Be sure of the cut you want to make before you begin. Then cut fairly firmly—it doesn't take much pressure—rolling the blade away from you. Be definite about the cut, but don't get overconfident. Cut out your pattern pieces slowly.

Also don't cut through untrimmed pattern paper and fabric at the same time. Trim the pattern to the cutting line with the cutter and then cut next to it so the pattern doesn't shift around. This way it's not even necessary to pin the pattern to the fabric. Just weight it down—I use my collection of rulers and designer's curves as weights.

Because fabric layers will tend to buckle a little and slide away from the rolling blade, hold them down behind the blade to keep them flat. Cutting next to a straight edge holds the fabric perfectly, so I always cut straight lines with a ruler. For cutting long, slow curves, you can also grab both layers in front of the blade and slightly slide the fabric in the direction you are cutting. This sounds complicated, but it isn't. Try it first without a pattern in place to worry about.

If cutting curves seems daunting, draw some on scraps of fabric or paper and practice. It's just like driving—it's easier to turn the wheel when it's rolling, so keep it moving. Fifteen or twenty minutes of sincere effort will convince you that this is the best tool for curves. As with cutting straight lines, it's a good idea to cut slowly, but try to keep the cutting motion smooth.

Don't try to cut notches or clip with the cutter. It's too hard to know where the cut stops. Instead, clip out the notches later with small scissors. Not knowing where the cuts stop makes cutting corners imprecise. I overcut slightly on outside corners, and undercut on inside corners, and then snip the uncut threads with scissors later.

If you notice that occasional crosswise threads are not completely cut through, try a little more pressure with the next round of cutting. If the uncut threads occur regularly, say, every 4 in. or so, that means that there's a nick in the blade. Since the blade cannot be sharpened, you'll need to change it. If you're careful to protect the blade with its cover when you're finished cutting (do this for safety's sake, too), the blade will rarely get nicked or dulled. I've cut out dozens of garments without needing to change blades.

When you remove a cut-out section of the pattern, do so slowly, checking as you go to see that all the threads have been cut through. If you have uncut threads and move quickly, you'll disarrange any other pattern pieces and the layers of fabric. If you find uncut threads, it's easy to snip them with a pair of scissors.

Of all the brands, I prefer the Olfa cutter and usually use either size of Olfa with an adjustable guide. You can set the guides to make the cut at a certain distance from a reference line, like a ruler or pattern piece. I cut my basic stiff-cardboard patterns without a seam allowance, then set the guide on the cutter to accommodate the seam allowance I want. I trace around the pattern with the guide butted to its edge, and the cut is made with the seam allowance provided for. This is particularly useful when working with collars, as you'll see in Chapter 7, and for cutting out shirts from the same pattern that need different seam allowances. Once you try one of these cutting setups with cutter, mat and guide, you may become as thrilled with it as I am — and bother all your sewing friends until they try it too!

OTHER HELPFUL TOOLS. In addition to the rotary cutter, there are a few other optional tools that I find quite useful. A *sleeve board* will prove very helpful for

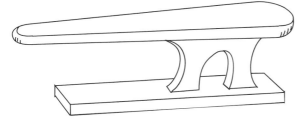

ironing curved collars and cuffs. *Fraycheck*, a liquid that retards fabric fraying, is great for slightly stiffening buttonholes before you cut them out.

A *walking foot* (A) will help you match patterns and topstitch collars. And a *button cutter* (B), which is like a small chisel with its own little chopping block, is the best tool available for opening buttonholes. A *buttonhole spacer* (C) can be handy too. For accuracy, spread the spacer out fully and then compress it back to the size you want. I also love my *magnetic pin holder*. It's very efficient to be able to toss pins

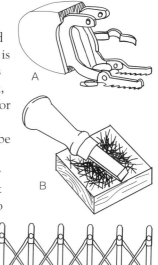

at it without looking and know that they won't get lost. I position it right behind my machine so I can toss the pins as I stitch up to them.

A *corner radius template* is a handy device for shaping rounded corners or pocket and cuff patterns (the one I like is Template Designs #TD 108, which is available from a drafting supplier). When I'm topstitching a rounded shape, I'll sometimes mark the stitching line by tracing it with this template. If you like this approach, check out the other curve templates at the same source, like the 60° ellipse, which is a very attractive alternative to the partial circle.

CHAPTER THREE

THE CLASSIC SHIRT

In this chapter, I'll discuss the various elements of the classic dress shirt in some detail. Bear in mind that the shirt under analysis here is the traditional, conservative shirt produced by fine shirtmakers and clothiers in the United States and much of Europe. The details discussed below are standards established by long practice and common use that, of course, can be varied as choice and taste dictate. The traditional shirt makes a good point of departure for style changes — as you will see in Chapter 9 — but, before departing from tradition, let's consider what may be sensible reasons for staying with it.

ANATOMY OF THE CLASSIC SHIRT

Every classic dress shirt has the following elements: a one-piece, pleated or gathered back; a narrow, one- or two-piece double yoke; two front sections that overlap; flat-felled armscye, side and underarm seams; one-piece sleeves with plackets; either barrel or French cuffs; a collar on a separate stand; and a rolled hem. That's it.

One-piece back

A one-piece back can be cut in a single piece, folded along the center-back line. Pleats or gathers in the back provide a little extra room when the arms are raised or reached forward. Gathers are traditionally placed 3 in. to 4 in. in from the shoulder seams above each shoulder blade, or the entire back can be gently and evenly gathered into the yoke along its entire bottom length. Alternatively, a pleat turning outward can be placed over each shoulder blade, or a pair of opposing pleats can be positioned together at the center back to form a box pleat.

This last arrangement is perhaps the most common, at least on American shirts, and I think it's the most attractive. It places the pleat in the natural hollow of the back, allowing the rest of the shirt to lie smoothly across the back and turning a purely functional device into a natural design feature that doesn't call attention to its function. The box pleat is also the easiest of these alternatives to make, although it's vital that it be perfectly centered and equal in depth on both sides.

Regardless of how you handle the ease in the shirt back, at least 1 in. should be taken in on each side. A Brooks Brothers man's shirt in my collection — a classic shirt if ever there was one — has a 1¾-in. wide box pleat, with 1¾ in. of fabric pleated into each side. A woman's shirt can, but needn't, have a narrower pleat. Or a woman may prefer gathers instead of pleats. It's up to you.

Some shirts have a so-called locker loop at the top of the box pleat. In my opinion, this is a totally useless and undesirable feature, particularly if you are the shirtmaker, since it's time-consuming and tricky to sew correctly and looks dreadful unless it's held taut and close to the yoke. A small, badly centered box pleat with a drooping loop is a definite eyesore and serves no purpose but to announce poor workmanship and gratuitous design.

Since I'm already indignant, I'll move on to discuss back darts, particularly as they're used in men's shirts. They're not a feature of any shirt I'd consider a classic, but some custom shirtmakers offer them, and lots of ready-made shirts have them,

ONE-PIECE BACK WITH EASE VARIOUSLY HANDLED

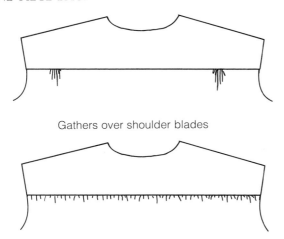

Gathers over shoulder blades

Entire back gathered

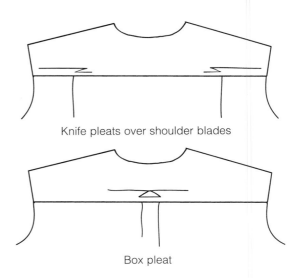

Knife pleats over shoulder blades

Box pleat

usually without accompanying pleats or gathers at the yoke. These darts normally start right under the shoulder blades and run straight down the shirt back for about 14 in. to 16 in., tapering to nothing at the top and bottom and taking in about 2 in. on each side at the widest point. The reason for back darts is purely cosmetic — to make the shirt follow or suggest an idealized shape, that is, the triangular back of the classically proportioned male. In the process, these darts turn a garment that's traditionally loose-fitting and drapes smoothly into one that's form-fitting and falls awkwardly on the body.

To my eye, the need for darts is merely evidence of ill-cut side seams. Besides creating chevrons out of any vertical stripes in the fabric, darts call unwelcome attention to themselves by visibly doubling the often somewhat transparent fabric. They also make ironing the shirt back a complex chore by ensuring that it will not lie flat. Whereas in a well-made shirt, every seam is either edged or topstitched to create a flat, crisp look, darts often create ugly wrinkles down the back since they distort the fabric. Worst of all, while a shirt needs to hang somewhat loose at the back to allow the wearer to sit down without pulling out the shirttail, darts usually release just at this point, causing the shirt to look as if an invisible vest that's too short is being worn, below which the shirt bags out.

If you still dare to put in darts after all this, please make sure that they conform exactly to the shape of the wearer's body since nothing is more unsightly than darts straining against a form that they don't fit.

FINISHES TO HANDLE EXCESS FABRIC ON A SLIM FIGURE

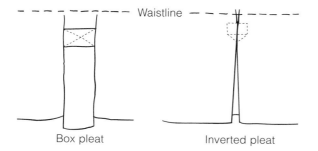

These finishes are suggested only to reduce fabric on a slim figure. They are not part of a traditional dress shirt.

If you must take in some material at the back, try stitching the box pleat down at a point that will always be tucked in, allowing the pleat to release again over the hips, as shown in the drawing below, and resolve to reshape the side seams on the next shirt. (A box pleat can also be inverted if you prefer, as in the blue corduroy shirt on p. 138.)

Thank you for bearing with me through this tirade. I have more to say on back pleats and darts but will reserve it for the discussion of fitting in Chapter 4. Meanwhile, suffice it to say that the traditional and tasteful shirt back is simple, functional and otherwise unadorned.

One- or two-piece double yoke

A yoke is vital to a shirt. It provides extra strength in the area bearing the weight of the shirt. It conceals the seams at the shoulder, keeping them away from the top of the shoulder, where they might rub uncomfortably. It allows the front and back to be shaped to the wearer's shoulders without darts. And it serves as a basic design detail of the shirt. It's usually only the least expensive woven dress shirts that are made without yokes.

By "double yoke," I mean that two complete yokes are cut, and the front and back seam allowances are sandwiched in between the seam that joins them. The classic shirt has a narrow yoke, measured from front to back at the shoulder. Wide yokes that fall lower on the back shoulder are distinctly sporty in effect. They can also interfere with the ease of movement offered by the shirt back by positioning the pleat, and thus the give, below the area where moving the arms forward creates tension across the back. My Brooks Brothers shirt yoke is only 1⅝ in. wide at the shoulder. A yoke more than 2½ in. wide at the shoulder seems to me too sporty for a dress shirt for a man. A woman's dress shirt could certainly have a wider yoke — up to 5 in. — but narrower is still dressier.

Shirt advertisements nowadays occasionally mention two-piece yokes, as if everybody knows how desirable these are. In fact, there are only three reasons for cutting a two-piece yoke: first, to allow each half of the yoke to be cut differently to accommodate unequally sized shoulders (obviously

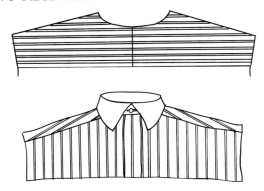

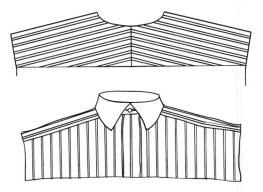

Grain parallel to back edge of yoke creates angled stripes at front seam. (Grain on one-piece yoke is same as shown.)

Grain parallel to front edges on two-piece yoke creates chevron on yoke back and parallel stripes at front seam.

not a feature of ready-made shirts and a very tricky and questionable business anyway); second, to permit the seam of a yoke front in a striped fabric to be on grain so that it will run parallel to the stripe (a distinctly British touch that looks quite odd — but not uninteresting — to the American eye and causes a sort of chevron effect at the center back); and third, to save material (four small yoke pieces can be cut out of smaller scraps than two large yoke pieces). The seam at the back touted in the advertisements thus is almost certainly a bogus indicator of quality or extra care, especially if the shirt fabric is unstriped. Yet it is a simple touch to add and *is* economical of material, so why not?

However, although I don't recommend cutting the yoke halves differently (for more on this, see p. 42), the British touch of aligning the yoke front with the fabric grain can be fun on a striped shirt. And the seam, centered above a box pleat, adds an attractive touch, but nothing more. In the end, it's entirely up to you. Since I enjoy machine-embroidering the name or initials of the wearer on the inner yoke as a kind of label, I would find the seam an interference. Yet you could certainly cut only the outer yoke in two pieces, because the seam is only decorative. If you decide to do this, just remember to add a seam allowance to both sides.

Shirt fronts

The shirt fronts on a contemporary dress shirt are totally separated neck to hem by a button front, traditionally lapped left over right for men and vice versa for women. (A popular variation on the dress shirt, the pullover tunic shirt, uses a single-piece front with a placket just like a long sleeve placket and made the same way. This placket is centered down the shirt front, creating an opening from the neck to about the waistline. Nowadays this tunic design is reserved for sportshirts. See p. 130 for more information on this variation on the classic shirt.)

There are two possible finishes for the full-length front opening: with and without a front band. Using a front band is the American standard; leaving it off yields a more European feeling and is simplicity itself to construct. Whether or not to use a front band is entirely a matter of personal taste, and it's debatable which style is more formal. I feel "with" is sportier and "without" dressier, but I'm very possibly biased because of how much faster "without" is to make. There's no question, however, that an Ivy League look requires a front band, so I wouldn't leave one off a button-down shirt.

A classic front band should be 1½ in. wide, topstitched ¼ in. along each side. On a fine-quality shirt, and anywhere the pattern is intended to match across the band, the band should be cut separately and attached to the shirt.

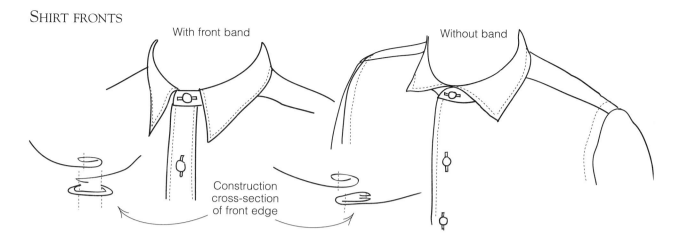

With front band

Without band

Construction
cross-section
of front edge

Flat-felled armscye and side seams

Wide, flat-felled armscye seams of about ⅜ in. to
½ in. are essential to a dress shirt, and they're easy to
sew (as you'll see on pp. 94-97). The flat-felled seam
effectively interfaces the armscye seam, adding shape
and firmness to it and finishing the sleeve perfectly
all at once. The procedure for sewing this seam
makes it the fastest way of attaching a sleeve I know
of. Only one pin is required.

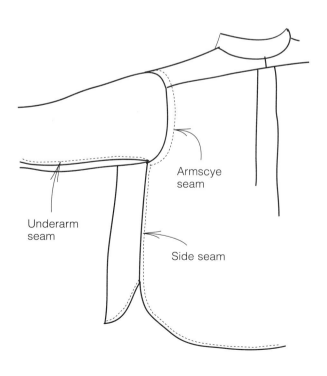

Underarm
seam

Armscye
seam

Side seam

Flat-felled side and underarm seams are also easy
and very gratifying to sew when you own a felling
foot, which can easily be obtained for all domestic
machines but which, for some reason, is almost
universally unknown. This foot creates a tiny,
elegant and completely finished seam identical to
that on the most expensive dress shirts made.
Although not quite as effortless as armscye seams,
flat-felled side seams are well worth the effort and
work beautifully, even on quite curved seams. The
technique is sure to become part of your frequently
used sewing skills. Non-flat-felled side seams are ugly
and shapeless, and there's really no excuse for them.
If you insist on not using a felling foot, don't even try
to fell the seams by hand as described in commercial
patterns. It's an exercise in futility that will turn you
away from shirtmaking forever. Instead, finish the
seam with a zigzag stitch or a serger, then topstitch
the seam to the rear, which makes what's called a
welted seam. All this is likely to look hand-done and
irregular, so at least try the felling foot.

One-piece sleeves with plackets

Because shirts are made to be assembled flat and to
have flat-felled seams at the armscyes, the sleeves
must be added before the side seams are sewn. For
this reason, sleeves on the classic shirt must be one-
piece. Two-piece sleeves, of course, are found on
tailored jackets and are set into the body of the
garment after the sleeve seams and side seams of the
body are sewn together.

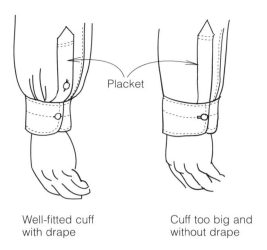

Well-fitted cuff
with drape

Cuff too big and
without drape

The sleeve placket is a distinctive feature of good-quality shirts and essential to any shirt aspiring to "dress" status. It should be at least 1 in. wide on a man's shirt but can be a little narrower on a woman's; its length depends on several factors, all based on personal preference. If you want to roll up your sleeves occasionally or if you like a sleeve-placket button—or need one because you like the sleeve to hang with a little drape at the cuff—then you'll need a fairly long placket of about 7½ in. with a 5¾-in. to 6-in. opening. (The placket button is not actually a mere designer's touch, but a rebirth from the days when men wore their sleeves with drape, allowing a custom-fitted cuff to stay put when the arms were raised. The drape caused the placket to gape open, hence the button.)

If you don't want any of the above, the placket can be shortened, but it should be at least 6 in. long, with a 4½-in. opening (remember, though, the shorter the placket, the harder the cuff is to attach). Don't be apprehensive about making the placket—it's quite simple (see pp. 102-105). Go through a sample, once, slowly, and you'll look forward to every other one you make. It is such a satisfying and professional detail and requires no practice, only an understanding of the steps.

The sleeve is traditionally cut wider than the cuff, so it must be gathered or pleated down to size. The width of the sleeve depends upon the amount of drape you want at the cuff and whether you want to use a barrel or French cuff. These are all matters of

personal taste and have some bearing on the masculinity or femininity of effect, at least in my mind. I find pleats somewhat more masculine, dressier and certainly easier to produce than gathers, although some fine men's shirts are made with gathers, especially, for some reason, when they have French cuffs. If the sleeve is to be gathered, the gathers must be equally distributed along the entire cuff. If the sleeve is pleated, the pleats are either concentrated on both sides of the placket or equally spaced around the cuff, as you please.

Barrel and French cuffs

A barrel cuff is made to button with one cuff end tucked under the other, matching the placket construction. This cuff can be made with a built-in curve around the wrist and can have (in descending order of choice for traditional effect) rounded, square or diagonal corners. The standard cuff length is 2⅝ in., with 2¼ in. the minimum.

French cuffs, also called double cuffs, cannot be shaped to the wrist since the halves on either side of the fold curve in opposite directions. They are made to close with cufflinks, with both sides of the cuff lying together and pointing away from the wrist. This arrangement requires an adjustment of the placket: The underneath part of the placket must be folded toward the inside of the sleeve, so that the placket

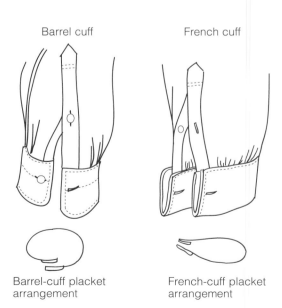

Barrel cuff

French cuff

Barrel-cuff placket
arrangement

French-cuff placket
arrangement

will close without overlapping. This correspondingly reduces the width of the sleeve end (see the bottom drawing on the facing page). However, French cuffs should be looser than barrel cuffs can be, so that they lie smoothly and don't strain at the wrist. Also, the fold of the double cuff is not at the halfway point but just slightly above it, toward the sleeve, so that the top part of the cuff is slightly larger than the bottom part and, when folded back, conceals the seam joining the cuff and sleeve. The top part of the cuff should be 3 in. long when folded over. The placement of the cufflink holes determines the fold, since they must naturally match, so position them carefully, after establishing the fold. Like barrel cuffs, French cuffs can also have (in descending order of preference for this type of cuff) square, rounded or diagonal corners. However you topstitched the collar, match this stitching on the cuffs, preferably at ¼ in. from the edge.

French cuffs, of course, produce a much dressier effect than barrel cuffs and must be beautifully ironed and starched because they call attention to themselves far more than their plainer counterpart. The eye is drawn not only by their greater bulk but also by the flashiness of the cufflinks used. Understatement, as always, is I think in the best taste. I find French cuffs rather cumbersome and showy for my taste and lifestyle, but I do like the choice of wearing simple cufflinks. Consequently, I've occasionally opted for *single* French cuffs, that is, a cuff that's not folded back but whose sides lie together, pointing away from the wrist, held together by a lightweight cufflink. I've devised several pairs of cufflinks out of appealing buttons. I attach them together with colored silk twist, using different buttons on each end so that they are reversible — very low cost, versatile and fun.

Collar on a stand

A collar without a separate stand, that is, a collar and stand cut in one piece, cannot be made with any built-in curve for the neck, because folding the one-piece collar and stand would cause the curve to go in opposite directions, just like French cuffs. Even the least expensive "dress" shirts have no way around this and are made with a separate stand and collar. On traditional dress shirts, the collar is topstitched at ¼ in. from the edge. Stitching closer to or actually on the edge inclines, in my opinion, toward a cheaper effect. Nowadays, some button-down shirts come with both top- and edgestitching, about ¼ in. apart. I think this is overkill and, for home sewers, an invitation for trouble, but perhaps you'll like the challenge of keeping the two rows of stitching exactly parallel.

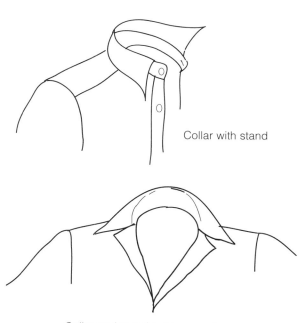

Collar with stand

Collar and stand cut in one piece

Rolled hem

A rolled hem is also basic to traditional shirt finish. It's easy to sew with the rolled hemmer foot and very tricky and discouraging to do by hand, as advised in all commercial patterns. The technique is discussed in detail on pp. 91-94.

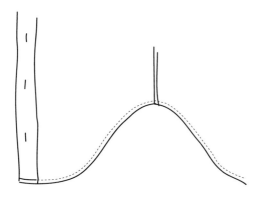

Sundry details

You may have noticed that I did not include a pocket in the list of elements of a dress shirt, simply because a pocket is not part of the traditional dress shirt. This may come as a shock to you, as it did to me when I bought my first Brooks Brothers shirt in the early 1960s when I was in high school. It was my first brush with a "gentleman's dress shirt," a gentleman presumably being someone who would never put anything in his shirt pocket even if he had one. Why? Because he had plenty of other pockets on his jacket and vest, and because he would never be seen in just his shirt sleeves anyway.

It's true that tailored outer garments can support any bulk or weight without distortion better and more sensibly than a shirt. It's also true that, once you get used to it, the absence of a pocket makes for a more elegant, smoother and simpler shirt front. In addition, it's a great boon to the shirtmaker to leave off the pocket, since making and applying it require refined skills in shaping, edgestitching and often pattern matching. Since all custom shirtmakers ask their clients whether a pocket is required and its absence is something of an indicator of custom work, I suggest you pass on a pocket. However, even Brooks

Brothers puts a pocket on these days, capitulating to popular demand, and so must you, very probably, if you're sewing for someone who can't imagine a shirt without a pocket. And it will only add to your skills to be able to put one on.

The classiest shirt pockets have rounded bottom edges, which are harder to make than pockets with square or pointed bottom edges, the round bottom serving no other purpose than to demonstrate beautiful sewing skills. Once committed to pockets, you can, of course, shape them any way you like as long as the pocket is closely edgestitched all around and reinforced at the corners with two rows of stitches. Look at your own ready-made shirts and see what you like best. Don't get too complicated, and you'll do fine. I've included a pocket pattern or two with some topstitching guidelines on pp. 77-78.

Since topstitching is such a prominent part of a well-made shirt, stitch length is of some importance. The longer the stitch length, the cheaper the look. Also, a short-stitched seam has more stretch than a long-stitched seam. The reason for this is that the shorter the stitch, the longer the path the thread has to travel over a given distance and, thus, the more give the seam has. Not only does a short-stitched seam (at least 16 stitches per inch) look better than one with a long stitch length, it's also easier to sew accurately, because the sewing proceeds more slowly. On very fine shirting materials, even 24 stitches per inch may not be too many. Whatever stitch length you decide upon, use the same length throughout the shirt, whether you're construction stitching or topstitching. When turning corners and rounding curves that will be turned inside out, like collar and cuff ends, use a stitch length as short as possible.

With regard to thread color, always use an exact match with the fabric or a slightly lighter color; try a grey in the same value range if you can't find a match. If the material is multicolored, match the thread with the lightest color. If there's any white in the fabric, use white thread.

PART TWO
PATTERNMAKING

CHAPTER FOUR

MAKING SHIRTS FIT

*T*he classic shirt we've been discussing is a man's garment that looks great on a woman. And while there's basically only one shirt style for men, with minor detail variations and two collar types (one with a stand and one without), there are dozens of ways in which elements of a man's shirt have been adapted to women's blouses, which are a much bigger category of garment. A woman might find a dress-shirt collar and stand designed for a tie on a pleated, ruffled and darted blouse with set-in sleeves and no yoke. Virtual facsimiles of the man's dress shirt with all the parts and details scaled to fit a woman are commonplace. Or a woman can simply wear a man's shirt, as many have done and everyone agrees looks wonderful. The point is that the classic shirt evolved to fit a figure without a bust. Coming up with ways to accommodate and flatter the bust has given rise to endless options for a woman's shirt/blouse, and so, for women, there's no simple answer to the question, does it fit?

Because the dressmaker's method of fitting the bust — by adding darts — isn't a very shirtlike solution to the issue, a basic shirt pattern for a woman with a C or D bust can get additional fullness by replacing the darts with shoulder pleats or gathers, or with dropped-shoulder seams, deep armholes and a very loose fit. The easiest way to get this look is just to use a man's shirt pattern, possibly recutting the sleeves and/or collar to fit a bit more closely. In short, there are a lot of ways to adapt the classic shirt for a woman.

For that reason, I've aimed the following discussion of fitting and my fitting process in Chapter 5 at fitting a man. This is not because those sewing for a woman shouldn't read and use the information — they should — but simply because there are so many more options for a woman's "shirt." Those sewing

for women are also much more likely to have dealt before with fitting in general and to have already arrived at some solutions to individual fitting problems, like a basic fitted shell or an adjusted shirt-style pattern. I'll have some more comments on fitting with my method when we get to Chapter 5 on draping a pattern. Meanwhile, let's look briefly at the evolution and salient features of fit in a man's dress shirt.

THE WELL-FITTED SHIRT

The dress shirt is a subtle garment evolved from a very simple one, which still reflects some of its simple origins. The first woven "tops" were made entirely from rectangular pieces, with no shaping for body curves at all. A shirt was thus a long rectangle of fabric with a hole in the middle for the head, two small rectangles of fabric for the arms and side seams that stitched it all together.

EVOLUTION OF THE CLASSIC SHIRT

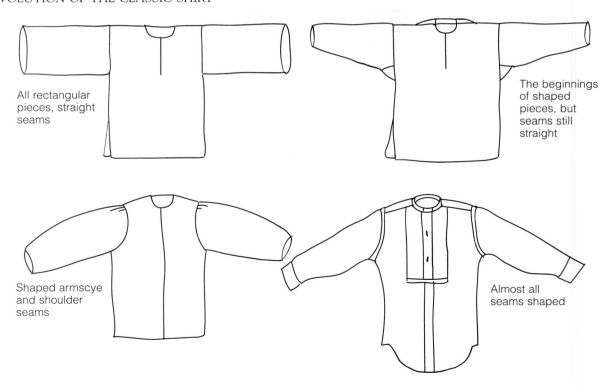

All rectangular pieces, straight seams

The beginnings of shaped pieces, but seams still straight

Shaped armscye and shoulder seams

Almost all seams shaped

Gradually those charged with making garments noticed that people's shoulders sloped, that their arms and torsos tapered and that they generally kept their arms down at their sides, not held out straight. As a result, shaped seams began to emerge. Chief among these was the shoulder seam, and today a well-fitted shoulder is the primary indicator of a well-fitted shirt. With a well-fitted shoulder there are no wrinkles along the line from armpit to neck, either in front or in back.

Shaped clothing from woven materials has, of course, evolved way beyond even the modern shirt, which still uses a one-piece sleeve and has no darts front or back, relying instead on shaped side seams to achieve a good fit in the torso. The shirt has lagged behind, for instance, the suit jacket, allowing

comfort and utility to take precedence over style — that is, the shirt's rectangular fit allows for maximum movement at the expense of a smooth, body-shaped fit. The shoulder is, in fact, the only part of a modern shirt whose fit is definitive since even the fit of the collar and sleeve are subject to personal preference. I think you'll agree that shirt collars that are too tight to button or sleeves that don't reach the wrist simply don't fit, regardless of current style. Beyond that, however, there is quite a range of possibilities in terms of fit, and what follows is liberally laced with my own opinions.

Collar fit

Starting at the top and with the most complex part of the shirt, the chief attributes of collar fit are the tightness or looseness of the collar band and how high the top of the collar rests on the wearer's neck. Neither of these factors should in any way affect the fit of the shoulders and body, which are fitted first. Once these areas are well fitted, the neckline seam is established to rest comfortably on the neckline.

Mind you, the "neckline" is not really a line. It's an area — where the neck can be said to stop and the body begin. The main issue in establishing the neckline on a shirt is that it not be so high on the neck that it pulls the shoulders or front of the shirt away from the body. This problem can be caused by a collar that's too tight. Because the neck tapers toward the head, an overly tight collar must be positioned higher and higher in search of a comfortable diameter.

For a man, the size and fit of the tie is very important to the fit of the collar, and these two things should be considered together. The tie should never be pulled tighter than the collar stand, which produces unsightly wrinkles in the collar and shirt fronts. Thus, the fit of the collar determines the maximum tightness of the tie.

Some people like a tie to stick out a bit from a firm, snug knot; others prefer a soft, loose knot that lies flat against the chest. The first requires a snug

SHOULDER FIT

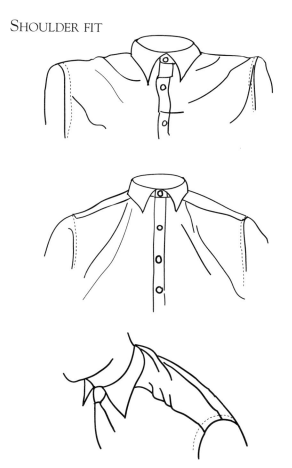

Shoulders that are square (top), sloping (middle) and forward-thrust (bottom) all cause ugly wrinkles when yoke is ill-fitting.

Varying height of collar affects look of tie.

*High, tight-fitting
collar allows firm knot
of tie to stick out.*

*Low, loose-fitting collar
allows soft, flat knot of tie.*

*Varying size of tie and tightness of
knot affects look of collar.*

collar, the second a loose one (see the drawing above). But there's more to this than just diameter. The snug, brisk look is associated with a higher collar, the loose look with a lower one. These variations are determined by the height of the stand and the shape of the collar itself, as adjusted to match the stand.

The size of the preferred knot also affects the proper amount of gap at the top of the stand, between the ends of the collar. The tie should not distort the graceful lay of the collar by being too large for it, nor should the tie be so small that the collar seems disproportionately large. All this is irrespective of the collar style chosen, whether rounded, cutaway, button-down or other, although the button-down collar is traditionally made with a ½-in. to ¾-in. gap. The choice, however, is entirely yours and depends on the current style for, or your taste in, necktie widths.

Shoulder fit

I've discussed the slope of the shoulders but not their length. For a man's shirt and a woman's shirt that aims to look like one, the yoke/sleeve seam should rest just on the shoulder point, neither falling off the shoulder onto the arm nor causing the sleeve to reach up over the arm to get to the yoke. The shape of your shoulder determines whether this point is, in fact, a point or more like an area. If it's hard to pick a precise shoulder point, tend toward a narrow fit if you're slender and a wider one if you're not.

Sleeve fit

Proper sleeve length is actually based upon cuff style and fit. A ready-made shirt has to have a loose-fitting cuff so it can accommodate, if necessary, a larger than average wrist. In effect, this results in people with average and smaller than average wrists wearing cuffs that don't fit. In a custom-made shirt, the cuff is made to fit the wearer properly, and consequently the sleeve can be long enough to provide a slight fullness or drape just above the cuff. This fullness is called wearing ease and allows the cuff to stay put even when the arms are raised or extended. Were wearing ease provided in a sleeve with a cuff that was too large, the cuff would dangle below the wrist. The standard then is that the sleeve length is right when the cuff hangs just where you want it, regardless of how you move your arms.

If you prefer a French cuff, which should be worn looser than a barrel cuff so that it lies smoothly, you'll probably have to make the sleeve a little shorter than you would for the barrel cuff. This prevents the French cuff from hanging too long when the arm is held down at your side. Since a suit jacket usually has a two-piece sleeve and inevitably moves up the arm as it is raised, the French cuff, which is not snug to the wrist, will move with the jacket. The barrel cuff, on the other hand, tends to stay with the wrist.

Of course, a dress shirt doesn't always have to have long sleeves, though a short-sleeve shirt is not as dressy with a suit coat since no cuffs show. If you want a short sleeve, its bottom edge should reach the inner joint of the elbow, breaking over the forearm as it's raised. A short sleeve usually has a simple turned-up hem about 1 in. wide.

Sleeve width can vary greatly and is a matter of personal taste (see the drawing below). The traditional standard of sleeve width, however, is quite loose, with minimally shaped seams—recall the rectangle—producing the gathered drape at the wrist mentioned above. The more rectangular the sleeve's shoulder seam, the more loose folds will appear in the underarm and biceps area when the arm is at rest, and the greater the range of comfortable motion will be. This ease can be taken up by shaping the seam a bit more, which, in turn, correspondingly limits motion. Ideally, the wearer should be able to move freely without disturbing the fit of the shirt body, and for this, considerable wearing ease is required at the shoulder. A short sleeve is usually a little narrower than a long sleeve.

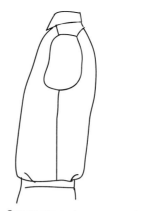

Snugness or looseness of shirt body is a matter of personal preference, but wrinkles at side seams are a sign of poorly fitted posture.

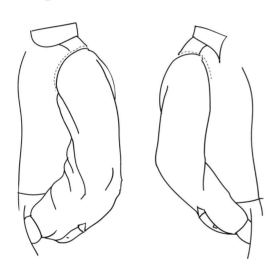

Width or looseness of sleeve is a matter of taste.

Side-seam wrinkles from slouched posture   *Side-seam wrinkles from very erect posture*

Body fit

The fit of the shirt body is based on two arguable points—comfort and fashion—and one indisputable factor—posture. Let's look at posture first.

How you hold your body, whether upright or slouched, stiff or relaxed, greatly influences the fit of your shirt and must be taken into account if that fit is to be accurate. Posture also affects the positioning of the shirt's neckline from front to back, which I adjust simultaneously with the shoulder fit when fitting the shirt's yoke (see pp. 43-44). The fit of the yoke, which should lie smoothly, is also affected by

the subtle postural effect of carrying the shoulders forward or keeping them back. The adjustment for this effect is made in the fit of the shirt's front and back, as you'll see in Chapter 5.

Posture has its most pronounced effect in the hang of the shirt's front and back. If you're wearing a ready-made garment and you slouch, you'll have diagonal wrinkles at the side seams. A custom shirt, however, will be properly fitted to accommodate your posture, preserve the correct hang of the shirt front and prevent wrinkles at the side seams.

Comfort and fashion are often at odds with each other in many articles of clothing but should be reconciled in a traditional shirt. This shirt hangs smoothly and freely on the shoulders and over the chest, and then never again conforms tightly to the body. It hangs in a subtle balance between snugness and bagginess, and yet is neither. And where that point is differs for each of us. You'll find it for yourself when making a pattern in Chapter 5.

The length of the shirt—or more accurately the length of the side seam—is determined by where you like to wear your waistband. You should be able to sit down and raise your arms straight above your head without pulling the side seams of your shirt up out from your trouser tops or skirt bands. Incidentally, the looser the shirt is at the waistline, the less tightly it should be tucked in so that the looseness will hang or drape smoothly around the waistband in a similar fashion to the sleeve draping around the snug cuff. The actual length of the shirttail hanging below the end of the side seam is a matter of personal taste. The best way to determine shirttail length is by measuring a shirt whose length you like.

In summary, a well-fitted garment of any sort looks as if it were made for your particular body, whereas a poorly fitted one looks like the wrong person is wearing it. A well-fitted garment never calls attention to itself and never emphasizes but always conceals variations in the wearer's body from the ideal.

ACHIEVING GOOD FIT

Fitting is the hardest part of sewing. In fact, it's a whole separate subject usually handled in books about nothing else. There are plenty of books on fitting, all aimed at the frustrated sewer for whom other fitting methods have failed. This abundance of books is not because the world is still waiting for a good fitting method, but rather because the problems of fit are complicated and unique to each person. That is to say, every body truly is complex and different; what constitutes good fit can be endlessly disputed; and there are countless variations in construction and style that affect where alterations are to be made. It's fitting expertise (and an eye for figure-flattering shapes) that makes fortunes for great tailors and dressmakers, not skill with the sewing

machine—*that* can be relegated to the sewing room, while "the master" cuts the pattern. Fit comes first because it's fit that makes people look good. Good sewing techniques only make garments look good. So even if you have no glaring defects of build and fit pretty well into ready-made clothes, you'll have to analyze your body and then face the fitting problems you do have if you want a true custom fit.

Nonetheless—and despite the elaborate descriptions you've just read of the ways the various parts of a shirt need to fit—you can relax. Shirts are simply not hard to fit. As I've been hinting all through the preceding material, I've got a fitting method that makes fitting the neckline, shoulders and body of the shirt to your unique posture easy and intuitive. This method is described beginning on p. 42. You'll need no body measurements, and you can even get along, if you want to, without buying a pattern. All the other fitting issues described above you can handle with simple measurements, so that your first shirt will fit well enough to wear with pride. You may want to refine the details, but you can do that to your heart's content as you make more shirts from the initial pattern. Fitting issues are complex, but, fortunately, shirts are not.

Understanding fit is largely a question of raised awareness. All of us, particularly men, are more or less used to the fit of ready-made shirts. We don't think about fit much, provided we can button a shirt and move comfortably. Once you start sewing, however, it's inevitable that your attention is drawn more and more to clothing, and fit—or the absence of it—increasingly becomes an issue. Nowadays whenever I see someone wearing a shirt, I automatically notice how the shoulders hang and the yoke rests, and where the garment is straining.

If you're new to questions of fit, I suggest that you spend some time in front of a good mirror investigating how your clothes—particularly shirts—fit. Move about in them, slouch, puff up your chest or tummy, square your shoulders and raise your arms. Move in all sorts of ways to see how various body shapes and postures affect the fit of your garment.

You may start to feel, as I did, that you don't have any shirts that really fit well, even though the sleeves are the right length and nothing is too tight. Don't worry; all the more reason to make your own. Try to find the posture that the shirt you're wearing was made to fit. Then, when you return to your normal posture, you'll see what this position does to spoil the effect. We'll be aiming at a solution that looks relaxed and appropriate to your normal stance. But notice that even minimal movement spoils any garment's fit, and the more fitted the garment, the more easily its fit is disturbed. You'll probably also notice, paradoxically, that you have lots of shirts that *almost* fit well, but they seem to look good in subtly different ways. Different fabrics and different styles can create substantially different effects within a basically similar family of garments, but getting a grip on that is where your lifetime of future sewing pleasure comes in. For now, if we stick to classic dress shirts, we can get off to a sure start.

DEVELOPING A SHIRT PATTERN THAT FITS

Since shirts are the only garments I can think of for which yokes are a basic element and not just a decorative possibility, let's start with the yoke. Every fitting method I've seen either regards the yoke of a shirt as an alterable piece, suggesting that it be cut, spread, trimmed and so on, or adjusts a basic shirt shell with no yoke, only a front and back and a single shoulder seam. In the latter method, a yoke is simply drawn in on the basic shell to replace the single shoulder seam with two new seams, as if the yoke itself did not affect fit at all. Neither approach makes sense to me as a way of fitting shirts. Both seem like attempts to make a yoked garment adapt to general fitting solutions. In contrast, we're going to adapt the fitting solution to the yoked garment.

The yoke is a fashion detail that's recognizable to most eyes, and for that reason its shape cannot be altered appreciably. In any case, you need not change the yoke's shape since you can make any necessary fitting adjustments with slight, unnoticeable

alterations in the shirt front and back. Thus, my first rule for fitting a shirt is: Start with a yoke that fits across the shoulders, and don't adjust its shape unless you want to change its width from front to back. The yoke should be straight across the back edge, angled across the front edges and more or less square at the armscyes.

Of course, the yoke also includes the back of the neckline seam. That area can and should be adjusted to fit the neck, but we'll deal with the neckline later, once you've settled on a yoke that fits the shoulders.

BUILDING SHAPE INTO YOKE SEAM

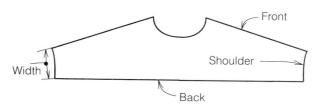

Unshaped seam

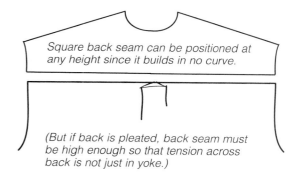

Square back seam can be positioned at any height since it builds in no curve.

(But if back is pleated, back seam must be high enough so that tension across back is not just in yoke.)

Shaped seam

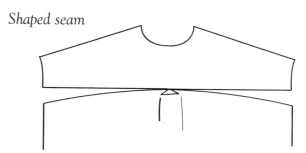

A rounded back sewn to a straight-bottomed yoke acts as two darts that meet in the middle, and seam must be positioned at curve in wearer's back.

SHAPING SHOULDER SEAM

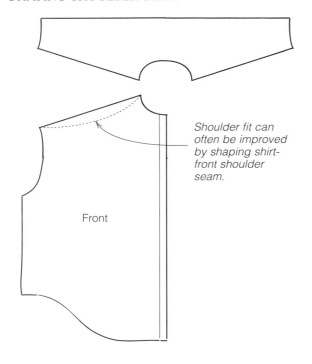

Shoulder fit can often be improved by shaping shirt-front shoulder seam.

Front

My second rule of shirt fitting is: Always adjust the shoulder seams of the front and back to fit the yoke. These seams can be easily shaped to accommodate the complex curves of the shoulders and upper back. For example, if the top edge of the shirt back and the back of the yoke are both perfectly straight, the seam would likewise be straight and not shape the back at all. But if you curve the back's top edge and leave the yoke unaltered, as in the bottom drawing on p. 35, the resulting seam joining them essentially incorporates two horizontal darts pointing to the middle, adding shape to the back of the shirt. Where that curve occurs—and the extent of it — greatly affects the fit of the shirt. The narrow yoke of the classic shirt described earlier puts the curve at a good place for most people, but other widths can work too. We'll determine how much to curve the seam and whether to change the width as we fit.

The shirt front's shoulder seamlines are the place for adjustments for shoulder slope, which almost everyone requires to some degree or another. This is by far the easiest place to provide it. We can also shape this seam with a slight curve if needed to fit the hollow between the shoulder and the chest better, as shown in the drawing at left.

Let's now consider the pattern as a whole. There are four basic approaches to developing a shirt pattern: adjusting a commercial pattern; drafting your own pattern; copying an existing shirt; or combining the best of the first three methods. I propose the combined approach, but let's look first at each method separately.

Adjusting a commercial pattern

At the heart of adjusting a commercial pattern is fitting a trial garment based on the selected pattern. The problems inherent in this method are what size pattern to get and how to adjust it once you've made a muslin version and can see that it doesn't fit. These points are covered in the standard books on fitting and adjusting patterns, which I'm proposing we just ignore, at least long enough to consider my alternative method. For my method, we'll take full advantage of the fact that patterns provide you with a coherent set of shapes whose seams are all matched in length and whose details are already established and drawn. We can get these shapes from a pattern we buy, or from one we make, as described below, whichever seems easier. After doing it a few times, I'm convinced that making your own is much easier, but both ways can work well.

If you choose to buy and alter a pattern, I recommend that you first measure a few significant places on one or several of your comfortable shirts so that you begin to know what measurements you'll need on your own pattern. With the shirt laid flat on a table and the arms outstretched, measure the width of the body a little below the armhole, the body's

MEASURING FIT OF COLLAR STAND

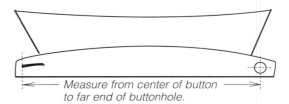

Measure from center of button to far end of buttonhole.

length at center front, the width of the sleeve and the width of the yoke. Then, on a shirt whose neck fit you like, open the neck straight out and measure from the front edge of the buttonhole to the center of the button on the opposite side, as shown in the bottom drawing on the facing page.

Drafting your own pattern

Drafting your own pattern depends on having access to a draft, that is, a set of instructions to follow for a generic shirt into which you plug various measurements, whether your own or a standardized set, representing sleeve length, chest measure and so on. The draft produces basically the same kind of pattern as a commercial pattern, with the measured items already adjusted, except that most commercial patterns have been styled or refined by a designer to a certain degree, while the drafts I've seen are very basic. They're also relatively hard to locate and don't represent much of an advance, if any, over commercial patterns, so I suggest skipping this approach unless you happen to find a draft that appeals to you.

Nonetheless, drafting a pattern gives one a great sense of power over patterns in general. It makes it forever impossible to be afraid of changing them. I've tried to incorporate a little of this spirit into all of the fitting work to come, particularly with regard to simple shapes like cuffs and collars, and I encourage you to change any pattern shape once you see the need for it, or if you have an idea you want to try.

Copying existing shirts

There are lots of complex methods for copying or making patterns from existing garments, but you don't need any of them to copy most shirts. Here I describe a method you can use to copy any simple, undarted, ungathered garment whose parts will lie flat. You'll need some large sheets of paper, at least as big as your shirt from center front to side seams, and from collar to hem. You can use bona fide pattern paper, available from some fabric stores (see the Sources of Supply on pp. 164-167), which is marked with a grid that's a big help in keeping the garment sections straight and on grain, but any paper will do — try rolls of wrapping paper, shelf paper or butcher's paper.

The general idea is to tape or pin the paper over a thick, folded towel or similar padded surface, then simply lay down the garment section to be traced, anchor it so it doesn't move and poke a pin through both the seamlines and the pattern paper into the towel or padding below. Continue pricking along all the seamlines and when you've finished, you'll have a silhouette of the pattern piece marked with pinhole dots, which you then connect in pen or pencil.

To copy a shirt, you need to make only half of all the pattern pieces (front, back, yoke, collar, stand and cuffs), except for the sleeves. Start by folding the shirt exactly along one side seam, so that the entire back is out of sight. It doesn't matter which side you pick. If you want to mark a pocket position, copy that side. Then make sure the center front is as straight as possible. Pin it securely to the towel so you can smooth the front out, using the center front as a grain reference (Step 1 in the drawing on p. 38). Don't worry about the shirt back underneath, just pin through it. Copy the back in the same way, but first pin out any pleats from top to bottom, and pin-mark the center back so it's easy to follow (Step 2). Repeat the process for half of the yoke, again marking center back (Step 3).

Even though you need a full pattern for the sleeve, you can copy only half of it at a time. Start by folding the sleeve along the underarm seam and smoothing it over to find the center line that runs on grain from the top of the sleeve cap down to the cuff. Pin along this center line, keeping it as straight as possible and working down the sleeve until you're about 2 in. from the cuff and any gathers or pleats at the cuff have started to spread apart (Step 4). Smooth back the fabric to the underarm seam and pin down from the armscye to the same point from the cuff. Then check along the armhole seam to see that the fabric is on grain. Feel through the fabric to find the back half of that seam; it's often a different curve. If so, pin-mark both front and back armscye curves on your pattern paper without moving the sleeve.

Next mark along the cuff/sleeve seam, and extend the center line down straight to meet it. Continue the curve of the seamline smoothly down to meet the

COPYING A SHIRT

1

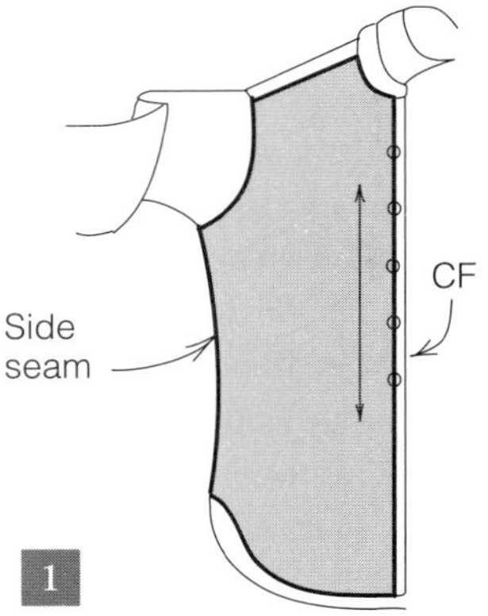

Side seam — CF

With shirt positioned over pattern paper and padded surface and anchored with several pins, poke a pin through seamlines to transfer pattern shape to paper. First pin through center front (CF) in a straight line, smooth out front to side seam and pin at corners, keeping fabric on grain and unwrinkled.

2

Pin closed any pleats in back and repeat process for half of back. CB — Side seam

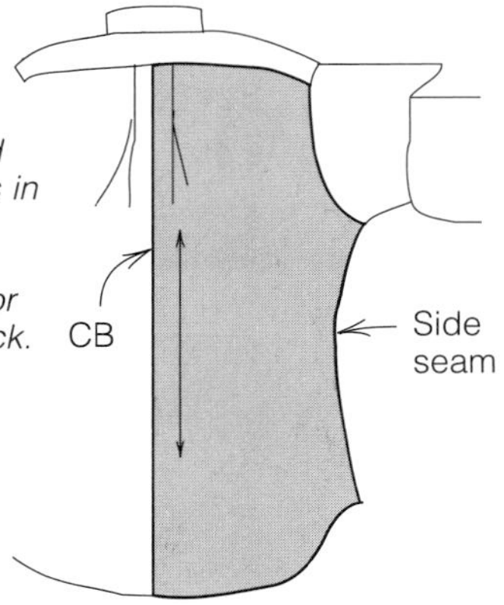

3

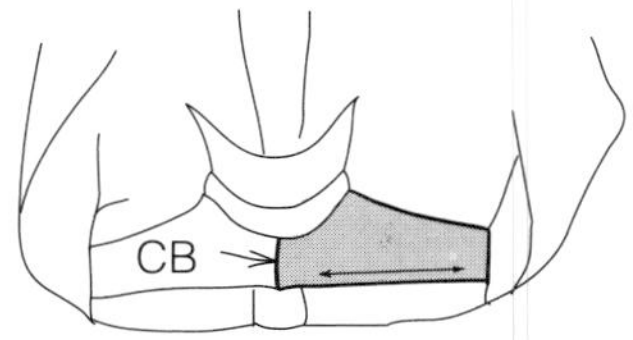

CB

Pin half of yoke down flat, disregarding how rest of shirt falls, and pin around shape, marking center back (CB).

5

CL

CL

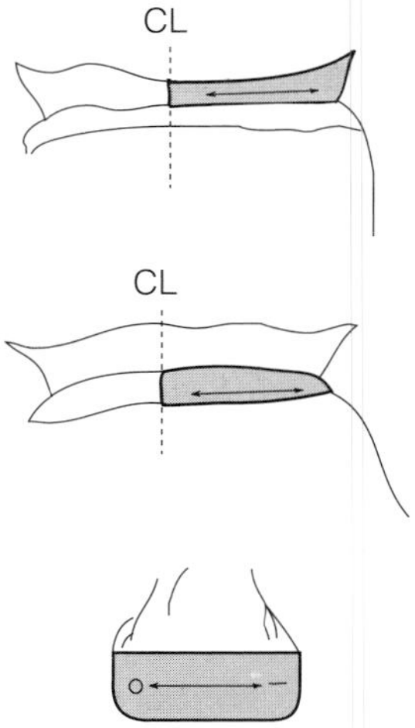

Find center of collar and stand. Arrange each separately on grain and pin around. Be sure to pin collar and stand separately to preserve grain. Pin around complete cuff, if possible.

4

CL — Back half of armhole seam — Underarm seam

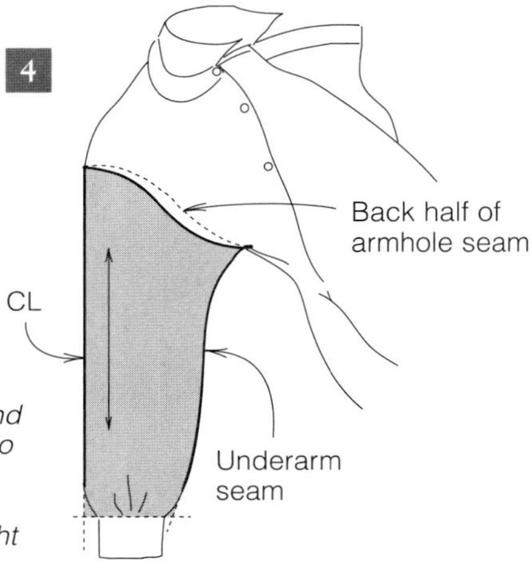

Fold and pin sleeve at underarm seam, and smooth over to center line (CL) from cap to cuff. Pin down center as far as possible toward cuff. Pin-mark sleeve-cap curves, front and back. Estimate position of straight line through top of cuff.

cuff on the other side. If the cuff seamline seems curved or different front and back, find a midpoint compromise and draw a straight line through it at right angles to the center line. Draw a center line the length of the sleeve on another piece of pattern paper and line up your half-sleeve pattern along it. Trace around it and flip the pattern over to trace the back half of the sleeve, noting any differences in the shape of the sleeve cap, front and back. The slash for the placket should be centered above the cuff seam on the back half of the sleeve.

When you take a pattern of a collar and its stand, adjust each piece separately on the pattern paper for straightness of grain since the seam connecting them is usually shaped rather than flat (Step 5). This is how I derived the patterns included in Chapter 6.

For the most accurate results, take a pattern by this method from a woven plaid, checked or striped shirt so the grain is always easy to see and you can immediately tell if you're distorting the shape of the garment section as you smooth it out flat. Just keep the lines straight and the checks square. If your shirt has no plaid, try to keep the threads themselves straight. If you can't see them well enough, just watch out for tension in the fabric. You don't want to stretch the fabric, just keep it smooth and relaxed. Don't worry about getting every last inch and apparent subtlety of the shape perfect. All you need is a basic outline to start the fitting with.

When you've got all the parts transferred to paper, straighten and smooth the lines with a straightedge and a dressmaker's curve. Then check and correct the lengths of the seamlines to make sure they'll fit together.

Combined patternmaking method

The combined method of patternmaking is what I call the drape method. It's different from classic draping because we won't start quite from scratch. Instead, we'll work around a few pattern shapes, like the yoke and matched armscye and sleeve cap. You can either pick a shirt whose yoke, sleeve fit and general shape you like and copy the yoke and shape of the armscye and sleeve cap, or select an appropriate traditional commercial pattern and use these parts of it.

Determining the size of commercial pattern you need to get can be a little tricky. For both men and women, the easiest dimension to match to your actual measurements is the length of the yoke. None of the shirt parts is really difficult to alter, but it's useful to start with the yoke because the shoulders generally suggest the size of the frame. If you get the yoke right, you've got a good chance of keeping the rest of the shirt in proportion. The trouble is that patterns don't, as a rule, tell you the yoke length. So unless you can open up the pattern at the store and measure it, you'll have to revert to chest measure.

To find your own yoke size, measure across the top of your shoulders at the back just below your neck, from the point where you want the armhole seam to rest to the same point on the other side. If you find you're too big or too small for the yoke in your commercial pattern, see the drawing above for some suggestions about altering the yoke.

ALTERING A YOKE PATTERN

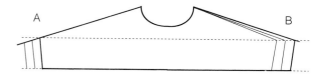

If you need to alter biggest or smallest available yoke to fit your shoulders, note that alteration A changes height of yoke end and hence armhole size. Alteration B does not change yoke's end height but does change yoke's length. If you alter yoke, make corresponding changes in front and back (done automatically in the drape method) and recheck sleeve cap to see that it still fits yoke.

Once the yoke is settled, we're going to proceed as follows: Instead of making a muslin version of our pattern, we're going to construct a pattern on the person for whom we're sewing — which may be ourselves — by pinning lengths of gingham (or any lightweight cotton or blend whose woven pattern clearly shows the grain) so that it drapes smoothly over the body. Then we'll trace the armscye seam shapes from the shirt whose yoke you copied or from the commercial pattern onto the fabric. After we perfect the body shape, we'll alter the remaining pattern pieces to match the new pattern we're draping.

This approach is a great improvement over pinning a paper pattern together and holding it up to the body to check for fit. In the process, we'll gradually produce, piece by piece, a well-fitted "muslin" gingham shirt, which we'll then trace to create our pattern. This entire process will take some time, so set aside an afternoon, and ask a friend to help if you're fitting yourself.

A final word before you move on to Chapter 5 and try out this method. I would be the last to suggest that my drape method is the best of all possible pattern-fitting techniques. It is only the best method I've found, and it's very specific to shirts. This method is based on my experience, and so it seems easy to me. By all means, use any method you like to fit your pattern, but please don't fiddle with the yoke!

CHAPTER FIVE

DEVELOPING A BASIC PATTERN

he purpose of the drape method described in this chapter is to fit the yoke, fronts and back of the shirt to a man's body, especially in the shoulders, so that the yoke lies smoothly across the shoulders and against the neck, and the fronts and back fall without wrinkles from the yoke. The method for developing a woman's shirt pattern is the same as that for a man's, except for some bustline and shoulder-length details, which I'll discuss immediately following the man's drape (see pp. 48-51).

Before we get into the draping process, a word on symmetry. Almost no body is perfectly symmetrical, and the most typical, and critical, asymmetry is found in the shoulders. Unequal biceps or wrists don't present a problem. You can ignore the biceps and fix the cuff with button placement or two different cuff patterns. But if your shoulders are unequal, you must decide whether you want a symmetrical pattern (and the garment it will produce) or an asymmetrical one. You've probably never had an asymmetrically fitting garment, so you can't really answer the question. But if an asymmetrical pattern gives you a good fit for the first time in your life, you'll probably find it hard to go back to a symmetrical pattern.

On the other hand, a symmetrical pattern enables you to cut out identical halves on a fold or through two layers of fabric, and you'll thus need only half-patterns. If your pattern is asymmetrical, you'll need separate patterns for both fronts, a full back and so on. You also need to remember that you cannot cut out an asymmetrical pattern on a bold plaid fabric and have the seams and other details fall at the same place in the plaid on each side. Such fabric calls attention to asymmetry. Yet if you've really got your heart set on a bold plaid, I'd say use it—a poor fit will be even more noticeable than an asymmetrical plaid.

My opinion has wavered over the years from favoring a symmetrical pattern at all costs to voting definitively for asymmetry. These days I'm tending toward asymmetry because there's no question that the fit is more exact, and I don't think differences in the way the fabric is cut are usually very obvious. The drape method automatically provides an asymmetrical pattern if your body is asymmetrical, so you have to go back and adjust it to find a working compromise if you want identical sides.

Ideally you should perhaps have two patterns if you're only slightly asymmetrical: one that's asymmetrical for plain, narrow-striped or subtly patterned fabrics; and one that's symmetrical for big plaids and strong patterns that might make the asymmetry more obvious. If you never make shirts from such fabrics, the choice is easy. In any event, I advise you to stick to my policy of having a symmetrical yoke. Also keep the armscyes the same

so the sleeves can be the same, at least in width. Different sleeve lengths would not be very obvious, and it would also be easy to trim one sleeve shorter after cutting them out together for efficiency.

If you're an inch or more different on opposite sides of your body, I think you're better off with an asymmetrical pattern, especially if you like a fairly fitted shirt. Less than that, and it's probably worth the added efficiency to try to find a good symmetrical compromise. It's not hard, just a matter of trial and error. Start by folding front and back patterns in half and finding the midline between unequal seams. When you're in doubt, favor the larger or longer side. Then draw new seams, baste them up and take a look.

THE DRAPE METHOD

To drape a pattern, you'll need the following:

- A commercial shirt pattern that includes a yoke you like that fits across your shoulders, or a yoke that you'll copy from a shirt whose fit and style you like.
- About 3 yd. of shirtweight cotton or cotton blend that has a woven plaid or check, so that you can tell at a glance whether the fabric is on or off grain. Gingham would be a good choice for this test fabric, but any similar remnant-counter fabric will do.
- A tight-fitting T-shirt (not a turtleneck) that will not shift around on your model and to which the yoke can be pinned.
- A couple of sharp permanent markers in different colors that you can easily see on your fabric.
- A good mirror.
- Scissors.
- A straightedge and a dressmaker's curve for truing up and smoothing lines.
- A work surface for tracing pattern shapes on the test fabric.
- A friend to help you if you're draping the shirt pattern on yourself (these directions assume that you're draping the pattern on someone else).

STEP 1. *PREPARING THE TEST-FABRIC YOKE.* Draw the seamlines of the yoke on the test fabric, mark center back, and cut out the yoke with a ⅝-in. seam allowance all around except at the neckline, where you should allow about ¾ in. Press under the front and back seam allowances, then the armscye ends, but leave the neckline unpressed. (If you're copying a yoke from a shirt you like, start by making a paper pattern of the yoke, as described on pp. 37-38, which you can then cut out in gingham, as described here.)

PREPARING THE YOKE

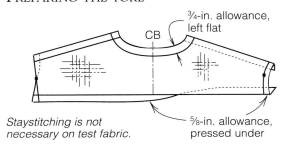

¾-in. allowance, left flat

CB

Staystitching is not necessary on test fabric.

⅝-in. allowance, pressed under

STEP 2. *POSITIONING THE YOKE AND CHECKING THE BACK NECKLINE.* The model should be wearing the T-shirt, which should be pinned tight if it's loose. Position the test-fabric yoke at center back, which you establish visually. Smooth the yoke across the shoulders, ignoring the neckline until the shoulders of the yoke look okay. If the neckline seems to be interfering with positioning the yoke, snip into the allowance a little so it can spread.

When the yoke is smooth, turn your attention to the relationship of the neck and neckline allowance. The allowance should be too small rather than too big, since in the latter case you would need to cut another yoke to add more fabric. Cautiously snip into the seam allowance until it seems to rest at a good place for the neckline, which may or may not be where it was indicated on the pattern. Try not to snip into the neckline allowance any more than is necessary to get it to lie smooth around the sides of the neck and still allow the yoke to lie smooth too.

POSITIONING YOKE ON MODEL

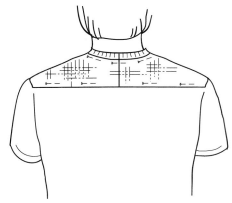

Arrange and pin yoke to T-shirt so fit looks good and yoke is entirely free of wrinkles.

Looking from the side, make sure the neckline does not drop down much below the high point of the shoulders (see the drawing below). Imagine the straight section at the center back of a collar sticking up from the neckline. Would it lie against the back of the neck, or would it tend to pull away? To check this, try wrapping a folded strip of fabric around the neck. From the front, do you like the position of the yoke fronts against the shoulder? If you're not happy with the way the yoke looks, mark a new line (the same on both sides, so the yoke remains symmetrical) and press the seamline again.

If the shoulders are very hollow, the yoke will not be able to follow them without wrinkling, but that's life. You can't really fix this problem without padding

CHECKING NECKLINE FROM SIDE

Neckline should not dip too low in back.

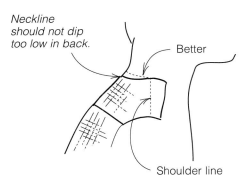

Better

Shoulder line

the shoulders. You can experiment with a slightly narrower or wider yoke from front to back, which might help, but the weight of the fabric when the shirt is complete will help too. Does it look as though the ends of the back neckline could join the front neckline in a smooth curve? If not, redraw them. Do you like the position of the ends of the yoke? If not, mark and press new ends. When all is well, proceed to the next step.

STEP 3. PREPARING THE TEST-FABRIC FRONTS. Cut off a length of test fabric that's long enough to go from neckline to hem, plus about 3 in. Hold it up to your model and measure the width by eye so that it's more than wide enough to go around the front of the chest — or waist if that's bigger — and cut it. Fold the test fabric along a center-front line that coincides with a prominent vertical line of any pattern on the fabric, and mark center front.

Hold your thumb and forefinger up to measure the width of the neck from side to side, then transfer this rough measurement to a ruler and halve it. Mark this half-measure at one end of the center-front line, then reduce it about ½ in. so it's definitely smaller than the model's neck. Draw a U-shaped neckline from this mark so that it's centered on the center-front line, as shown in the drawing at left below. Then cut out the neckline on the fold.

STEP 4. DRAPING THE FRONT. Hold the neckline U up to the model's center front, which you establish by eye. Then pin the center front to the T-shirt when the bottom of the U is snug against the model's neck in front. Pin the center front at the waistline too.

Pick one side to start on, then lift up the top corner of the test fabric on that side until the grain is straight and horizontal from the center front out to the edge. Without allowing the fabric to droop, lay it down over the shoulder. Check the grain again, and when it's horizontal, pin the muslin to the middle of the yoke and out in both directions until it's smooth from neck to armscye. Clip the neckline seam allowance minimally, if necessary.

CUTTING MUSLIN FOR FRONT

Unfolded width equals chest measurement plus 4 in. to 5 in.

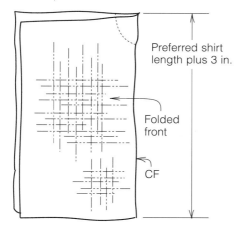

Preferred shirt length plus 3 in.

Folded front

CF

Cut rectangle on lengthwise grain, mark center line and fold along line. Cut semicircle at top ½ in. less than half neckline measurement.

DRAPING THE FRONT

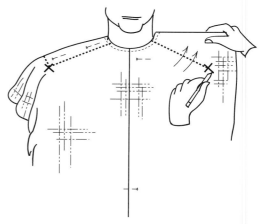

Position front so it's centered and snug to neckline. Lift and pin corners of rectangle to make front hang smoothly, and trace yoke's pressed front edge onto front.

Feel through the test-fabric front to find the pressed front edge of the yoke, and mark it on the front with dots from the neckline to the armscye end. Make a crossmark at the end. Repeat the procedure on the other side, then recheck the grain across the whole front, correcting it if necessary.

STEP 5. ESTABLISHING THE FRONT NECKLINE. Look at the neckline from the front, and clip around it wherever necessary to get the test fabric to lie flat at the neckline. Don't get carried away with clipping. You want to produce what looks like the snuggest-fitting neck the model can stand. Draw the ends of the front neckline to blend smoothly into the back neckline.

STEP 6. DRAPING THE BACK. Cut another big test-fabric rectangle for the back, and mark center back on it. Pin the test fabric to the center back of the yoke with about a 1-in. overlap at the seamline, and then pin the center back at the waist too. Don't worry about adding a pleat or gathers to the back yoke while you're draping the pattern, which should fit well without either. If you want a pleat or gathers, add it to the pattern before cutting out your real shirting fabric.

Next, lift up the corners of the gingham and mark the yoke edges through the test-fabric back for both sides, just as you did on the front. Put a crossmark at the armscye ends of the yoke.

If the model's back is rounded so it sticks out beyond the bottom edge of the yoke, the fabric will want to fold into a little dart as you try to smooth it to meet the yoke, as shown in the drawing at right. You can put the dart in with pins if you like, which could become gathers or pleats in the finished shirt, or you could cut another, wider yoke that extends to the point of the dart (see pp. 35-36 for more information on shaping the back/yoke seam). Cutting a wider yoke would allow all the needed dart shaping to go into the back/yoke seam.

DARTING BACK YOKE ON ROUNDED BACK

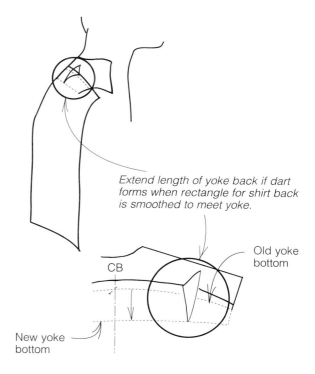

Extend length of yoke back if dart forms when rectangle for shirt back is smoothed to meet yoke.

Old yoke bottom

CB

New yoke bottom

Position new yoke bottom at point of dart and recut back to eliminate dart.

I should add that if you're making shirts for someone who slouches, you might notice that even after you've draped a shirt body the neckline (and often the whole yoke) tends to pull away from the neck toward the back, as shown in the drawing on the next page. One solution that's worked for a friend of mine is to take a horizontal fold out of the chest area of the shirt body from armscye to armscye. This adjustment works because slouching reduces the length of the chest, while stretching the back length. The fold reduces the front armscyes and the chest fabric in between, which will hold the neckline and yoke down against the body. Anywhere from ¼ in. to ¾ in. may need to be folded out, and trial and error is the only way to be sure. Pin out a small fold first, and give it a try.

ADJUSTING A PATTERN FOR FIGURES THAT SLOUCH

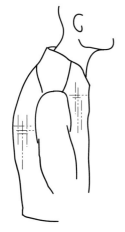

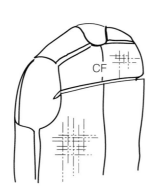

If neckline (and perhaps yoke) pulls away from neck toward back…

…try pinning a horizontal fold across front.

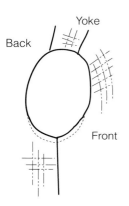

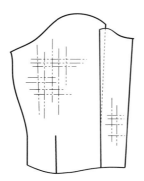

To make sure sleeve still fits after adjusting front, either drop armscye at side seam…

…or slash sleeve in front and pivot from cuff to armscye to reduce sleeve-cap length in front only.

This adjustment makes the armscye smaller. So you can either lower the armscye a little at the side seam to return it to its full length (that way the front half of the seam is still shorter than the back), or you can slash the sleeve in front, as shown in the drawing above, and pivot out the amount of the fold. To decide which correction to make, have the model wear the adjusted body drape around for a few minutes to see if the shorter armscye is too short.

DRAWING AN ARMSCYE

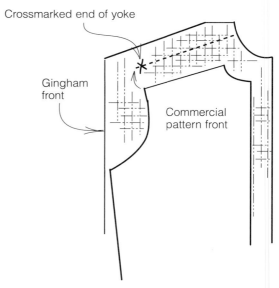

With commercial pattern front laid on top of draped front, match top of armscye to crossmarked end of yoke. Trace armscye onto gingham, extending seamline if necessary.

STEP 7. *TRANSFERRING THE ARMSCYES FROM THE PATTERN TO THE TEST FABRIC.* When you're sure the front and back test-fabric rectangles are clearly and accurately marked, label and unpin them and then lay them flat on your work surface. Starting with the front, align the point on the pattern where the armscye and yoke seams cross with the crossmarked point on one side of the test fabric. Then pivot the pattern from that point until the center fronts on both pattern and test fabric are parallel. They may not be in the same place, but they should be parallel. Trace the armscye seamline onto the test fabric, then repeat this process for both sides, front and back.

If you notice any asymmetry in your work, don't worry about it for the time being. Draw a straight vertical line down from the bottom of each armscye to the hem as a reference line for the side-seam adjustments. Smooth out (but don't flatten) the curves you marked at the yoke seamline on the front and back pieces with your dressmaker's curve. You can't have any wavy lines. Trim the yoke and armscye seams to create about a 1-in. seam allowance, but don't trim the side seams if you think the waist is bigger than the chest (see the discussion below). Otherwise, go ahead and trim those seams too.

Swinging out side seam to accommodate full waist

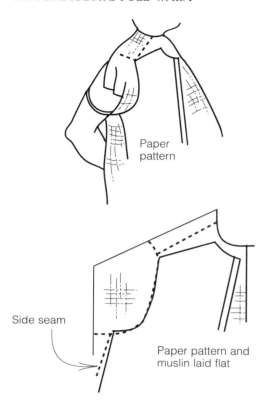

Paper pattern

Side seam

Paper pattern and muslin laid flat

Altering front neckline

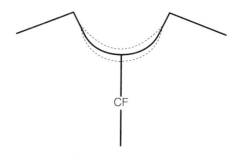

CF

To make circumference changes of less than ¾ in., raise or lower front neckline. This change is automatically made in the drape method. On commercial patterns, redraw pattern's neckline.

STEP 8. CHECKING YOUR PROGRESS AND ADJUSTING THE SIDE SEAMS. Unpin the yoke and machine-baste the back and front to it, with right sides together. Slit the center front about 6 in. so it will slip over the model's head, but pin a fabric scrap to one side of the slit so you can pin the front closed once it's on the model. With the front closed, pin the side seams at the bottom of the armscyes and at a few points down the lines you drew. Then stand back and check your work.

If you're not happy with the yoke/shoulder fit, ignore it for the moment and concentrate on the side seams. What you want here is for the circumference of the shirt to skim the girth of the body with the closeness of fit the model prefers, while also making sure there are no obvious diagonal wrinkles emerging front or back across the side seams. If there are, you can probably correct them by shifting the seams up and down a little in relation to each other so they no longer match at the armscye. If there's a big belly to

accommodate, the front side seams will have to be off-grain, swinging outward as they near the waist, as shown in the drawing at left.

When you like the fit, mark the new seams front and back, deciding at the same time how long you want them. Now back to the yoke. The most likely problem here, if there is one, is overfitting of either the curves or the shoulder slope. It's a good idea on every pattern, especially if the shoulders slope a lot, to add a little ease to the seam, tapering from nothing at the neck to ⅛ in. or ¼ in. at the armscye, front and back. This may be all the help you need. Also try flattening out the usually concave curve you drew for the front shoulder seamline. If none of this helps, check your work, because if the yoke was smooth when you draped the fronts and back to it, it still should be.

Now consider relaxing the neckline fit a little by dropping it in front, up to ¼ in., if the wearer wants an easy fit there, which most people do. You can check this fit and find the collar stand's length by folding a thin strip of fabric to about a 1-in. width, then wrapping it around the neckline and carefully pinning its edge, first at center back, then along the neckline in one or two places, then crossing it at center front.

Finally, decide where you want the hem to be. It's usually a little longer in back than in front, since it's most likely to pull out in back, but that's up to you. You can always cut the hem another way on subsequent shirts, but for the moment pick the hem shape you think you'll want on most shirts.

STEP 9. MEASURING SLEEVE LENGTH AND COMPLETING THE BODY AND YOKE PATTERNS. The basic steps of draping the shirt body are finished at this point. The way you'll treat the center-front opening depends entirely on the kind of opening you want on your shirt (for information on the classic construction of the center front, see pp. 116-117; for more center-front options, see Chapter 9). The rest of the shirt, that is, the sleeves, cuffs and collar, can be fitted with measurements (we'll look in greater detail at making collar patterns in Chapter 6), but you might like to try the effect of the adjustments described below on one or both sleeves in test fabric, machine-basted in place. I wouldn't bother to put cuffs on the test sleeves, but you could. In any case, the next step is to measure from the top of the armscye seam to the point on the wrist where you want the cuff to end. Add 1 in. for ease, then subtract the cuff width, and that's your sleeve length (see the drawing below).

When you've finished testing, unbaste the seams and fold the front and back along their respective center lines. Then note the degree of asymmetry and decide whether you're going to make a symmetrical or asymmetrical pattern (see my guidelines on p. 42 for help in making your choice).

Before we discuss ways to refine a sleeve pattern, let's look at how a woman's drape would proceed up to this point. Then I'll come back to sleeves to tell you how to perfect a pattern. And, for anyone having trouble with the sleeve who wants to create a pattern from scratch, I'll discuss some sleeve-pattern basics. In Chapter 8, I'll give you some guidelines on cutting out the pattern you've just draped in your shirting fabric.

DRAPING A WOMAN'S SHIRT PATTERN

The only reason for a woman's shirt drape to differ from a man's is if the bust is full enough to require additional fitting. Typically, a shirt with fitted shoulders (which is what we've been talking about up to now) fits loosely enough in the chest to accommodate a size A or B bust easily without darts or other means to provide more room. A size C or larger bust, however, usually needs the extra room that darts offer. Of course, if you've got a shirt you like that fits and has no darts, just copy that, drape the shoulders to customize the fit and skip this section.

The contemporary manufacturer's solution to fitting a wide range of women's sizes has been to make women's shirts so big that bust fullness isn't an issue. This is the "big shirt," or dropped-shoulder look. Dropped, or "extended," shoulders are made with yoke/shoulder seams that extend 1 in. or 2 in. beyond the actual shoulder point, as they would if the shirt were way too big (extending the seams any less would just make the shirt look misfitted). Since the armscye drops more or less straight down from the end of the yoke/shoulder seam as usual (in other words, it doesn't swing back in toward the chest to compensate for the extra-wide shoulder), the shirt body is wider, too, providing plenty of room for the bust.

MEASURING SLEEVE LENGTH

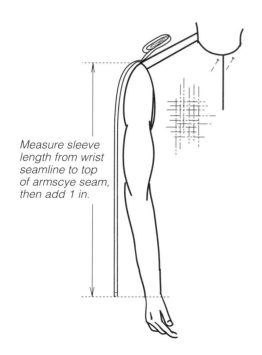

Measure sleeve length from wrist seamline to top of armscye seam, then add 1 in.

The dropped shoulder is simply one way of handling the fullness. It makes a virtue of this fullness, adding more all around to give the garment a balanced look. At the other extreme is the closer-fitting shirt with shoulders that match the body underneath, and darts, if necessary, to provide room at the bust. I don't think bust darts are any more appropriate on a classic shirt than back darts (which I discussed on pp. 20-21), and for the same reason: Shirts should fall loosely and smoothly from the shoulders, not mimic the contours of the body. Horizontal side-seam darts also obstruct the smooth vertical drape of the fabric. But anyone can still have fitted shoulders without all these problems. If you need a dart, you can simply pivot a horizontal bust dart to the shoulder seams or armscye and turn it into a seam, gathers, a pleat or a vertical dart. At least at the shoulder seam or armscye, the fullness will be handled vertically, like the flow of the fabric.

In any event, it's good to be able to fit both a shirt pattern with a dropped shoulder and one with a classic fitted shoulder. In either case, the place to start, as with a man's shirt, is with a pattern you make from a garment you like or with a commercial pattern. Again, all you really need from either pattern is a yoke you like and a matched armscye and sleeve cap. If you want shoulder pads, arrange them as you want them, either under the T-shirt or pinned to it, before you start.

A *pattern with extended shoulders*

These directions apply for a man's shirt used for a woman and for a woman's "big shirt" (they also apply to an extended-shoulder shirt for a man). Pin the yoke at center back as I explained above for the man's drape. (For any of the unexplained steps below, the procedure is the same as for the man's drape.) Fit the neckline, and make the test-fabric rectangle for the front. When draping the front and you get to the end of the shoulder, as you're feeling along the yoke's front edge, hold up the part of the yoke that's drooping off the shoulder. Extend the front yoke/shoulder seamline in a straight line out to the end of

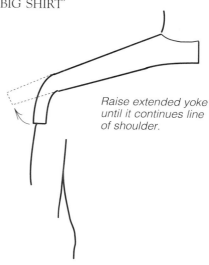

Raise extended yoke until it continues line of shoulder.

the yoke, as shown in the drawing above, keeping the angle you've established for the seam unchanged to the extended end point. Start the armscye, tracing from the end point as usual, and that's all there is to it. Continue the drape as described for a man, and when you get to the back, extend the back yoke seam as just described for the front yoke seam.

A *pattern with fitted shoulders*

To drape a shirt with a fitted shoulder and darts, fit the yoke, shoulders and neckline as described above for a man's drape, making sure that the front rectangle fits around the fullest part of the bust and reaches comfortably to the side-seam area. With the front fabric marked at the yoke and pinned in place, position the commercial front pattern or the front pattern you copied from the shirt you like so that the top of the armscye on the pattern meets the end of the yoke on the fabric, as described for a regular drape on p. 46. Pivot the front so that the side seam is in a reasonable place. Try also to keep the center fronts on the gingham and pattern parallel, but don't worry if you can't. The side seam and armscye are the important lines to position, and you'll use the center front on the fabric in the final pattern. Trace the front pattern's armscye onto the gingham and down the side seam a couple of inches, then trim away the gingham fabric beyond the armscye, leaving about 1½ in. of seam allowance, so you can redraw the line later if you want.

Working each side separately, pinch out a horizontal fold at the side seam in line with the bust point on that side. You want to gather up enough fabric in the fold so the front hangs straight down and on grain from the level of the bust point, wrapping smoothly around the circumference of the bust. But don't gather up so much fabric that the front pulls in toward the waist. Pin the fold to the inside as you would with a regular dart so that it tapers to nothing about 1 in. to 2 in. from the bust point. Then repeat the process on the other side.

Unless you actually plan to make a shirt with darts in this position, it doesn't matter whether both darts are on the same horizontal level or if they're otherwise identical. But if they're not, this is all the more reason to shift the darts to the shoulder, as shown in the drawing at right, where the differences will be less obvious. Next check the drape of the front below the bust, adjusting the darts if necessary to get the fabric on the straight grain. Then mark the darts carefully with your marker, and also mark the bust points to which the darts should point. Next, drape the shirt back, and pin and mark the side seams that you want.

At this point, take a look at the armscyes again and decide whether you like their position. When the model's arms are down at her sides, does the vertical part of the seam fall more or less on top of the little crease above the armpit without a lot of excessive wrinkling? If not, smooth the fabric out and redraw the curve the way you want it. And does the horizontal part at the bottom swing below the armpit about where you want it—about 1½ in. to 3½ in. below, depending on the proportions of your model? Again, if necessary, redraw the line where you think it will be best. (This is still an experiment; you can change your mind later.) Adjust only one side, since we're trying to keep the armscyes the same.

DART PIVOTING

1 To pivot bust dart to shoulder, cut pattern from midpoint of shoulder seam to bust point.

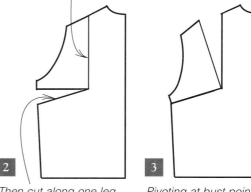

2 Then cut along one leg of dart to bust point.

3 Pivoting at bust point, close dart and open new dart at shoulder.

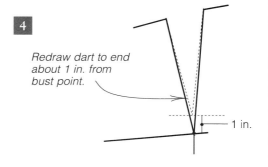

4 Redraw dart to end about 1 in. from bust point.

1 in.

Dart can be gathered out, pleated or seamed.

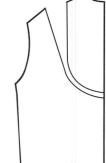

When you've got something you're ready to try, make sure that all the darts, seams, bust points and neckline are clearly marked, especially where the side seams cut across the ends of the darts. Also make sure that the fit is comfortable across the chest, and then unpin the front and make a careful tracing of the marks on a piece of paper. If after folding the fabric on the center front you decide that the front is quite symmetrical, then you need only trace one side of the fabric onto paper. Otherwise, make a full-front paper pattern with two darts and a center-front line.

Finally, you want to transfer, or pivot, the fullness provided by the darts to the shoulder/yoke seam, where it can be gathered, pleated, turned into a seam or left as a dart. The drawing on the facing page shows the steps involved in dart pivoting. The rest of the pattern should look and fit unchanged.

To test the fit and look of your pattern, cut out a test-fabric version of your adjusted tracing. Then press the fullness at the shoulder into a pleat and baste the front to the yoke and back (you can decide later whether you actually want a pleat, gathers or a dart at the shoulder; this is just to test-fit). If you're unsure about the position or shape of the armscye, make a test sleeve and baste it into place so you can check that too.

SLEEVES

Shirt sleeves are just like shirts in terms of fit: They're pretty basic and easy to alter, but subject to a good deal of refinement. By far the most important fitting issue for sleeves, whether for a woman's shirt or a man's, is length, and that's probably the only part of the shirt sleeve that's bothered you if it wasn't right. The next most bothersome fitting problem is an armscye that's too tight. If the one on the shirt you copied was too tight (if you didn't work from a commercial pattern), I hope you've already made the armscye longer on your drape.

Cuffs and sleeve length

Before you can measure your sleeve length or make a sleeve pattern, you need to know exactly what size your cuff will be. The best place to start is with a cuff you like the look of. Simply measure it all around, trace off any curves or shaped edges, then measure your own wrists. Measure both wrists since they may be different. If they are, use the larger measurement for your cuff, or make two different cuff patterns. Consider the size of any wristwatch or jewelry that will be worn with the shirt, and allow for that too. The around-the-wrist, or length, measure of the cuff is equal to your measured circumference, plus some ease (1 in. is a good place to start), plus 1 in. for the button overlap, or 2 in. if the cuffs are for cufflinks. These are guidelines.

If you decide later that you want a different fit, simply make a new pattern. The hand-to-sleeve distance of the cuff, that is, its width, is whatever your chosen cuff has, or you can look in the Catalog of Pattern Details on pp. 75-76 for a few classic cuff patterns. Use this measurement when you're taking your sleeve length (the drawing on p. 48 shows the two points to measure between).

When you make or correct your sleeve pattern, you need to decide how much fabric you want to gather or pleat into the cuff, in other words, how much bigger the sleeve needs to be at the cuff seam than the cuff itself. I like a lot of pleats, so I allow about 5 in. for them in the sleeve pattern; anywhere from 3 in. to 6 in. makes sense. Then there's the sleeve placket to consider, which adds about 1 in., unless you make French cuffs, in which case the placket adds only ¼ in., since it gets folded differently for them (as described on pp. 24-25).

The reason I'm being vague here is that you don't really need to know how big this sleeve-end seam actually is until you've made it, that is, with the sleeve seamed, the placket in place and folded back if necessary for French cuffs. Then I measure it exactly and figure out how I want to deal with the excess fabric in the sleeve, based on my cuff pattern. Maybe there are stripes, and I want to put a pleat the width of the stripe at every third stripe. I like to integrate the fabric design into the details like that, so I stay flexible. As you work around the cuff seam making pleats or gathers, you can change or break the pattern at the underarm seam, if convenient, since it will not be very visible there. As long as I've allowed about 5 in. extra for the bottom of the sleeve at the cuff seam, I wait to see how I'll deal with it when I get to it. It all works out.

Now back to the question of sleeve length. To sew a sleeve to an armscye, the sleeve cap and armscye need to be the same length. There's no need for any ease in the sleeve cap. I've never put any in and never missed it or had a complaint about it, so if it's

ADJUSTING SLEEVE-CAP LENGTH

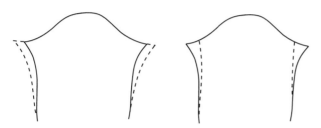

*Add or subtract up to 2 in. from sleeve cap.
Distribute total change equally on each side.*

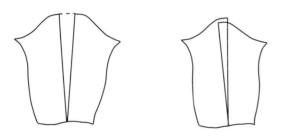

*To add or subtract more than 2 in.,
slash to cuff and spread or overlap.*

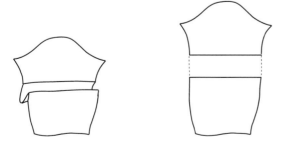

*To lengthen or shorten sleeve, fold or slash
in center and redraw underarm seamline.*

in your pattern I suggest you take it out. If after carefully measuring the adjusted cap and armscye you find that they no longer match, and you like the feel of the armhole on your drape, the easiest place to change the cap length is at the ends of the cap. You can add or subtract up to a total of 2 in. by simply drawing more length or cutting it off equally on each side (see the drawing at left) and redrawing the underarm seams to coincide. Add or subtract more than that by slashing down the middle of the sleeve and spreading or overlapping the two halves, as shown in the drawing. To change the length of the sleeve, simply fold out or slash and spread across the width of the sleeve at the center, then true the side seams. If you basically liked the sleeve you started with, that's all you have to check: the length and sleeve-cap measurement. If you want more information on the fit of a shirt sleeve, I suggest some further refinements you can make below.

The drawing at left on the facing page shows how all the seams on a sleeve that's almost working can be recontoured without significantly altering their length to produce subtle but real effects. The change at the cuff end is too subtle to affect the fit significantly, but it's worth doing. Reshaping the cuff angles it forward, making it conform better to the curve of the arm, without making it much more difficult to attach.

If you're satisfied with your sleeves at this point, you can stop here. But before you do, take a moment to find and mark the midpoint of the sleeve cap and the armscye (probably somewhere on the yoke) so that you can match them when sewing them together.

If you're still having trouble with your sleeve pattern, let's back up and look at how sleeves are designed, and how they interact with armscyes. I should add that the discussion below of sleeve patterns is by no means exhaustive. If you want to explore the subject even further, look at the books on pattern drafting listed in the Bibliography on pp. 168-169.

Back

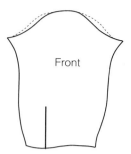

Front

This change increases pull across chest or back; sleeve-cap change is minimal.

This helps reduce tightness in chest or back; may add to cap length, so remeasure.

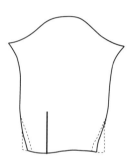

This increases or decreases for biceps or forearms; be sure to keep same side-seam length.

This adjusts for larger or smaller cuffs, or for more or fewer gathers at cuff.

Changing sleeve end for angled cuff

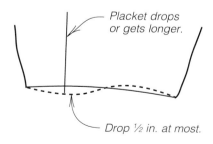

Placket drops or gets longer.

Drop ½ in. at most.

Each of these major variations on regular sleeve shape (shown as a heavy line) has same length from shoulder to cuff, and each can be made to fit same shape of armhole.

Sleeves and armscyes

Lay out flat a few shirts from different makers, and you'll notice at least two things. One is the excess material at the armpit that will not lie down flat when the sleeve and body are smoothed out; another is the various angles at which the sleeves join the bodies. This angle is probably different on each shirt. Some sleeves stick out almost at a right angle to the center front, and some slope down at almost 45°. The different angles are caused by the shape of the sleeve caps, not the shape of the armscyes, which are probably more or less the same.

If you wanted to design a shirt sleeve from scratch for a fitted shirt body such as we've just draped, one way you could do it would be to lay the body out flat (whether you're copying a shirt or using a commercial pattern), as just described, so that the front is flat and the armscye is divided in half between the front and back. Then trace around the armscye from the top at the yoke to the side seam, following its shape in back and ignoring it in front, as shown in the drawing on the next page. You could now take your sleeve-length measurement and use

Relationship of sleeve cap to sleeve angle

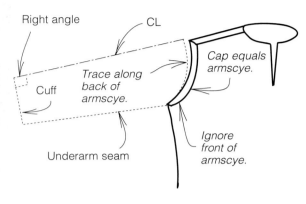

Right angle

CL

Trace along back of armscye.

Cuff

Underarm seam

Cap equals armscye.

Ignore front of armscye.

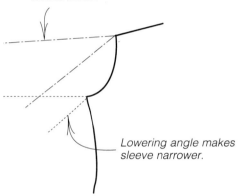

Raising angle makes sleeve wider.

Lowering angle makes sleeve narrower.

Adding a sleeve 'gusset'

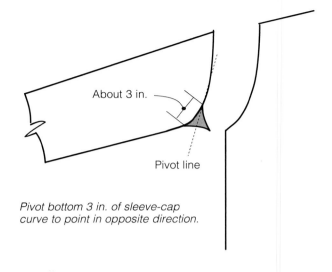

About 3 in.

Pivot line

Pivot bottom 3 in. of sleeve-cap curve to point in opposite direction.

it to draw a straight line out from the edge of the yoke at the top of the armscye to indicate the center line of the sleeve. You'd have to decide on an angle for your line, but if you just extended the shoulder line, as shown in the drawing above, that would be a good place to start.

At the cuff end, you could drop a perpendicular line down from the sleeve's midline, half the length of the cuff seam, which is the length of the cuff, plus whatever ease you want for gathers or pleats (see p. 51). Next you could draw an underarm seam coming out of the side seam and tapering up to meet the bottom of the cuff seam. The shape of your sleeve cap could be exactly the same as the back half of the armscye. You would now have a very basic but totally usable outline for half a sleeve.

What would have happened to the shape of the resulting sleeve if you had picked a different angle for the center line of the sleeve? As you can see in the drawing at left, if you raise the angle, the sleeve gets wider, the underarm seam gets longer and the cap (whose curve stays the same shape) pivots at the end of the center line, making the angle there wider. If the sleeve swings down, it gets narrower, the underarm seam shortens and the angle at the cap gets narrower too. In other words, the greater the angle, the looser the fit and the easier it is to raise the arms without pulling the shirt out of the waistband, but the more underarm bulk there is when the arms are at rest. The question the sleeve maker has to answer is, what angle offers the best compromise between a loose, comfortable fit and excess fabric at the underarm?

Enter the underarm gusset. Remember the rectangular shirt, described on pp. 30-31? Its sleeves stuck straight out at right angles to center front, with a straight line for an armscye. To strengthen the underarm seam, a little square of fabric called a gusset was inserted in the corner formed by the body and sleeve. It didn't add any reaching room, but it protected the seam from ripping. In modern shirts, that gusset has been built into the sleeve pattern, and it allows the sleeve to be put in at a nice, sleek angle and still have some reaching room.

SLEEVE-CAP VARIATIONS

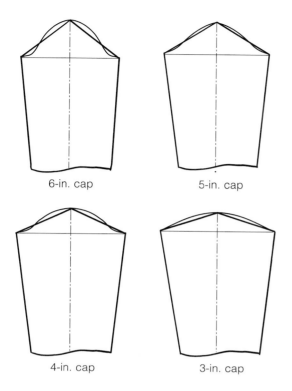

6-in. cap 5-in. cap

4-in. cap 3-in. cap

It's become that little bit of extra fabric you could not lay flat when you spread your shirts out to check the sleeve angle.

I'd venture to say that you've never noticed any difference in comfort from the various angles you saw when you spread your shirts out, unless you've tried climbing ropes and swinging from tree limbs in all your shirts. One reason they're all comfortable enough is that little bit of sleeve gusset. It's like having a hinge at the underarm. The drawing at right on the facing page shows how you would add gussetlike shaping to the rudimentary sleeve that we just drew.

Patternmakers describe the sleeve angle in terms of the height of the sleeve cap, that is, the difference between the length of the sleeve's center line and the length of the underarm seam. When the cap height changes, the length of the cap nonetheless stays the same — in order to fit the same armscye still — but the sleeve width has to change: the higher the cap, the narrower the sleeve and the smaller the sleeve angle. It's like an archer's bow: The length of the bow doesn't change, but when you bend the bow by pulling the bowstring, the bow seems to get shorter because the ends come closer together.

Workable sleeve-cap heights range from about 2 in. to 6 in. The important thing to realize about all this is that each of the sleeve-cap variations in the drawing at left can be sewn into the same armscye. In practical terms, the sportier the shirt, the greater the sleeve angle and the lower the cap. The likelier the sleeve is to be worn under a suit (where underarm bulk would be uncomfortable), the lower the angle and the taller the cap. A typical dress shirt has about a 5-in. cap, which means that the sleeve angle is lower than the average shoulder angle. If you can see the grain of the sleeve fabric on a shirt you're examining, you can get a quick idea about the cap height by looking at the sleeve grain at the armscye seam at chest level. If the seam is nearly on the cross-grain, the cap height is very shallow.

In summary, if you want to play with your shirt-sleeve pattern, a good way to start is by fitting the body, finding a comfortable armscye and measuring it. Then use the armscye length to lay out different sleeve-cap curves, and for each one, drop sleeve-length midlines down from the center of the curve, draw cuff seams at right angles to the midline, draw in underarm seams, add the gusset, cut out the pattern and try it on. You can refine your results using the ideas in the drawing at left on p. 53, which shows how to make subtle sleeve alterations. Or use the understanding you've now gained to copy a different sleeve from a shirt you already have, and adjust its cap length to fit your draped shirt-body's armscye.

CHAPTER SIX

COLLARS, PLACKETS, CUFFS AND POCKETS

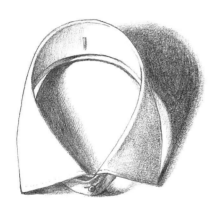

ou can change the entire character of the most basic shirt pattern in countless ways without changing the shape of the body and sleeves at all, merely by choosing different finishing details, such as collars, plackets, cuffs and pockets. This chapter contains a collection of classic and not-so-classic patterns for these details, which you can use on shirts of any cut, fit or style, and also on nonshirt-like garments, like blouses and dresses.

I hope you'll also feel free to make any changes you like to these details, whether big or small, subtle or severe, so that you get just the effect you're after. Keep your eyes open for other details to add to your collection—look to magazine photos, commercial patterns, your own clothes and garments you can borrow long enough to copy (you'll find some of the nonclassic details I've collected in the Catalog of Design Ideas at the end of Chapter 9). I like to scan pattern books, because once I spot an interesting detail I can get the construction information from the pattern and change its shape or proportion to my own liking. I look in most sections of pattern books for shirt-related details, but especially the designer sportswear.

COLLARS

Collars offer the most options for variation, so let's start with them. You may have noticed that the pattern we made in the last chapter did not include a collar. This is because the shape of a shirt's collar is a fashion issue and has little bearing on the fitting problems we addressed in making the basic shirt pattern. In fact, once you've found a collar stand that fits, it's a simple matter to design a collar for it. The size of the collar is adjusted the same way as the collar stand or band—by lengthening or shortening it at the center back. In the Catalog of Pattern Details beginning on p. 64, I've provided a variety of patterns for collars I've come across, as well as the collar stand that goes with each.

Of course, you can substitute an alternative collar stand or design a new stand for any of these collars, provided the collar covers the stand when folded over on it. Finding or drawing your own collar patterns and experimenting with various effects is probably the part of shirtmaking I find the most fun, and I recommend you try it too. You can cut collar patterns out of white paper and hold them up to your neck to get an idea of how they'll look before cutting them in fabric.

First consider the geometry of collar bands around the neck: If you cut a strip of paper the length of your neckline plus 2 in. for an overlap, then bring the ends together, you'll get a cylinder, as shown in the drawing above. Necks are more like cones, in that they get smaller toward the head. To make your paper strip take a conical shape, pull the ends

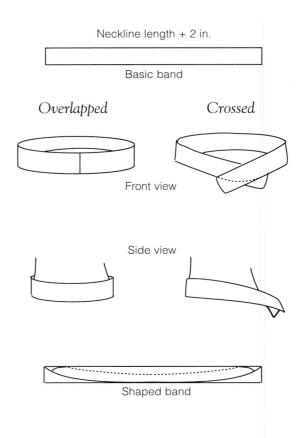

Neckline length + 2 in.

Basic band

Overlapped *Crossed*

Front view

Side view

Shaped band

down so they cross at an angle instead of exactly overlapping. This angles the front of the band inward, while leaving the back straight—not exactly a cone but very like a neck. If you trim off the corners that stick out and create a curve, you'll wind up with something like the bottom (neckline) edge of a collar band or stand.

Collar designers have come up with a variety of shapes for the top edge, as you'll see in the patterns at the end of this chapter, and so can you merely by drawing a new shape for it. You can make the top narrower or wider than the bottom, parallel to the bottom or entirely different from it. Cut out a paper shape like a collar—the part that falls from the top edge of the stand—and notice what happens when you play with it, as we just did with the band to form a cone (see the drawing on the facing page). Collars usually don't overlap in front, so just pinch the corners together at the top edge. Then pull the front of the collar down and see that the points swing farther apart. Push it up and the points come together. In other words, you can control the point spread of a single collar shape by changing the shape of the stand: the higher in front, the narrower the spread, and vice versa.

You'll notice that the classic collar shapes shown in the Catalog of Pattern Details have lots of subtle curves. These add distinction and finesse, so observe them, experiment with them, borrow them. But above all, don't be afraid to change them. As you can

PLAYING WITH THE POINT SPREAD

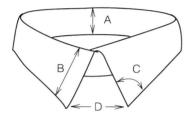

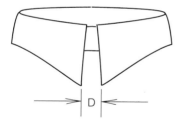

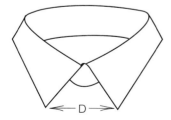

A, B and C stay the same. D changes as you raise and lower stand.

see in the drawing on p. 60, it's pretty simple to alter the design of a collar. The pattern for the collar I evolved in this drawing is shown on p. 71, and an example of the finished collar is shown in the middle photo on p. 145.

If you wear a tie, I recommend that you consider a separate collar rather than an attached one. There are several reasons for this: First, having one shirt with several different collars is simply more fun. Second, if the collar's attached, it's the first part of a shirt to wear out (along with the cuffs). Third, collars are harder to make than shirts, so you can separate the tasks and wait for your collar-making skills to catch up with your shirtmaking abilities. Fourth, if you keep a little extra fabric around, you can make new styles of collars for old shirts as fashion or your taste changes. You can, of course, replace an attached collar with a little more effort, but a separate collar lends itself to much more change and experiment.

The reasons for *not* choosing a separate collar are almost as many and as compelling: First, buttoning on a separate collar when dressing is a fussy business that's not suited to some temperaments. Second, it's not really possible to wear a shirt with a separate collar without a tie, unless you also wear it without a collar—not an unpleasant look but, again, not for everyone. I've come up with a few ways to attach a separate collar so that the shirt can be worn open at the neck (see one example in the drawing on p. 145), but these require even more fussing and are just for the diehards among us. Nor can you wear your tie with the collar unbuttoned, which is a serious problem for some. Third, if you have your shirts professionally laundered, it will cost more to do the collars separately. On the other hand, since hand laundering causes less wear on shirts and hence is the best way to care for them, you might send just the collars to the laundry if you can stand washing the shirt body yourself and if you can find a laundry that will shape the collar for you—the older ones may remember how. I finally bought a mini-press, which I find the best way to put a professional finish on collars, so I even launder the collars at home.

Designing a collar

I wanted to make a stock collar to go with my black silk shirt (shown on p. 145). I began with this drawing of a traditional stock collar.

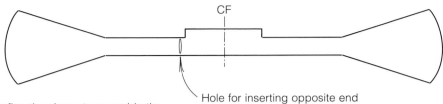

Hole for inserting opposite end

But I wanted to refine the shape to resemble the drawing of the complex wing collar on p. 129...

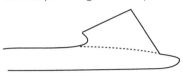

...which looks like this when folded:

So I redrew the stock like this...

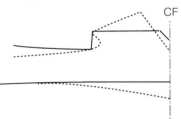

...and reshaped the tie section like this.

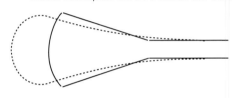

Then I decided to make a regular collar pattern from my new design. So I redrew the stock to have an overlapping front and a closed back. The final pattern can be found on p. 71.

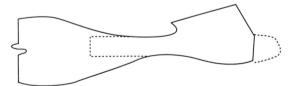

Another variation I designed (shown in the bottom left photo on p. 127) evolved from the pattern on p. 71. By extending the overlaps in front, a mock bow tie was formed.

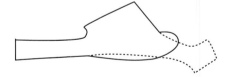

I reshaped the CB fold line on the pattern so the finished collar hugs the back of the neck and forms an interesting point.

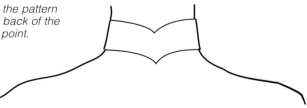

SEPARATE COLLAR

A separate collar can have an extended and shaped stand on overlap end, which needs to be about ½ in. longer than band to fit around it.

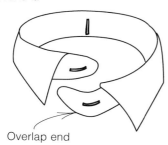

Overlap end

Collar buttons like the traditional front-collar button (left) and button for back of neck (right) are used to attach separate collar to shirt neckband.

For a more comfortable fit, choose a smooth and rounded-edge button for neck side of your double-button collar 'stud.'

If the idea of a separate collar appeals to you, make your first shirt without a collar because getting the collar just right, both in terms of style and sewing perfection, can take some experimentation. The collar band is essentially a collar stand whose top edge has been cut down, as you'll see if you study the collar band and stand patterns in the Catalog.

With the following minor exceptions, collars (and stands) are cut the same way, whether they're going to be separate or attached. If the collar is attached, the neckline seam on the bottom of the collar stand can always be the same. In other words, once you settle on a shape for this seam that works, you can use it at the bottom of any collar stand. You could also experiment with other shapes, like those you'll find among the patterns in the Catalog or elsewhere.

If the collar is separate, the bottom edge of the stand does not have to duplicate the neckline seam on the band exactly. The only important thing is that the stand cover the band when buttoned on. Also, a separate collar must be cut ½ in. longer than one that's to be attached in order to accommodate the band. Both the collar stand on a separate collar and the attached band on the shirt have two buttonholes at center front. To attach the collar to the band, these buttonholes are filled with a single separate collar button (which can sometimes be found at vintage clothing stores) or a cufflink-like assembly of buttons sewn together, which I find the more comfortable alternative (see the drawing at left). To secure the collar in back, a button on the band at center back fits into a corresponding buttonhole on the stand.

In the collar patterns in the Catalog, I've provided no seam allowances, because the technique I use for making collars starts with interfacing cut exactly at the seamline without a seam allowance. The collar stands all have ¼-in. seam allowances. I cut each pattern out of stiff, thin cardboard so I can use its edge to guide my rotary cutter. In the collar-making discussion on pp. 106-109, you'll see that the amount of seam allowance at the free edges is not critical since we don't use it for guiding the actual sewing during collar construction.

PLACKETS, CUFFS AND POCKETS

Sleeve plackets (which can also be used for neckline openings, usually at center front on a pullover shirt) look complex, but they're laid out on a very simple grid. You can easily design your own placket or modify the ones given in the Catalog, using nothing more than a ruler and ⅛-in. graph paper. The drawing on p. 62 shows the general scheme for a placket, which you can vary in length and width, provided the underlap is narrower than the overlap. The shape of the finish at the end of the overlap is usually just a triangular fold, but it can be anything

PLACKET SCHEMATIC

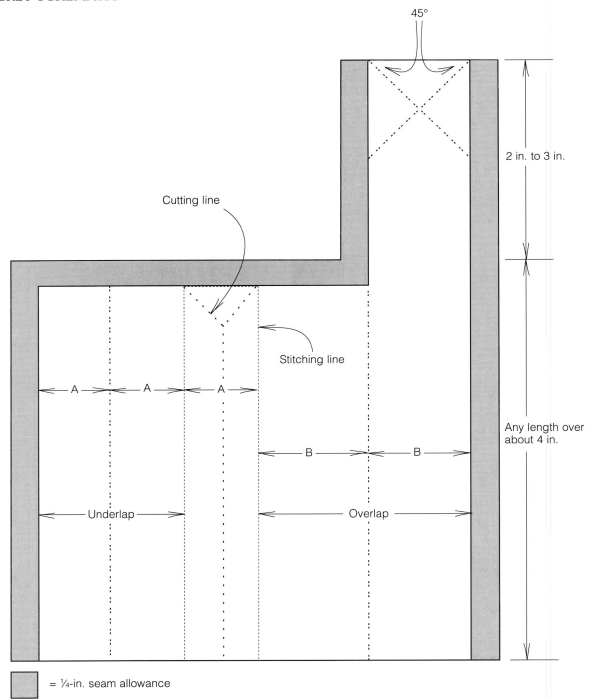

45°

2 in. to 3 in.

Cutting line

Stitching line

A   A   A

B   B

Underlap

Overlap

Any length over about 4 in.

= ¼-in. seam allowance

you like. The triangular shape is a classic shirt detail, and it's very simple to make accurately, as you can see in the drawing at right. I've also included a pattern for a center-front placket opening in the Catalog (see p. 74). An extreme version of a placket that I like and have included a pattern for on p. 73 incorporates an elbow patch (you'll see a shirt I made with this elbow-patch-and-placket combo on p. 140). The patch portion of the pattern is a template and could be shaped in any number of ways.

Cuffs are pretty basic in design. The cuff patterns on pp. 75-76 are classics. For more ideas, see the Catalog of Design Ideas at the end of Chapter 9.

The pocket patterns I've included in the Catalog are the ultra-traditional patch pockets found on classic dress shirts. You'll find more pocket ideas in Chapter 9, but, in fact, you can put any kind of pocket you like on the front of a shirt. The most interesting thing about the pocket patterns shown on pp. 77-78 is that they're actually templates, that is, they're construction tools as well as cutting guides. Let me explain.

When you're sewing a layer of fabric down by edgestitching along a fold, as you do with patch pockets, you've got to establish the fold first, which is usually done by ironing. If the folded edge is curved or shaped in some way, it's hard to form precisely by eye, especially if it needs to be perfectly symmetrical. To simplify the process, I make a thin cardboard template the exact shape and size of the edge I want and use it as a form, ironing the edge over it. I can also use the template as a pattern by cutting a specific distance away from its edge, measuring either by eye or with the help of the guide on the rotary cutter. The "fold allowance" doesn't need to be exact. If some part of the piece needs a seam allowance instead of a fold, I cut that part of the pattern/template to be a precise cutting guide, like the collar edges mentioned above.

(Partial templates are useful, too. Once I've perfected a sleeve pattern, I make a template just for the seam at the armscye, so I can fold over a precise edge of the seam allowance for a clean, flat-felled seam finish, as shown in the sleeve-construction discussion beginning on p. 94.)

CREATING A SYMMETRICAL TRIANGLE ON PLACKETS AND BANDS

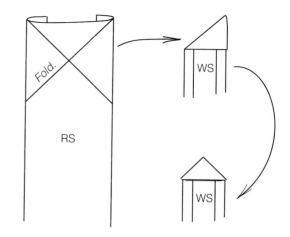

I like cardboard (shirt cardboard from the laundry, bristol board from an art store or oaktag from a tailor's supplier) as a folding guide because it's easy to cut and will not get hot under the iron. I make a typical shirt pocket with a template by first tracing the exact shape of the finished pocket onto my template cardboard, using rulers and French curves to make it perfect. Then I add allowances for the wide folded finish at the pocket mouth (see the pocket patterns on pp. 77-78), and cut out the template. I allow about ⅜ in. around the edge that I'll shape, then I fold and stitch the pocket mouth as planned. I take the incomplete pocket and the template to the ironing board and iron the remaining edges carefully over.

On curves, it's sometimes helpful to run a smooth tracing wheel along the edge of the template first, creating a slight crease at the fold line. When it looks good, I remove the template and iron the pocket from the front. A little glue stick helps hold unruly edges in place. I trim away the fold allowances at the pocket mouth, so they'll be concealed by the topstitched reinforcements, then I glue the pocket in position and carefully edgestitch it down.

A CATALOG OF PATTERN DETAILS

See pp. 61-63, and the appropriate construction sections, for instructions on using these patterns. All patterns are full-scale and alterable.

COLLAR STAND AND COLLAR PATTERNS   (Construction details on pp. 106-109.)

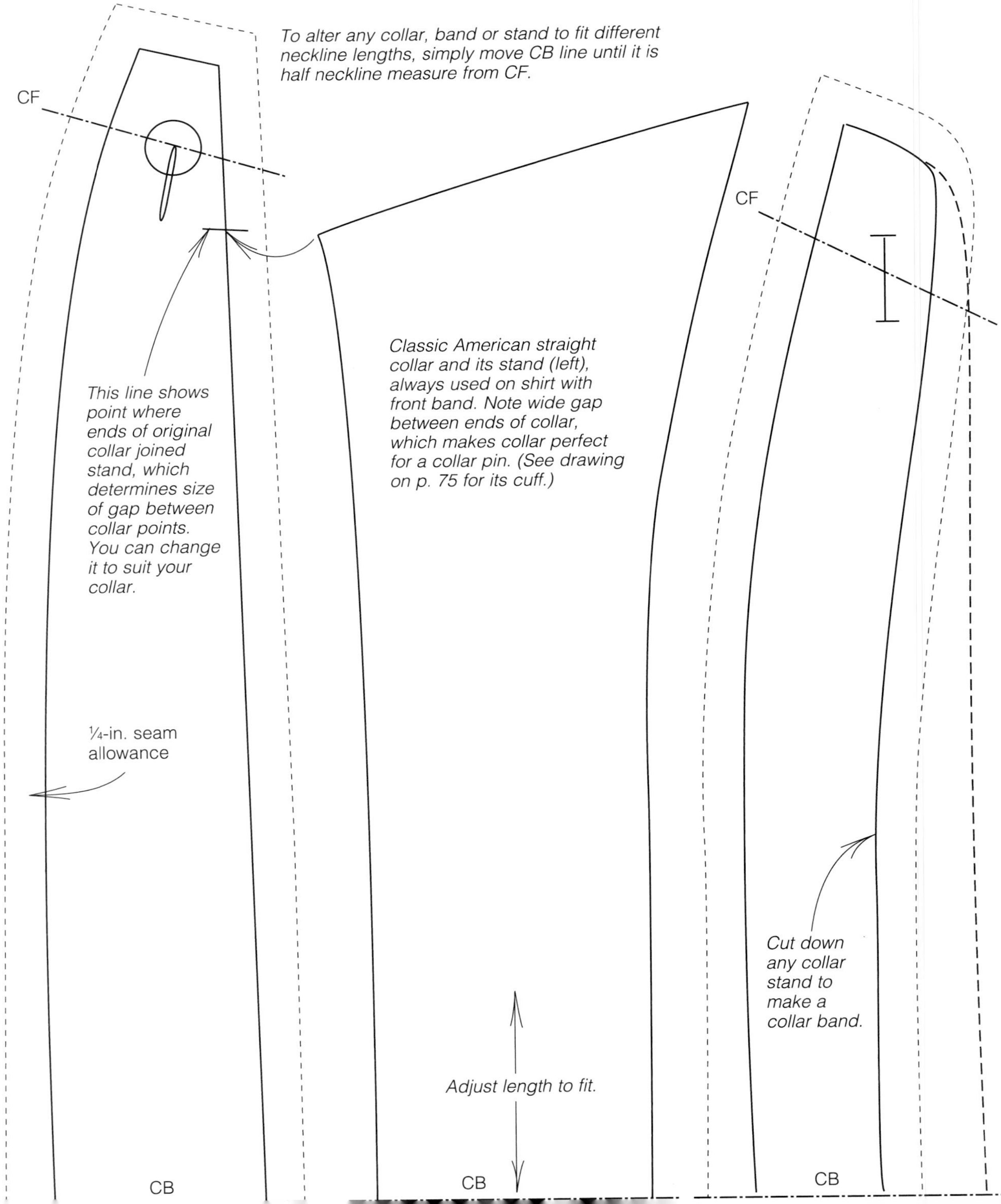

CF

To alter any collar, band or stand to fit different neckline lengths, simply move CB line until it is half neckline measure from CF.

CF

This line shows point where ends of original collar joined stand, which determines size of gap between collar points. You can change it to suit your collar.

Classic American straight collar and its stand (left), always used on shirt with front band. Note wide gap between ends of collar, which makes collar perfect for a collar pin. (See drawing on p. 75 for its cuff.)

¼-in. seam allowance

Cut down any collar stand to make a collar band.

Adjust length to fit.

CB   CB   CB

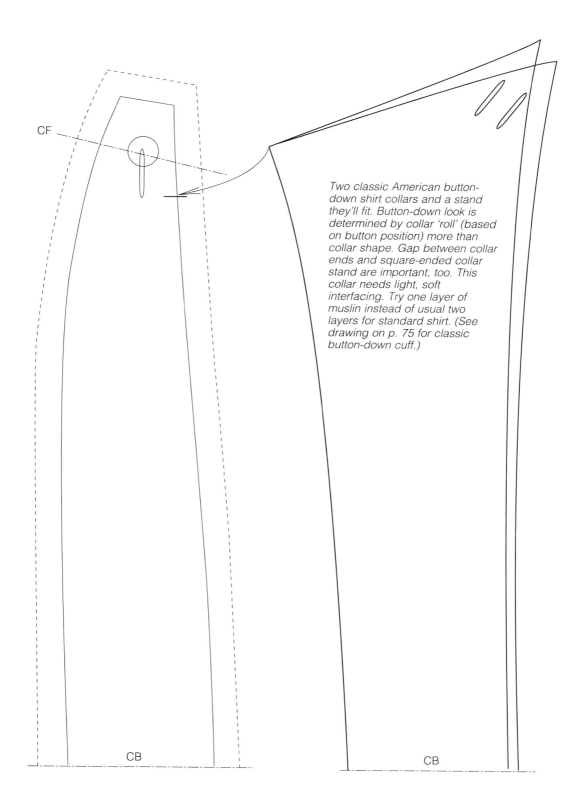

CF

CB

CB

Two classic American button-down shirt collars and a stand they'll fit. Button-down look is determined by collar 'roll' (based on button position) more than collar shape. Gap between collar ends and square-ended collar stand are important, too. This collar needs light, soft interfacing. Try one layer of muslin instead of usual two layers for standard shirt. (See drawing on p. 75 for classic button-down cuff.)

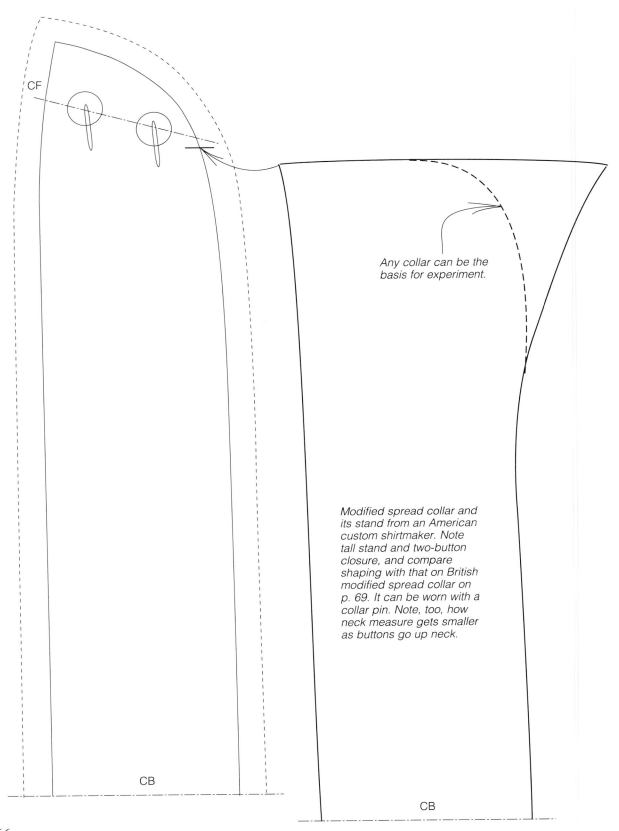

CF

Any collar can be the
basis for experiment.

Modified spread collar and
its stand from an American
custom shirtmaker. Note
tall stand and two-button
closure, and compare
shaping with that on British
modified spread collar on
p. 69. It can be worn with a
collar pin. Note, too, how
neck measure gets smaller
as buttons go up neck.

CB

CB

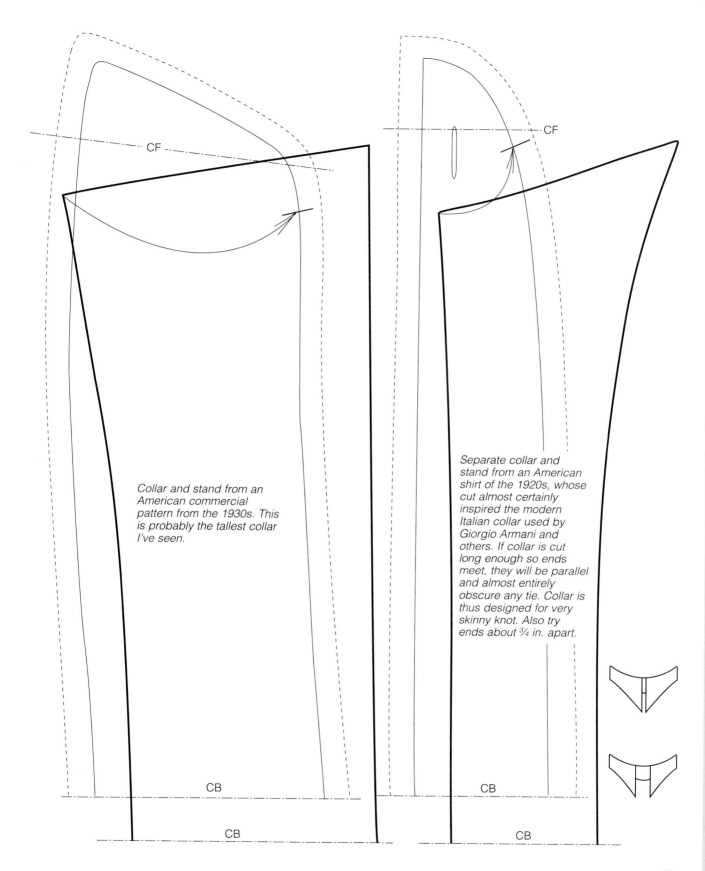

CF

CF

Collar and stand from an American commercial pattern from the 1930s. This is probably the tallest collar I've seen.

Separate collar and stand from an American shirt of the 1920s, whose cut almost certainly inspired the modern Italian collar used by Giorgio Armani and others. If collar is cut long enough so ends meet, they will be parallel and almost entirely obscure any tie. Collar is thus designed for very skinny knot. Also try ends about ¾ in. apart.

CB

CB

CB

CB

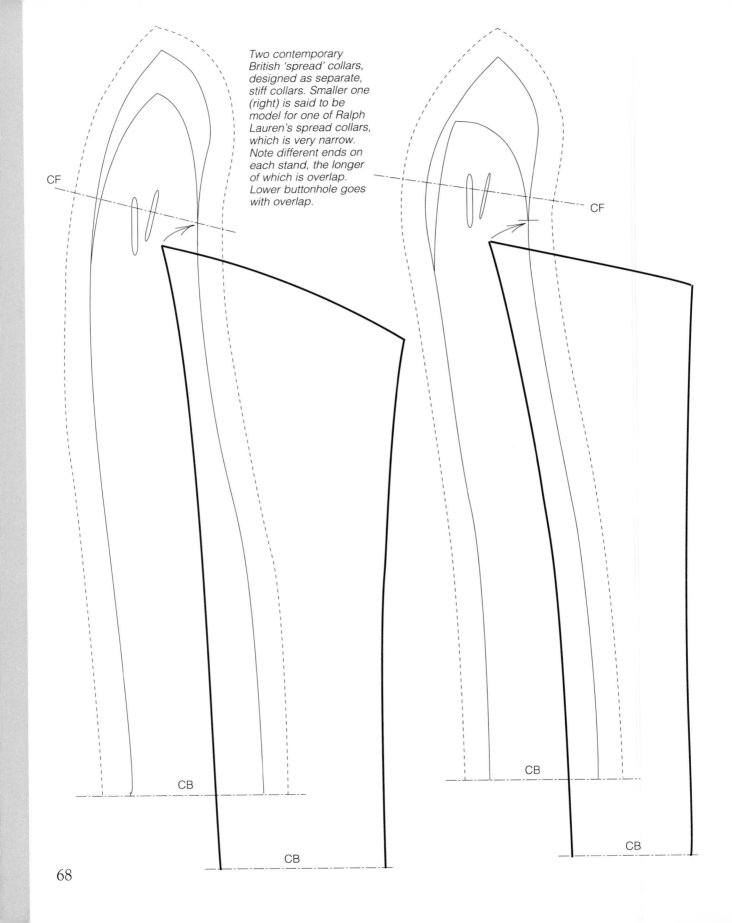

CF

*Two contemporary
British 'spread' collars,
designed as separate,
stiff collars. Smaller one
(right) is said to be
model for one of Ralph
Lauren's spread collars,
which is very narrow.
Note different ends on
each stand, the longer
of which is overlap.
Lower buttonhole goes
with overlap.*

CF

CB

CB

CB

CB

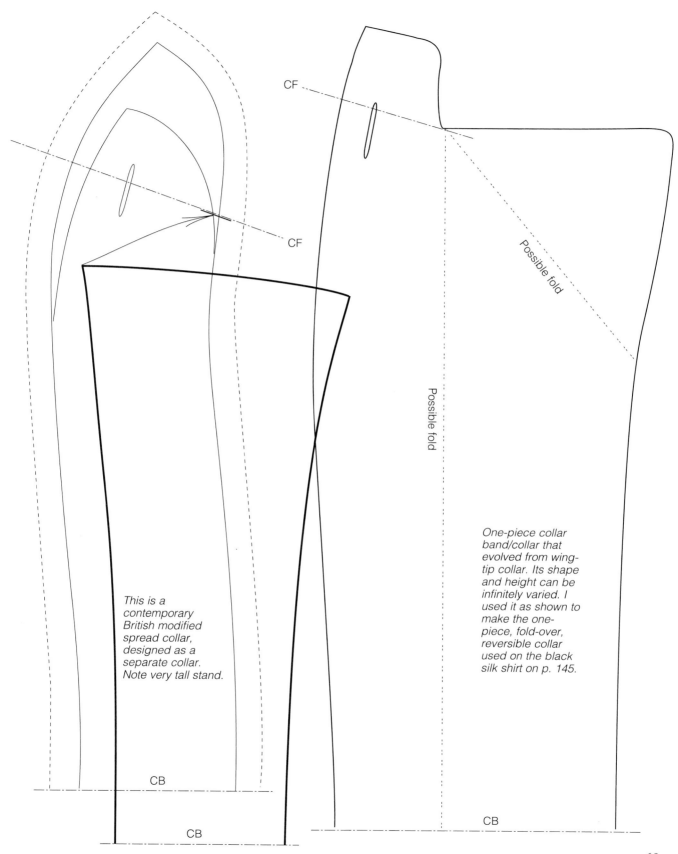

CF

CF

This is a contemporary British modified spread collar, designed as a separate collar. Note very tall stand.

Possible fold

Possible fold

One-piece collar band/collar that evolved from wing-tip collar. Its shape and height can be infinitely varied. I used it as shown to make the one-piece, fold-over, reversible collar used on the black silk shirt on p. 145.

CB

CB

CB

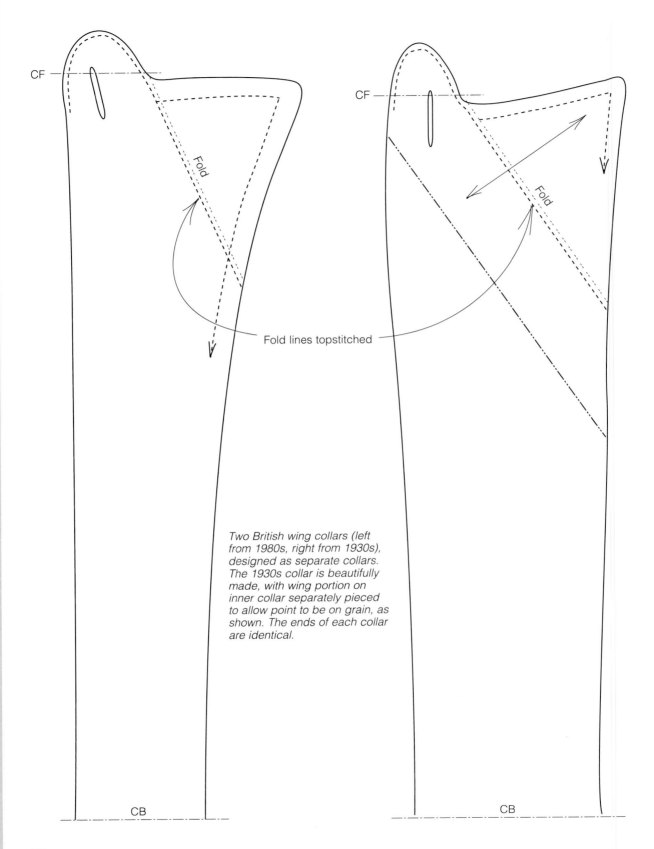

CF

Fold

Fold lines topstitched

CB

CF

Fold

CB

Two British wing collars (left from 1980s, right from 1930s), designed as separate collars. The 1930s collar is beautifully made, with wing portion on inner collar separately pieced to allow point to be on grain, as shown. The ends of each collar are identical.

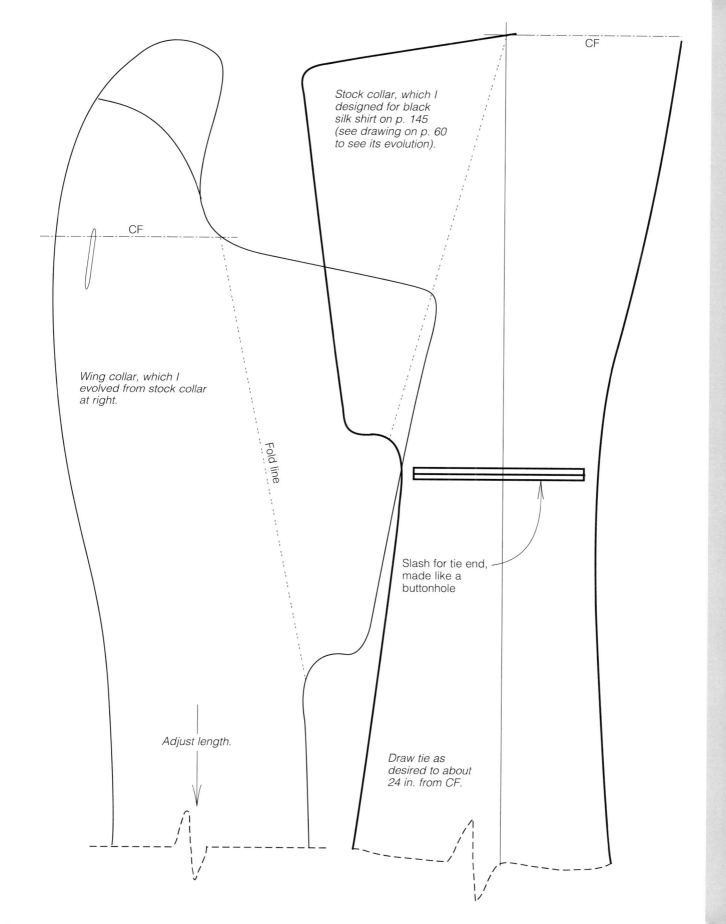

CF

Stock collar, which I designed for black silk shirt on p. 145 (see drawing on p. 60 to see its evolution).

CF

Wing collar, which I evolved from stock collar at right.

Fold line

Slash for tie end, made like a buttonhole

Adjust length.

Draw tie as desired to about 24 in. from CF.

PLACKET PATTERNS

(Construction details on pp. 102-105.)

To save fabric, a narrower sleeve placket could also be cut, or, for even greater economy of fabric, it could be cut in two pieces at this point.

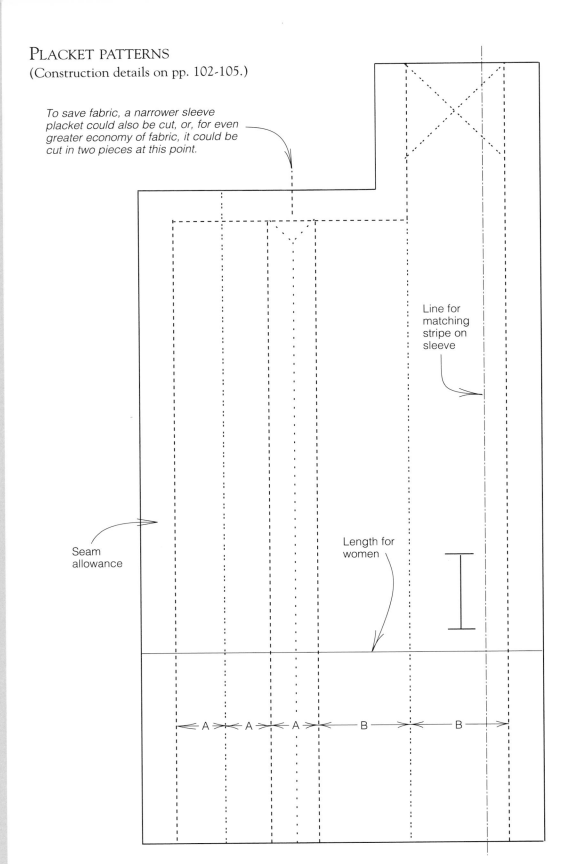

Line for matching stripe on sleeve

Seam allowance

Length for women

A → ← A → ← A → ← B → ← B →

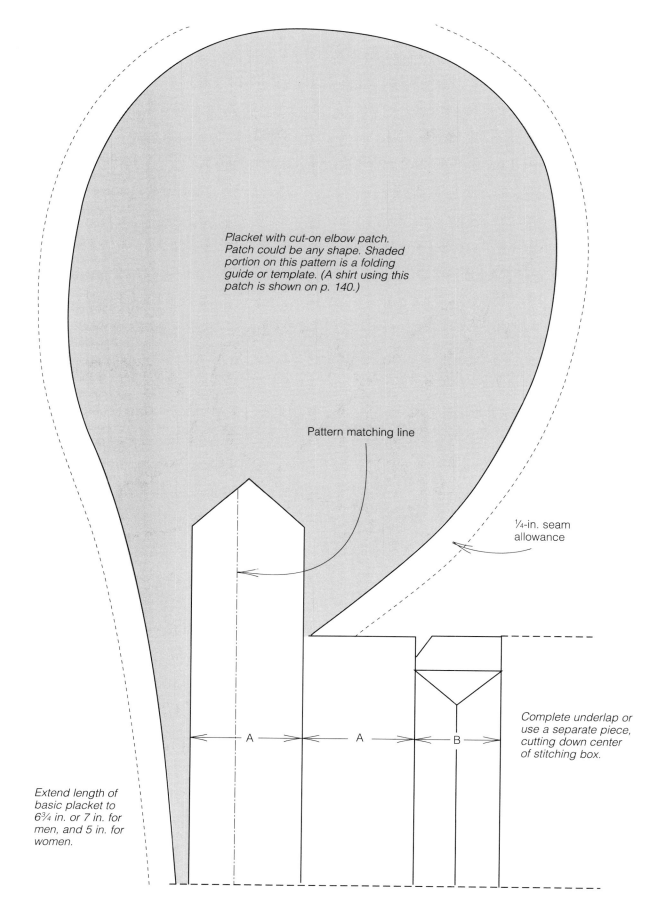

Placket with cut-on elbow patch.
Patch could be any shape. Shaded
portion on this pattern is a folding
guide or template. (A shirt using this
patch is shown on p. 140.)

Pattern matching line

¼-in. seam
allowance

A   A   B

Complete underlap or
use a separate piece,
cutting down center
of stitching box.

Extend length of
basic placket to
6¾ in. or 7 in. for
men, and 5 in. for
women.

Center-front opening placket (1¼ in. wide)

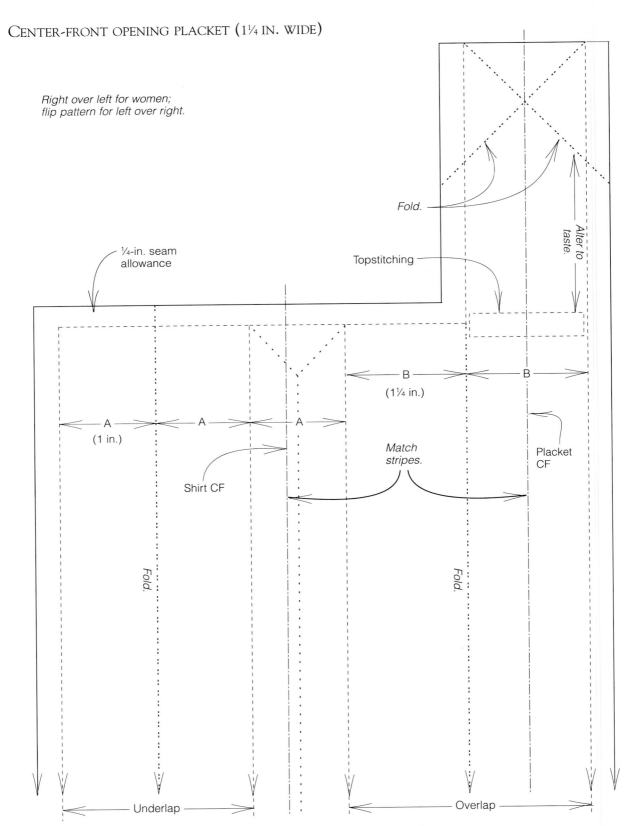

*Right over left for women;
flip pattern for left over right.*

Fold.

Topstitching

Alter to taste.

¼-in. seam allowance

B

(1¼ in.)

B

A

(1 in.)

A

A

Match stripes.

Placket CF

Shirt CF

Fold.

Fold.

Underlap

Overlap

Alter length to taste.

Overlap and underlap can be separate pieces.

Cuff templates and patterns

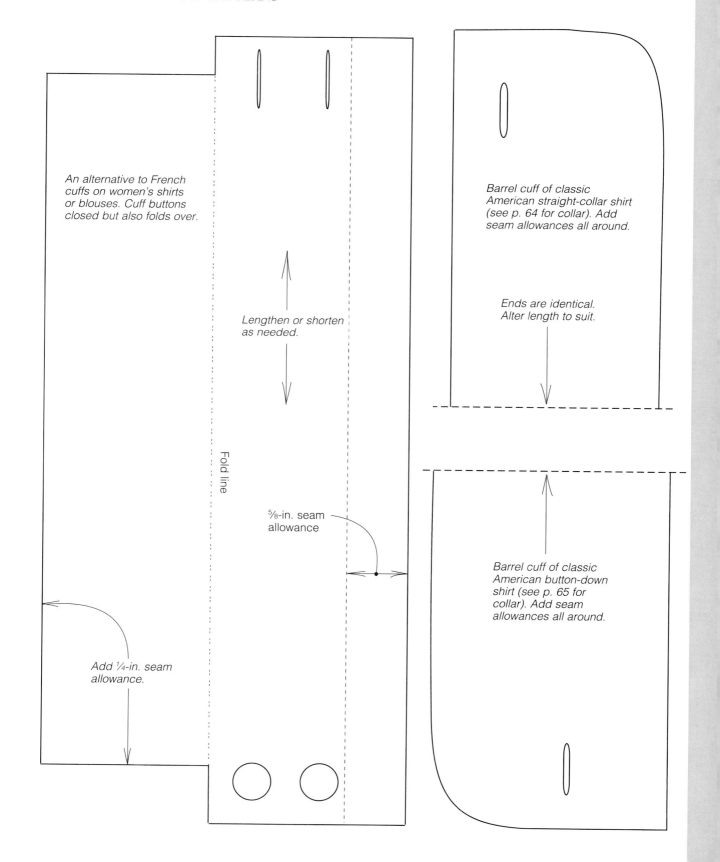

An alternative to French cuffs on women's shirts or blouses. Cuff buttons closed but also folds over.

Lengthen or shorten as needed.

Fold line

⅝-in. seam allowance

Add ¼-in. seam allowance.

Barrel cuff of classic American straight-collar shirt (see p. 64 for collar). Add seam allowances all around.

Ends are identical. Alter length to suit.

Barrel cuff of classic American button-down shirt (see p. 65 for collar). Add seam allowances all around.

French cuff

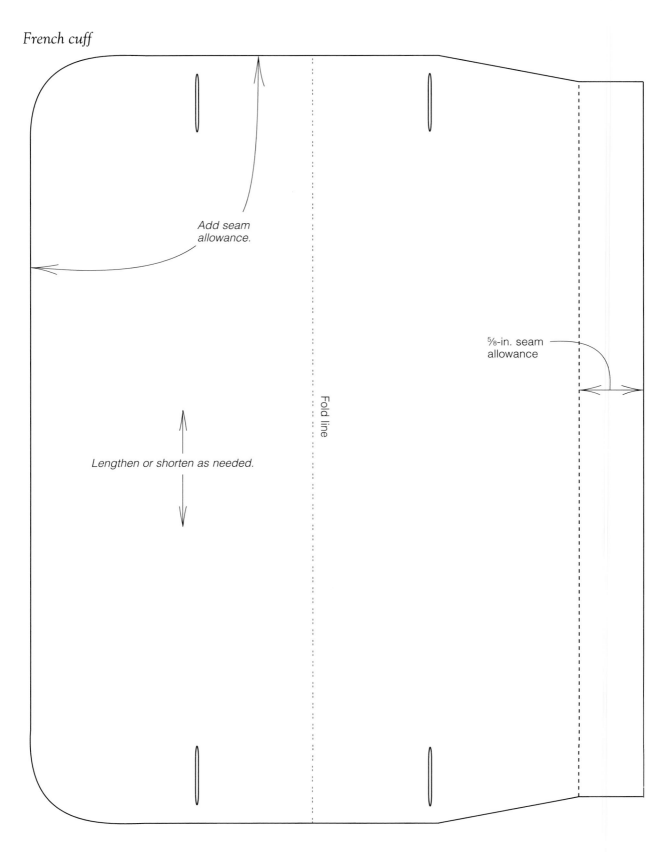

Add seam
allowance.

⅝-in. seam
allowance

Fold line

Lengthen or shorten as needed.

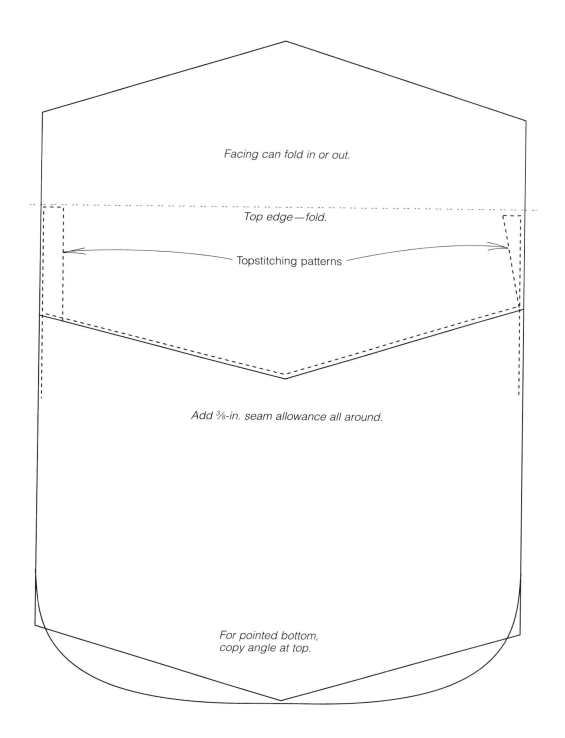

Facing can fold in or out.

Top edge—fold.

Topstitching patterns

Add ⅜-in. seam allowance all around.

For pointed bottom,
copy angle at top.

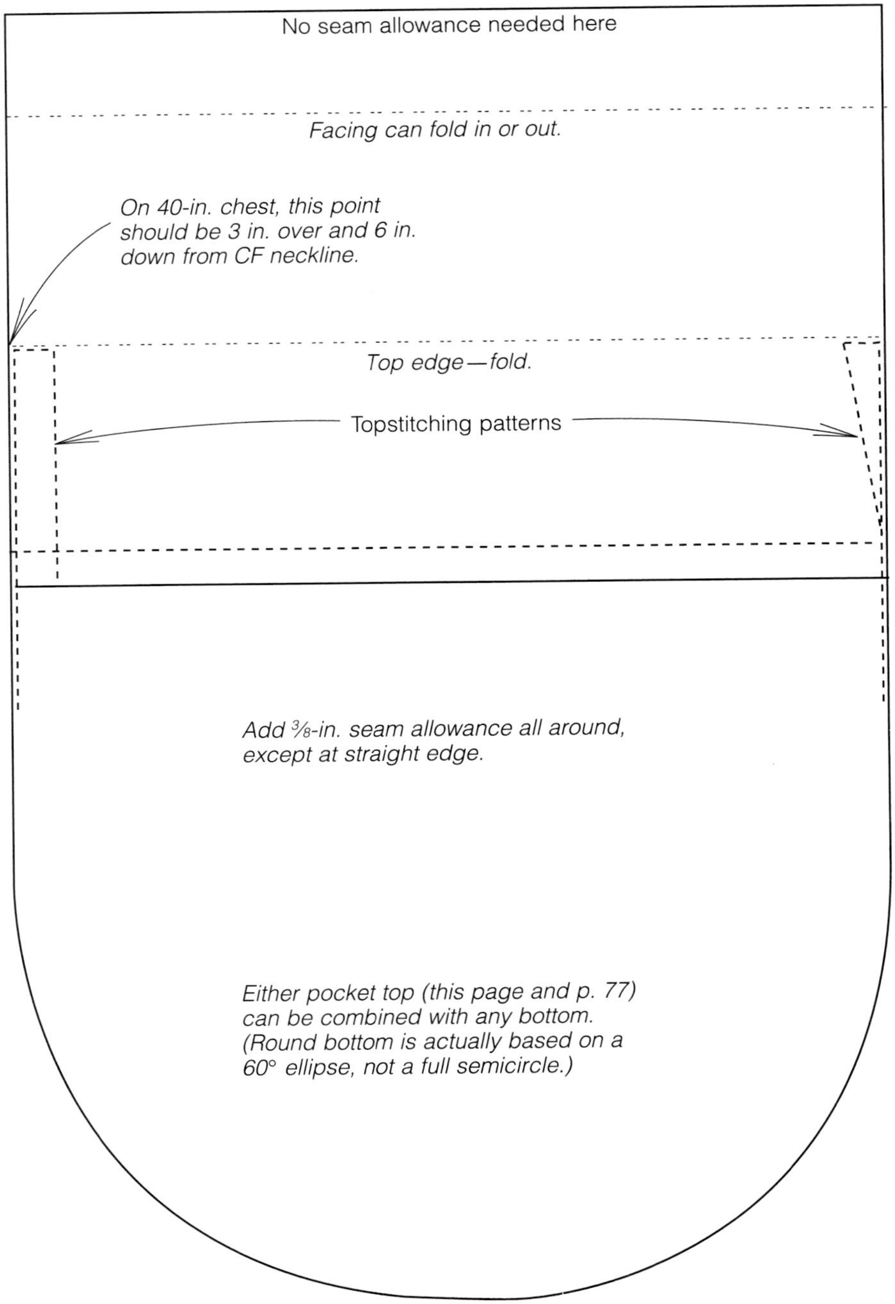

No seam allowance needed here

Facing can fold in or out.

_On 40-in. chest, this point
should be 3 in. over and 6 in.
down from CF neckline._

Top edge—fold.

Topstitching patterns

_Add ⅜-in. seam allowance all around,
except at straight edge._

_Either pocket top (this page and p. 77)
can be combined with any bottom.
(Round bottom is actually based on a
60° ellipse, not a full semicircle.)_

PART THREE

SHIRT CONSTRUCTION

CHAPTER SEVEN

A WORKSHOP IN PRECISION SEWING TECHNIQUES

The instructions that pattern companies provide with their patterns are a mixed blessing. At best, they can be a source of great insight into tricky constructions or a designer's procedures. But even at their best, they conceal the great truth about sewing: There are a lot of different ways to do things, each with a different effect.

Of course, the limits of space on printed patterns prevent them from showing more than one construction method, but that method is by no means necessarily the best to use for the task at hand. As you'll see, I often completely disregard the standard procedures in order to get the best results I can, rather than just something easier.

Pattern instructions are full of blind spots, too. Why, for example, don't the instructions for flat-felled seams or rolled hems at least suggest using a felling foot or hemmer foot since these accessories are inexpensive and you'll never produce results that are as uniform and attractive by hand? And do pattern writers really believe that a sleeve placket is better or more easily made if cut out first with a ⅝-in. seam, then hand-basted into shape rather than just ironed and then trimmed along the seams to ¼ in.? Happily, most shirt patterns nowadays show the sleeve placket with ¼-in. seams, but the point is still apt. If you blindly follow the pattern instructions for a shirt (or any other garment for that matter), you're almost guaranteed a homemade look because so little of the shirt is constructed the way a "real" shirt is made.

On the positive side, I've often bought a pattern just because it includes a designer detail I admire, like a concealed-button front or a formal shirt bib, and I want to see the patternmaker's suggested construction method for this detail, which I'll adapt for my own pattern. I usually save up a list of such patterns for pattern sales, but even at full price, sewing patterns are among the world's last bargains—provided you use them with a healthy skepticism.

Most of the skills required to make a shirt are the same as those needed to make any garment. In fact, since there's no hand sewing involved (with the possible exception of sewing on buttons), fewer skills are needed. But you'll probably find that some of the skills involved are new to you, and I suggest making sure that your skills are really skills—that is, that you've thoroughly understood and mastered these techniques. This is where practice comes in.

The skills you'll need are as follows: staystitching; sewing straight, curved and eased or shaped seams; construction ironing; trimming seam allowances; edgestitching and topstitching; making flat-felled seams and rolled hems; sewing the sleeve/body seam; attaching the cuffs and collar band; constructing a placket; and making a collar. To practice these skills as described in this chapter, I suggest you get a couple of yards of inexpensive shirt-weight, 100% cotton fabric from a remnant counter.

STAYSTITCHING AND SEWING SEAMS

Before you begin sewing any seams, you need to *staystitch* all curved or bias seamlines to keep them from stretching out of shape before or during sewing (seams parallel or perpendicular to the selvage don't stretch out of shape and hence don't require staystitching). The curved neckline seams on the yoke and shirt fronts are stretched straight when the collar stand is attached, and staystitching keeps the length of the stretched seamlines from changing. The collar stand itself, which is on grain, does not require staystitching. The shoulder seams on the shirt fronts also require staystitching, at least for beginning shirtmakers. Since these edges are on a slight bias, I've found that if the seams are not staystitched, they can stretch into ugly waves when sewn together.

It's important always to staystitch one layer of material at a time and sew with the grain of the fabric to minimize any distortion of the fabric (see the drawing at left on the facing page). Be careful to keep the fabric flat on the bed of the machine as it goes under the presser foot and not push or pull it. Let the feed dogs move the fabric, or you will stretch it while staystitching and defeat the whole purpose. Staystitch in the seam allowance just beyond the seamline, which is usually at ⅝ in., using eight to ten stitches per inch. The staystitching will be concealed in the seam allowance once the seam is sewn.

Staystitching should be followed by *clipping to the staystitching*. When clipping to the staystitching, make sure you do just that: Clip right to the stitching, not a little bit away, and do so without cutting the stitching. Take it slowly and be careful. If you cut the staystitching, the piece will stretch and you may ruin it. If you don't cut close enough to the stitching, the straight line you get will not equal the length of the matching piece. You don't want to sew right on the cuts, so staystitch in the allowance just beyond the ⅝-in. seamline, clip to the staystitching and sew the seam at ⅝ in.

STAYSTITCHING AND CLIPPING

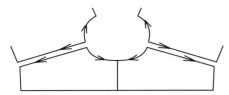

Staystitching stabilizes curved and bias edges. Staystitch shoulder seams on yoke and fronts. After attaching yoke and fronts, staystitch entire neckline. Note sewing directions.

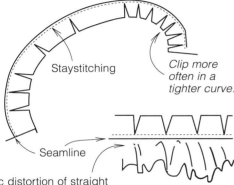

Staystitching

Clip more often in a tighter curve.

Seamline

Fabric distortion of straight edge below seamline joining it to clipped curved edge

On a curved edge, clip right to staystitching to straighten out and seam it to a straight edge.

You'll notice that as you straighten the curved edge, what was once a flat piece of material starts to bunch up and wrinkle below the staystitching. You should also notice, however, a smooth area about ⅛ in. wide right between the clips and wrinkles. That's where you should be sewing to avoid catching any folds of the staystitching.

Clipping right to the stitching applies equally to clip-and-turn situations, the classic example of which is the bound buttonhole. The opening for a sleeve placket is the shirt-related example. To get a smooth flat turn, you must clip exactly to the stitches in the corners of the opening.

Straight seams

Sewing straight seams involves more than just sewing in a perfectly straight line, which is not as easy as it sounds. You must also avoid having any ease in a straight seam, that is, avoid stretching one of the pieces of fabric more than the other as you're sewing them together. The sewing machine's feed dogs tend naturally to stretch the top layer more than the bottom, with the extent of the stretch depending on the presser-foot pressure and the slipperiness of the fabric. This stretching occurs because the feed dogs effectively grab only the bottom piece of fabric, while the top layer (or layers) gets shoved against the presser foot and slips over the bottom layer. A walking foot (see p. 17), whether built into the machine or a separate attachment, helps by putting feed dogs on top of the fabric too. Pinning, however, doesn't help, unless you pin every couple of inches. Otherwise, you simply get little bulges at each pin as you come to it.

To practice sewing straight seams, cut a few on-grain strips of fabric about 2 in. by 12 in. Carefully align two of these fabric rectangles, and start a ¼-in. seam. Sew about 1 in. in and stop with the needle down. Now grab the far ends of both rectangles with one hand and the near ends with the other, and pull slightly and evenly in opposite directions, creating a little tension without deflecting the needle at all. The trick now is to continue pulling

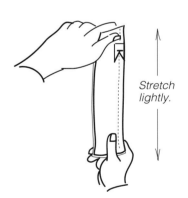

Stretch lightly.

evenly on each end of the strips and let the feed dogs move the fabric as they would normally, so that the stitch length is not affected. This is easier than it sounds. Remember, too, that your aim is also to keep the seams straight and even.

If the two pieces to be seamed are on the bias, you must staystitch both so that your pulling does not change the shape of the fabric pieces. If you're working with long seams, sew them in sections so that your hands stay no more than 12 in. apart, just as you've practiced with the fabric scraps. This technique also helps eliminate fabric puckering at the stitching line. Even if you have a walking foot on your machine, spend some time practicing this technique. It's the basis for another skill—eased seams—discussed on pp. 85-87.

Curved seams

Curved seams involve at least two separate problems: following a curve as you sew, and sewing a curved piece to a straight piece, for example, the collar stand to the neck. To follow a curve so that your stitching line is smooth rather than a series of small, straight lines, you have to move the fabric while the machine is running. The trick that works for me, especially when using exotic presser feet like hemmers and fellers, is to remember that most curves are parts of circles. If you can locate the approximate center of the circle that the curve is part of, you can use it as a pivot point while the feed dogs do the work.

Imagine that you've taped a thumbtack, point up, on the machine bed, just to the left of and about 2 in. away from the machine's needle. If you then pushed a square of fabric down over the thumbtack's point and slipped the edge of the fabric under the presser foot and started sewing, you'd find that the machine stitched a perfect circle. This is exactly the principle behind circular embroidery devices. Move the pin closer to the needle or farther away from it, and the circle will get smaller or larger, respectively.

When you're making clothing, you can't tape tacks on your machine bed and poke holes through your fabric, but you can use your hands to move the fabric *as if* it were held down at the pivot point so that the feed dogs move the fabric in a circle. Of course, this is easier when you're sewing outside curves whose pivot point is to the left of the machine needle. It's a little more difficult for inside curves since the pivot point is off the fabric. For these latter curves, keep the position of the pivot point in mind as you use your hands to move the fabric in a circle in relation to the pivot point.

Practice sewing curves in both directions by cutting pairs of S-shaped scraps of fabric and carefully seaming them together. Small curves are harder to sew than large ones, but using the circle

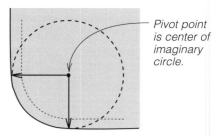

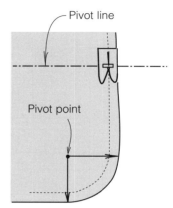

Pivot point is center of imaginary circle.

A curved edge is usually part of a circle.

Pivot line

Pivot point

To sew an outside curve, pivot fabric when pivot point hits pivot line.

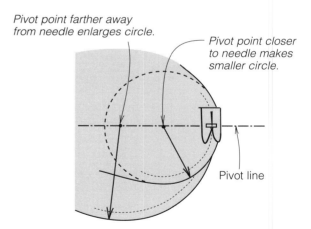

Pivot point farther away from needle enlarges circle.

Pivot point closer to needle makes smaller circle.

Pivot line

technique will make them a lot easier to work with. If you use the edge of the presser foot or the lines on the machine bed as seam-width guides, remember that only the part of the foot or line that aligns with the pivot point and the needle is an accurate guide when you're sewing curves, not the front edges.

When sewing a curved edge to a straight edge, you won't really be sewing a curve. Instead you'll first clip the staystitched curved edge and stretch it out straight to sew the seam joining the two edges as a straight seam. The point to remember in joining curved and straight edges is that the length of the seamlines is the same, even though one is curved.

To straighten the curved edge, clip the seam allowance at intervals ¼ in. to 1 in. apart, depending on the size of the curve—the tighter the curve, the closer the clips should be (see the drawing at left on p. 83). Then pin the straight and curved edges together, starting at the midpoint and working out to each end so that the seam-allowance edges match. Spend a lot of time getting these edges aligned—no clipped pieces should be dangling out. By carefully matching the edges, you'll get the staystitching to lie straight. This is usually a fairly awkward job, requiring lots of pins, at least one for every clip, but it works very well if you pin carefully.

Eased seams

By an *eased seam*, I mean one in which one edge is purposely stretched while it is attached to another unstretched edge. As I mentioned above, this happens automatically to a certain degree by the action of the feed dogs. What you want to do when sewing an eased seam is to control this action and use it to build shape into previously flat cloth.

To practice sewing an eased seam, take two more 2-in. by 12-in. fabric rectangles and align them so that all the edges match. Fold the rectangles in half lengthwise so that they're now 2 in. by 6 in., and mark the midpoint of the fold. Then hold the two ends of the strips together to make a circle and notice that the inner strip buckles a little bit. If you were to add a layer or two of interfacing, this buckling would become severe. The principle at work here is simply that for one thing to fit inside another, it must be slightly smaller. Thus, for one of two circles to fit inside the other, the first must have a smaller circumference—for example, an interlining must be smaller than the pattern piece it lines or it will wrinkle, an inner collar must be smaller than an outer collar, and so on.

By extension, if two pieces of fabric of unequal length are attached so that the shorter is stretched to match the longer, the shorter piece will pull the longer one into a curve. This is just what we're after when trying to get a collar to fit the curve of the neck.

To practice achieving this effect, unfold the two cloth rectangles, position them under the presser foot at midpoint and start a ¼-in. seam toward one end. Stitch straight for about ½ in., then grab the two layers together at the center with one hand and the bottom piece only with the other hand (Step 1 in the drawing on p. 86). Use two fingers of the second hand to keep the top layer aligned. Then continue stitching, but pull just the bottom layer taut, allowing both to feed regularly, just as for a straight seam, and trying to keep the seam's width even on both pieces. This is where your skill with straight sewing comes in.

A simpler way to sew an eased seam is to trim the bottom piece a little short (⅛ in. to ¼ in. on each end) before matching the midpoint. After sewing the first ½ in. from the midpoint, align the short edges and pull both pieces until the longer top piece lies flat and taut against the bottom piece, which has been stretched to meet it. This method is a good way to control the amount you stretch the fabric.

Try it both ways, however, and see how much extra length you can get out of the bottom piece by the time you're about ½ in. from the end of the unstretched piece (you should get at least ¼ in. to ⅜ in.). Then stop, needle down, turn the rectangles and sew the ends together, leaving them still unequal (Step 2). Try to make sure that the bottom edge sticks out the same distance all along the end.

Now return to the middle of the rectangles, and sew the other end in the same way (Step 3). You will, of course, be using the other side of the presser foot to guide your ¼-in. seam. You should see a distinct curve now built into the two layers (Step 4). Start thinking of this construction as a rudimentary collar. Trim the seam allowances at the corners (Step 5) and turn it right side out.

SEWING EASED SEAMS

1

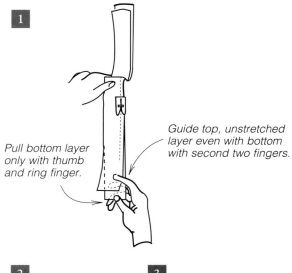

Pull bottom layer only with thumb and ring finger.

Guide top, unstretched layer even with bottom with second two fingers.

2

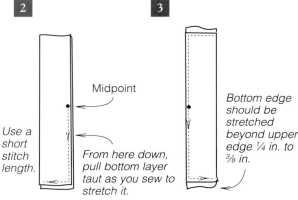

Midpoint

Use a short stitch length.

From here down, pull bottom layer taut as you sew to stretch it.

3

Bottom edge should be stretched beyond upper edge ¼ in. to ⅜ in.

4

Stretching bottom layer as you sew builds a curve into the two layers.

5

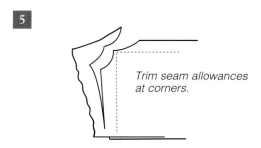

Trim seam allowances at corners.

When you iron this collarlike construction after turning it right side out, you should notice several things: the stretched piece (call it the "under collar" for now) lies smooth, while the "top collar" is loose and even wrinkled; the short seams at the ends tend to pull under toward the under collar; and, even under heavy pressing, the inward curve remains. All these effects occur because the stretched under collar refuses to stay stretched and relaxes instead. Had you measured the collar pieces before sewing them together, you would have also noticed that the collar's finished length is now slightly less than the original measured length of the top collar.

Why bother with all these "problems"? Well, first of all, we're going to try to turn these problems into manageable results. And, second, this is the best way I know of to get a beautiful collar without the elaborate machinery of the manufacturer. Let's consider these problems one by one.

LOOSE TOP COLLAR You've probably noticed when you iron some manufactured shirt collars that it's easy to get little creases around the topstitching at the front edges. You may even have thought it was a defect in the shirt. Far from it. Unless the creasing is excessive, it's one hallmark of a quality shirt because it means that the collar has been shaped, as we have just done, but in a controlled and precise manner, by a skillful maker.

The way to iron this collar, as you've probably discovered, is to start at each end and iron smoothly toward the middle so that the excess, which disappears when worn, is at the back of the collar. In the days of starched, detachable collars, it used to be standard practice to iron the curve back into collars and keep them in a rounded box (you can see one of these boxes at top right in the second photo after the Introduction). You may find it useful to let one end of a collar you're ironing hang over the edge of the ironing board so that it curves naturally. If you send your shirts out for professional laundering, you'll want very little excess material in the top collar because laundries iron collars flat.

SEAMS PULLED TO UNDERSIDE OF COLLAR   This, of course, is not a problem, unless the effect is extreme. A well-made collar has the edge seams somewhat concealed underneath the edge. Allowing the collar to curve helps to position the seam where you want it, just underneath the edge of the collar. Pressing the collar flat pulls the seam too far under the edge.

CHANGE FROM ORIGINAL MEASURED LENGTH   Now here's a real problem. How do you know how big to cut your collar pieces if sewing them together shortens the length? Obviously they have to be cut bigger, but how much bigger? The answer depends on how much you stretch the under collar, how much interfacing you use and how thick the shirting material is. The change in length can only be determined by trial and error. In other words, make a sample, measuring it before and after sewing to determine how much smaller the finished product is than the original top collar. Then add this difference to the top-collar pattern.

Control comes from managing to stretch the under collar by a fixed amount each time. Since the extent of the stretch determines the amount of curve in the collar and the consequent amount of trouble you (or your laundry) will have ironing it, the extent of the stretch is a matter of personal choice. I think you should stretch between 1/8 in. and 1/4 in. So the range of stretch is pretty narrow and determined principally by the thickness of the shirting and the amount of interfacing used. If you always use the same interfacing when making shirts from typical dress-shirt cottons, it's not hard to establish a fixed amount of pattern change and stretching for each collar. When you make a chamois cloth or wool sportshirt, make another sample collar. Making a second, rudimentary collar will be a good opportunity to test the interfacing you've chosen. When you determine the amount of stretch you're happy with, you can reduce each end of the under collar by that amount, as suggested above, centering the notches in the middle, sewing about 1 in., then matching the ends and pulling both top and under collar even. Working this way helps stretch the whole under collar, not just the long edge, and also ensures uniformity.

Now, just when you think you're finished with all this stretching, there's still more to do. A collar not only curves around the neck but also folds over at the neckline. So, right after turning the corner of the collar point when stitching up the collar's short end, you have a second seam to sew — that on the front edge — while stretching the under collar. In this case, however, you don't really want to produce an overall curve, especially if the collar is a long, pointed one. Instead, you just want to allow for shaping in the 1-in. to 1½-in. section that leads into the fold where the collar joins the collar stand. So stitch straight along this seam, without pulling, until the last 1½ in. or so, and then pull firmly. If the collar point is short, pull just the part near the raw edge joining the collar to the stand as much as you can, in either case stitching right off the end. When you can't grab the end because it is too small, just press it down against the bed of the machine, resisting the pull of the feed dogs while you pull both pieces from the back of the presser foot. It's more important to have a straight seam than a perfectly even stitch length.

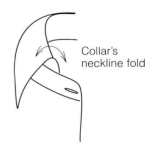

Collar's neckline fold

I urge you to try making several sample collars with scraps of shirt-weight cotton until the procedure becomes entirely familiar. On your first efforts, don't use interfacing or worry about the collar style. Try a simple rectangular shape, and then experiment with different angles for the collar's short ends (you'll discover that a bias angle stretches much more easily). The point of all this is simply to make the real thing with guaranteed success, especially when you're working with expensive or irreplaceable fabric. What you're doing is cumulatively gathering skills in preparation for making a real collar with interfacing, topstitching and so on, so that when you're actually making this collar, none of the separate steps is a problem. (You'll find more information about making a collar on pp. 106-109 — I saved the collar till last because it's probably the most difficult of the skills needed for shirtmaking.)

CONSTRUCTION IRONING

Construction ironing, that is, the way you use your iron when constructing clothing and forming garment details, is completely different from the kind of ironing you do in the laundry room when you're watching the soaps on TV. In the laundry room, your main interest is in making the clothes look good in any way you can. In construction ironing, you have to be much clearer about the effect your ironing has on the fabric. To see what I mean, take two more fabric strips and iron them, without using steam or spray. Now lay them side by side and spray one of them with water. You'll see that the water makes the fabric wrinkle up like a piece of bacon. The fibers are puffing up with moisture and pulling in, which makes the piece appear to shrink.

Iron the dampened fabric again, this time just laying the iron down on the fabric and applying only downward pressure, which you'll notice will produce lots of little puckers. To really iron the piece flat, you have to slide the iron a bit along the fabric, smoothing it and, in fact, stretching it out. That is, you have to iron the fabric, not just press it. With dress-shirt material, you need to iron, not press, for the most part.

Now spray the second piece and begin to iron one end. Then grab the other end and pull, while you iron toward it. You'll see that you can stretch the piece quite a bit and actually iron the stretch into it. If you slide the iron firmly sideways, you'll stretch the fabric more than if you use the iron's point without much pressure. It may occur to you that you can avoid the hassle of pulling the under collar while sewing it by just pressing a stretch into it beforehand. It almost works, and, in fact, may be enough for you. In my experience, however, you just don't get the right amount of curve this way. You end up having to pull it a bit anyway. But try ironing in the curve if you like, especially on cuffs.

The stretching that occurs in ironing is what pressing—that is, just laying the iron down on the fabric, applying only downward pressure—tries to avoid, particularly with woolens. If you've stretched shirting cotton, just spray it with water again, and the stretch will relax entirely. The point of stretching the fabric is to see what extremes are possible and to decide which you'll usually want to avoid and which, upon occasion, you may want to put to use.

It's important to keep grain direction in mind when you iron because woven fabrics tend to stretch much more on the crosswise (weft) grain than on the lengthwise (warp) grain. This is because the warp is kept under tension during weaving, while the weft thread that's woven side to side is only pulled smooth and not really stretched. Thus, for minimal stretching, iron with the lengthwise grain. (See also pp. 8-9 for information on ironing the fabric in preparation for sewing and p. 119 for information on ironing the completed shirt.)

When you're preparing details like plackets, bands and pockets for sewing, it's the iron that shapes the piece, primarily by creasing edges. (Be careful not to stretch pieces while you shape them, particularly the front bands.) This is the time for carefully positioning patterns and stripes, and making sure that the detail is just how you want it to look on the finished shirt before you commit yourself with the needle. I use a basting glue stick judiciously to hold down narrow folded edges and to position details on the garment. Ironing the glued spot dries the glue and makes it hold until wetted again, whether by spraying or washing.

It's my experience that you get much more predictable and desirable results from a dry iron and a spray bottle than from an iron set for steam. With spray, you have much better control of the amount and placement of dampness, and the steam is held to the fabric rather than being forced through it. I haven't put water in my iron for years.

When turning collars that have been eased together, you'll see that one of the seam allowances you're trying to iron down on the point presser (the top collar) is full of wrinkles. The remedy for these wrinkles is to lay the collar flat on the ironing board before ironing this seam, and iron-stretch the seam a little. Then the seam allowances will flatten much more easily. After turning the collar, just spray it to relax the stretch and then iron in the curve. At this point, the iron is what helps you position the seams by creasing the edge of the top collar when you have it just right.

Keep checking the two collar points for similarity and remember to press them inward toward the collar, avoiding any wrinkles by curling the collar around the top of a sleeveboard or off the edge of the ironing board. When the collar looks great, you're ready to topstitch.

TRIMMING SEAM ALLOWANCES

Trimming seam allowances is used both in grading straight seam allowances (that is, trimming each layer of allowance shorter than the previous one) and in clipping or eliminating curved and corner seam allowances. In both cases, the point of trimming is to remove bulk. In the case of graded seams, the widest layer of allowance lies against the outer side of the garment, thus covering and smoothing over the narrower seam layers to the inside. On shirts, seams are trimmed on the yoke, the straight sections of the collar, collar stand and cuffs. Other seams in the shirt are flat-felled.

Trimming seams is most easily done with the rotary cutter, which cuts both straight and fast. Scissors, in fact, are difficult to use to cut ⅛ in. to ¼ in. off a seam and keep the cutting line straight.

Clipping to curves is, I think, a much misunderstood procedure. Like clipping to staystitching or seam corners, it has a very specific task to accomplish — enabling a curved seam to turn smoothly — and if not done just right, interferes, rather than helps, with the task. The only curves in shirts that need to be clipped are those found in details that you've opted to make round: collars and cuffs and collar bands or collar stands whose ends are curved.

The curves in these optional details are all outward curves, and wedge shapes are traditionally cut out of the seam allowances to remove bulk, after trimming them to ¼ in. I propose that the seams here be sewn once with very small stitches, and that the allowances be removed completely — that is, cut right off just beyond the stitching line. The reason for this is that unless the little wedge cuts are very precisely made, they will either overlap or leave gaps in the allowance when the seam is turned back inside. Either effect ruins the flat seam you're aiming for. And worse, when turning the seam right side out, the points of the wedges tend to be visible along the curve. So instead of a continuous, smooth curved line, you get a series of lines and little corners. Try my method once, and if you don't agree, forget it. But please try it. You'll have an opportunity to do so when we discuss cuff construction.

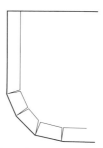

Clipped seam allowances in curves tend to create irregular edges.

Trim off seam allowance instead.

When trimming a collar point, clip straight across the tip, at most ¹⁄₁₆ in. away. Then pare away the sides so that there's no possibility of any overlap when the allowances are turned to the inside. Try to work with each collar point in exactly the same way since identical construction of the points each step of the way, even when clipping, helps to ensure that they'll look the same when you finally turn them right side out. We'll look in detail at the process of turning the points a little later (see pp. 105-106).

EDGESTITCHING
AND TOPSTITCHING

Edgestitching and topstitching are similar stitches in that they're not designed to be turned and pressed out of sight. Both serve primarily to hold seams and interfacing in place. Nonetheless edgestitching and topstitching are also decorative, so they must be beautiful, straight, even and uniformly distant from the edges of the details they adorn.

Edgestitching is a construction stitch used to attach sleeve plackets, pockets and the front edge of the yoke. It is also used on the back edge of the attached yoke to match the finish of the front, adding a desirable crispness to the look of the yoke, which is unhappily missing from many ready-made shirts. Accurate edgestitching is also an integral part of my procedure for collar making, as you'll see, so I heartily recommend that you practice it a bit if only to confirm that you can do it. A short stitch length slows the machine down nicely, and short stitches are a reliable indicator of high-quality construction. The exact distance you choose to edgestitch from the edge is less important than that you maintain that distance scrupulously. Stay well under $\frac{1}{16}$ in., however, or you'll be topstitching, not edgestitching.

The distance the stitches are sewn from the edge also makes a difference in how the stitching is managed. Edgestitching is done, as its name implies, by stitching alongside an edge, using the edge itself

Edgestitching should be right on edge. If stitching is more than $\frac{1}{16}$ in. from edge, it's topstitching.

Topstitching

Edgestitching

as the guide. Topstitching, usually at $\frac{1}{4}$ in. from the edge, involves using some other guide, usually the edge of the presser foot, to keep your stitching straight. In either case, refer to my discussion of curved seams on pp. 84-85. When topstitching curves, remember that you must use only the portion of the foot that lies exactly opposite the needle. You can use the front of the foot as a guide when sewing straight, but for curves you'll go wrong if you don't follow the directions on p. 84 exactly. It's also perfectly legitimate to mark the exact curve you want first, then stitch on the marking. All's fair in sewing.

The ultimate challenge for both topstitching and straight stitching is to pull tension into the fabric while ensuring that there is no variance in stitch length. You'll need to do this on collars and cuffs if you haven't got a walking-foot attachment and free arm on your machine to ensure that the loose top layer doesn't shift when you topstitch the long edge on these details. It's actually not that hard to do and you're the only one likely to notice. So don't get discouraged—just practice on a few scraps.

To topstitch a collar or cuff, start at one short edge of the collar or cuff and sew smoothly at the desired distance from the edge down to and a little beyond the corner, whether it's pointed or curved. Then pick up the two ends in front of and behind the presser foot and stretch them until the top layer is taut. Continue sewing to the other corner, maintaining even pressure, and relax, negotiate the turn and sew off the other end.

For both topstitching and edgestitching, it's important to adjust the thread tension so that the best-looking stitch is on the top of the collar or cuff as it goes through the presser foot. I don't mean to set the tension so that it's unequal but rather to adjust it slightly to favor the bottom, so that none of the bobbin thread is visible on top. Topstitched and edgestitched details are thick enough so that you may not need to make any adjustments, but do examine both top and bottom carefully to see which side of the stitch you like better. If it's the bottom, loosen the top tension a tiny bit, even on a self-adjusting machine.

It's also very useful—and great for one's confidence—to be able to adjust bobbin tension, which is very easy to do. You'll probably need to tighten the bobbin a little in any case as you begin to sew, particularly since you'll be using a slightly finer thread than for your usual sewing. The only tricky part in adjusting bobbin tension is not losing the little screw on the bobbin, so don't make the adjustment over a shag carpet.

The tension is right when you hold the full bobbin case by the thread, like a yo-yo by its string, and the case moves down the thread only if you bounce it slightly. If the bobbin slides down under its own weight, the tension is too loose, no matter how thick the thread. Conversely, if it doesn't budge when you bounce it, the tension is too tight. Make a little note and attach it somewhere on your machine to remind yourself which direction to turn the bobbin screw to tighten or loosen it. On most machines, turning clockwise tightens the tension, and counterclockwise loosens it.

FLAT-FELLED SEAMS AND ROLLED HEMS

Flat-felling seams and rolling hems on shirts should be done with special feet or, in my opinion, not at all. Unless you're making them at least ¼ in. wide, as you might on a heavy wool shirt, doing them by hand is a painful process that virtually guarantees sloppy results. The felling foot and rolled hemmer virtually guarantee beautiful results. They work very much the same way, by folding over a very narrow edge and stitching it neatly down at a precise distance from an edge. The difference in the two feet is that the hemmer folds the fabric twice, rolling the raw edge under, while the feller folds it once, flat.

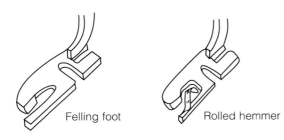

Felling foot   Rolled hemmer

Before you read any further, check to see whether your machine came with either of these feet. The rolled hemmer is more common, but some machine dealers, for example, Bernina, supply a felling foot as standard equipment on some of their machines, like the 830. If you don't have one or both feet, first check with the dealer for your brand of machine before resorting to other sources. Each foot will cost between $10 and $20, and you should get them both in the ⅛-in. size. You won't regret it. (Note that for the Bernina and other machines with metrically sized feet, you should get the 4mm rather than the 2mm rolled-hemmer foot since the 2mm is too narrow for working on shirting fabric.) If you can't find the feller, you can use the hemmer for both tasks, but it's not as easy to use for flat-felling seams.

To use either foot, the first step is to roll or fold by hand the end of the fabric (or layers of fabric) in the same way you want the foot to fold them. The feller takes a ¼-in. seam allowance and folds it over an ⅛-in. seam allowance, and then into an ⅛-in. seam. The hemmer rolls over about ¼ in. of raw edge, so the hem is ⅛ in. (See the Step 1 drawings of the flat-felled seam and rolled hem on p. 92, and form something approximating them by hand and with your iron.)

Next, place the folded or rolled edge under the foot as if it were a normal foot, positioning it so that the needle hits the inner edge where you want it; it should not be necessary to adjust the needle. Sew normally an inch or so, then stop, needle down, and raise the foot (see the Step 2 drawings on p. 92). Now bring the raw edge or edges up into the slot of the foot and over the inside lip or tab that curls the fabric. On the feller, this lip is flat. On the hemmer, there's also a sort of spiral into which you wind the fabric. (Using a pair of long, thin tweezers may help you get the fabric wound into the spiral.) Lower the foot and proceed, watching the foot do the work.

Your only job is to keep the same amount of fabric in the slot of the foot as the fabric moves forward so that the seam or hem is the same width throughout. Easy to do until you get to a curve! Here's where all your skill in edgestitching or topstitching curves comes in, and the principle is the same. Find the center of the circle the curve comes from and pivot from it so that the edge of the foot opposite the

WORKING WITH FELLING FOOT AND ROLLED HEMMER

Felling

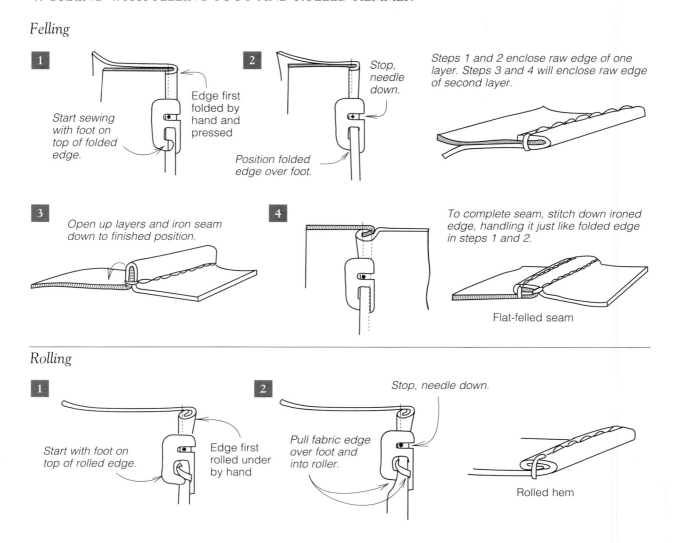

1 Start sewing with foot on top of folded edge.

Edge first folded by hand and pressed

2 Stop, needle down.

Position folded edge over foot.

Steps 1 and 2 enclose raw edge of one layer. Steps 3 and 4 will enclose raw edge of second layer.

3 Open up layers and iron seam down to finished position.

4 To complete seam, stitch down ironed edge, handling it just like folded edge in steps 1 and 2.

Flat-felled seam

Rolling

1 Start with foot on top of rolled edge.

Edge first rolled under by hand

2 Stop, needle down.

Pull fabric edge over foot and into roller.

Rolled hem

---

needle is always the same distance from the edge of the fabric. It's easier to do than to describe. Cut out some S-curved scraps of fabric and practice.

When rolling a hem, if you find that the raw edge starts to turn up and out, instead of down and under the roller, stop immediately and form a rolled edge for an inch or two in front of the foot, holding it down as it goes through the foot. You may also find that holding the folded edge up off the machine bed may encourage the roll to form correctly.

Both felling and hemming feet have a problem with bulk, especially when crossing other seams. For this reason, when you're hemming over the flat-

felled side seams or flat-felling over the sleeve/body seam, it may be necessary to stop just short of the seam, and start sewing again just on the other side of it, the same way as you began at the outset. When you're done, hand-form the skipped part and topstitch down to match the rest of the seam or hem.

Now that you've been introduced to these two feet, let's consider them separately. Rolled hems are likely to have much sharper curves in them than flat-felled seams, so your practice should involve different shapes for each foot. The side seam where you'll need the flat-felling foot is unlikely to have any sharp curves, so you don't need to practice anything but

Flat-felled princess seams

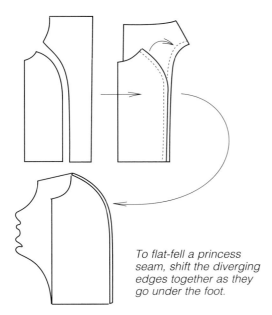

To flat-fell a princess seam, shift the diverging edges together as they go under the foot.

Shirttail hemline variations

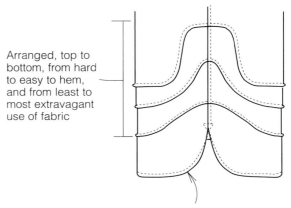

Arranged, top to bottom, from hard to easy to hem, and from least to most extravagant use of fabric

This hemline must be finished before sewing side seams. It should be reinforced at side seam, with topstitching or small triangle of fabric.

gentle curves with this one. You can nonetheless flat-fell sharp curves, as you can see in the drawing of princess-style flat-felled seams above.

The great thing is that on a shirt, you're in charge of how you shape your hems (see the top drawing at right). The sharper the curves you draw on your pattern, the harder they'll be to finish, so it's up to you. Fortunately the hems are mostly out of sight, even if the shirttails are worn out, so perfection is not required. Look at a few commercial shirts — they're not perfect either.

Flat-felling is a little more complex. Whereas rolling a hem involves stitching the edge down once, felling a seam involves stitching the edge down twice. In flat-felling, the two edges of fabric being joined are first positioned with right sides together and then passed through the felling foot, which folds one edge back over the other. Then the two pieces are opened out flat and the seam is ironed flat against one of the two pieces. With the two pieces still opened flat, the seam is again passed through the foot to sew an anchoring seam parallel to the first (see the drawing on the facing page).

You start out the same as in the first pass, with the edge you're going to stitch down under the foot. After sewing an inch or so, stop with the needle down and lift the foot. Then guide the fabric edge over the lip of the foot. Guiding the second seam is much easier than sewing the first since you just need to keep the first seam butted firmly up against the inside edge of the foot. As long as you do that, you'll sew the folded seam allowances down with a beautifully straight, perfectly parallel seam. Notice that it's just as nice on the top side as it is on the under side. Different but equally finished-looking. You can decide later which side of the seam you prefer to call the inside and which the outside, and sew your actual shirt seams accordingly, making sure

Either side of flat-felled seam can be used on outside of finished shirt.

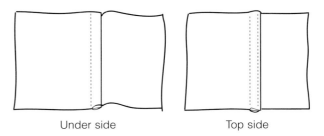

Under side   Top side

to treat all flat-felled seams on your shirt the same. You have to be careful to catch the whole ⅛-in. width of the top seam allowance in your first pass through the foot, particularly on any fabric that ravels easily. If this edge is not caught firmly, it will fray out at the seam.

Unfortunately, there is one aspect of flat-felling that is awkward. Consider your problem if the two edges being joined are the right and left sides of the same piece of cloth, instead of two separate pieces. This is the problem you'll encounter when seaming a sleeve. How, then, do you lay the fabric flat and sew the second seam? Well, you can lay only a small section of the seam flat at a time, and so you have to sneak in at it to sew it, while keeping the rest of the fabric out of the way of the needle. There's no way around it. It's awkward any way you try to do it.

Here's where you'll be glad you have a free-arm machine, or wish you did if you don't. Flat-felling a sleeve seam can be managed on a flatbed machine, but it's even harder. In either case, what you need to do is keep a short section of the seam, about 2 in. to 3 in., straight so that it can pass through the foot, while the rest bunches up behind the foot (on the flatbed) or bends 90° around the free arm. The wider your sleeve, and the longer the placket, the easier it will be. Be thankful that the felling foot works so well. You'll have no trouble keeping the seams even and straight, no matter how much you're working to manipulate the rest of the sleeve.

POSITIONING SLEEVE FOR
FLAT-FELLING SEAM

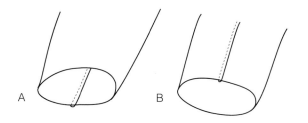

It's easier to flat-fell sleeve seam with sleeve turned inside out and extra fabric held above work, as in A rather than B.

On a flatbed machine, material will also be bunching up in front of the machine since the underside of the sleeve can't ever pass beneath the needle. For this reason, I suggest you roll up the excess material as you sew, going as far as you can and, if necessary, breaking the thread, repositioning the bulk of the fabric behind the needle and starting again to sew at the same place. You may find it easier to work with the sleeve inside out and with the sleeve material held above the seam rather than below it, as shown in the drawing below.

All this can be done, and it's not as difficult as it sounds. It's merely the most awkward part of making sleeves. You'll quickly see that it's worth the effort because the results look effortless and perfect, as if tossed off with an ease entirely at odds with the real challenge involved.

Finally, remember that since you want both your sleeves to look the same, you'll need to sew each of the two seams in the opposite direction so that both lie either toward the front or toward the back of the sleeve. Thus, start one from the bottom of the body, sewing onto the sleeve, and start the other from the sleeve, sewing onto the body.

SEWING THE SLEEVE/BODY SEAM

It was truly a joy to figure out a simple procedure for sewing the sleeve/body, or armscye, seam, which by ordinary methods is a bear to do beautifully. This seam needs to be flat-felled, but it's too big and curved for a felling foot. You can't get away with sloppy results, either inside or out, because the seam is so visible. On fine, light-colored fabrics, you can see right through the shirt fronts, and an irregular seam finish would ruin the shirt's appearance, even if it were beautifully topstitched. We're going to sew this seam using only one pin and the ordinary presser foot, by folding under the seam allowance before sewing. But before we construct a sample, look at the cross section of the sleeve/body seam in the drawing on the facing page to get acquainted with its anatomy and the basic steps it involves.

CROSS SECTION OF SLEEVE/BODY SEAM

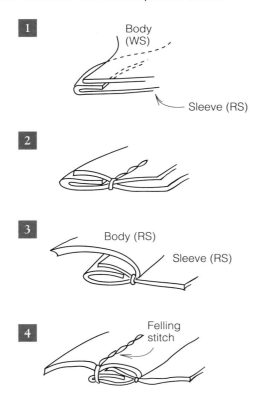

1 Body (WS)

Sleeve (RS)

2

3 Body (RS)

Sleeve (RS)

4 Felling stitch

To try out my procedure, prepare two rectangles of fabric, as shown in Step 1 of the drawing on p. 96. Draw a seamline on each that approximates the curves of the armhole and sleeve cap. To get the lengths equal, hold a tape measure at the length you want, say, 15 in., then arrange it on edge roughly in the shape of each seam and draw a smooth line to follow that shape on each rectangle (Step 2). Now draw a cutting line so that the seam allowance is ⅞ in. on the "sleeve" (Step 3) and ⅜ in. on the "body" (Step 4). Then cut off the excess on these lines.

At the ironing board, iron over a folded edge on the sleeve of about ⅜ in., starting at either edge, so the seam allowance is about ½ in. wide (Step 5). To simplify this process, I use a cardboard template the exact size and shape of the sleeve edge as a form (see p. 63). You'll notice that on the bias portion of the seam it's easy to follow the curve so that you get a smooth straight line at the fold. That's what we're aiming for. As you get to the top center, stop folding

and start again from the other side toward the middle. When you've ironed a folded edge on both sides, the fold may want to pucker at the top, but try to press out any little fullness in the seam allowance. What's important is that the folded edge be a smooth line, with no little corners. Basting glue is helpful here; you might also clip once cautiously at the center, stopping ⅛ in. from the edge. You shouldn't need the glue anywhere else since you're using all cotton, which takes a crease well. Use lots of spray or steam and get it crisp—but use the glue if necessary.

Now mark the midpoints on each seamline and lay the pieces together so the points match, with the folded edge upward, the body on top and the center lines parallel. The folded edge should stick out just about ⅛ in. from the raw edge of the body. Pin the two edges together, as shown in Step 6. On the real shirt, this would be with right sides together.

Next comes the fun part. Position this unit under the presser foot at the center dot and start a ⅜-in. seam (measuring from the body edge, not the folded sleeve edge) toward one end. Sew only as far as the two edges remain parallel to each other (perhaps an inch or so), then stop, with the needle down, and adjust the edges so that another few inches are parallel (Step 7). Continue sewing until you once again need to align the edges, working in this fashion until you get to the end (Step 8). The seams should end at about the same point, but complete accuracy is not important on this test.

Sew the other half of the sleeve seam the same way, which will mean using the other side of the foot since the body must remain on top in order for you to see how the edges lie. Don't worry about a little stretching. What's important is that the seamline be a smooth curve with no angles and the two seam allowances remain consistent, so do it carefully. On the real shirt, you'll match your seamline lengths carefully before cutting the pattern out, so the ends will match. For these practice pieces, just trim off any little discrepancies. Ignore pattern instructions to ease the sleeve seam.

Now unfold the two pieces and go back to the ironing board. Notice that you can't iron this seam flat except in sections. First, iron the sleeve from the inside, ignoring how the body folds. Make sure, however, that the folded edge is still in place and

CONSTRUCTING SAMPLE SLEEVE/BODY SEAM

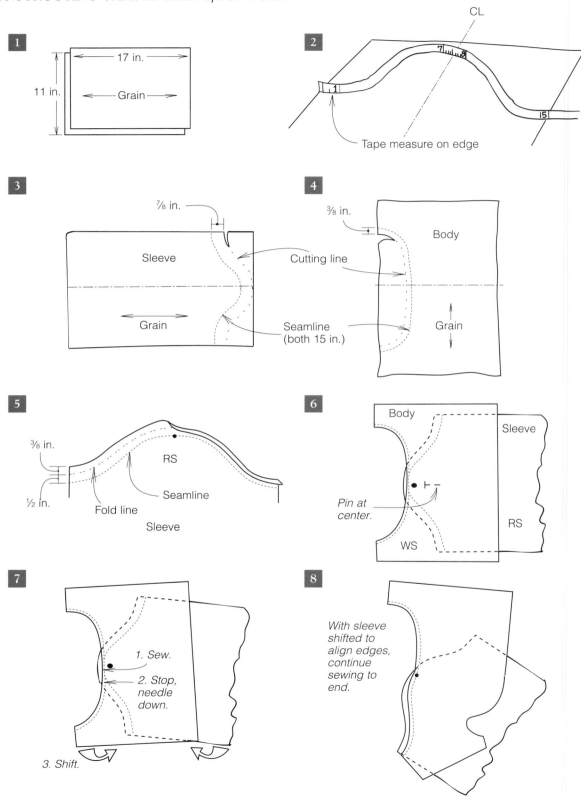

1

17 in.

11 in.

Grain

2

CL

7 8

1

15

Tape measure on edge

3

⁷⁄₈ in.

Sleeve

Cutting line

Grain

Seamline
(both 15 in.)

4

³⁄₈ in.

Body

Grain

5

³⁄₈ in.

½ in.

RS

Seamline

Fold line

Sleeve

6

Body

Sleeve

Pin at
center.

WS

RS

7

1. Sew.

2. Stop,
needle
down.

3. Shift.

8

With sleeve
shifted to
align edges,
continue
sewing to
end.

that the seam is smooth. Correct either or both of these now while you have the chance. Next, turn the seam in sections over a pressing ham and iron the body from the outside, ignoring the sleeve.

Iron the seam allowance toward the body, keeping it smooth. Check on the right side to see that the seam is pressed fully open. Now starting again at the midpoint, topstitch at a careful ⅜ in. from the first seam, off the edge, then turn and do the other half of the seam. If everything was done right, you'll have no trouble catching the folded edge of the seam allowance in the topstitching. On the actual shirt, the body will be a construction combining a front, the two layers of yoke and the back. You can trim away some of the thickness at the yoke ends, but no other trimming will be necessary. You'll start the topstitching at the back of the yoke rather than at the middle, so the join will be less obvious. Pull the threads to the underside before you start the second run in the other direction, ending exactly on top of the first line, and backstitch inconspicuously after a few stitches.

ATTACHING CUFFS AND COLLAR BANDS

Now we're going to try combining some of the above techniques with a new one. The technique I'm about to show you is so good that it almost belongs in the realm of trickery. It's a way of ensuring that the ends of collar bands and cuffs match the respective edges of front bands and plackets, while completely reducing the bulk of the combined seam allowances. I owe the idea for this technique entirely to a fascinating book called *Sewing Magic* by Barbara Hellyer (see the Bibliography on pp. 168-169). I send her a little heartfelt gratitude every time I make a shirt. With a little adaptation, her method was really the final touch that assured me that I could easily make professional-looking shirts. It's only one of many great ideas in her book, which I recommend wholeheartedly, if you can find it.

Here, in brief, is how the technique works. Instead of constructing a cuff or collar band before attaching it, hoping that it's just the right finished length (and invariably finding that it's not!), attach just the top cuff (or collar) to the sleeve (or neck), with right sides together, then attach the remaining cuff or collar piece plus interfacing to the first one, but only along the opposite long edge, leaving the ends open (see the drawing on p. 98). Now here's the trick: Arrange the sleeve (or shirt front) so that it's *inside* the cuff (or collar), still wrong side out, as I'll describe. Then you can finish off the ends exactly where the sleeve or body ends, going around the corner and restitching an inch or two of the sleeve/cuff seam (or neck/collar seam). Sew with a very short stitch length so that, before turning the cuff or collar inside out, the seam allowance can be graded or removed all the way around to the other long edge. Let's try a sample cuff. (Note that your sleeve placket may not be long enough to permit the cuff to lie flat. In this case, you'll have to work with each end of the cuff separately.)

Take a rectangle of scrap cotton about 10 in. by 15 in. I suggest you try roll-hemming the two long edges with the hemmer foot in order to give yourself a definite edge, like the edge of the sleeve placket or shirt front. Then cut two "cuffs" about 11 in. by 3 in. (Step 1 in the drawing on p. 98). I also suggest that you shape the short ends of the cuffs into curves so you can see how nice a curve you can get when the seam allowance is completely removed as described on p. 89. We'll forego interfacing for this sample, so lay one cuff piece against an end of the larger piece, with right sides together, and attach it with a ⅝-in. seam, starting and ending the seam exactly at the outside of the rolled edges on the larger piece (Step 2). Don't go beyond them, and leave about a 2-in. tail when you clip the threads, which will make the ends of the seams easy to see.

Next open the two pieces up and press the seams toward the sleeve (Step 3). Then lay the second cuff down on the sewn cuff, with right sides together, matching edges. In the absence of interfacing (which, were you using it, would now be facing up and cut to the exact shape of the second cuff and glue-basted in place), draw a seamline on the outer edge of the second cuff, about ¼ in. in from the edge,

MAKING AND ATTACHING CUFFS

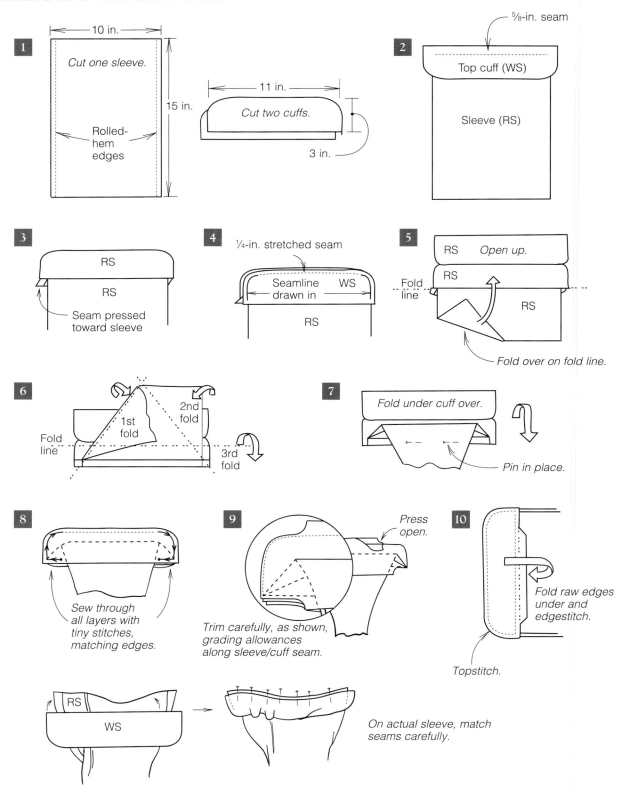

1 Cut one sleeve. | 10 in. | 15 in. | Rolled-hem edges

Cut two cuffs. | 11 in. | 3 in.

2 ⅝-in. seam | Top cuff (WS) | Sleeve (RS)

3 RS | RS | Seam pressed toward sleeve

4 ¼-in. stretched seam | Seamline drawn in | WS | RS

5 RS | Open up. | RS | Fold line | RS | Fold over on fold line.

6 1st fold | 2nd fold | Fold line | 3rd fold

7 Fold under cuff over. | Pin in place.

8 Sew through all layers with tiny stitches, matching edges.

9 Press open. | Trim carefully, as shown, grading allowances along sleeve/cuff seam.

10 Fold raw edges under and edgestitch. | Topstitch.

RS | WS | On actual sleeve, match seams carefully.

feeling through the top layer to find the rolled edges of the "sleeve" and bringing your drawn seamline right up to them (Step 4).

Starting at the top edge of the cuff where it begins to straighten out after the curve, stitch in about 1 in. and stop, with the needle down. Now grab the short end of the cuff and stretch the top piece about ⅛ in. to ¼ in. longer that the bottom piece, as described on pp. 85-86 in the discussion of eased seams. Stitch across to the opposite end of the top edge, stopping where the curve begins. Fold this seam open (Step 5).

Next look at steps 6 and 7 to see how you're going to arrange the sleeve inside the cuff. Since in actual practice there will be a shirt at the other end of this piece, you can't just roll it up. Instead, it must be folded as shown.

Fold back the "under cuff" and align the long edges at each end, then turn the cuff over so you can see the seam from Step 2. Starting at the base of the cuff, about 2 in. in from the outer edge, stitch with very short stitches, exactly on top of the ⅝-in. seam, going toward the outer edge and stopping to turn at the corner (Step 8). Then continue the seam smoothly around the curve, pivoting as you've learned to do, and blending it carefully with the seam already sewn at the top edge. Sew both sides the same.

Feel through the layers to make sure you've caught just the point in the sleeve and not any of the edge you've folded out of the way. When you're satisfied with this, trim off and grade the seam allowances to within 1/16 in. of the seamline, as shown in Step 9, press the remaining seam allowances back flat (stretching if necessary) and turn the ends out. The ends of the sleeve should be held firmly enough so that you can pull on them to turn them out completely. Work the edges of the curve all the way out by rolling them between your fingers. Fold in the unstitched edge of the whole thing. I hope you're as delighted as I still am when I do this. On the real cuff, of course, you would now edgestitch the cuff to close it up underneath and topstitch it all around (Step 10).

With one exception, the instructions for making and attaching the cuff and collar band are the same. That exception involves a point that may have occurred to you: A collar band is much narrower than a cuff, and a shirt front is much larger than a

ATTACHING A COLLAR BAND

Collar bands and cuffs are attached same way, except that shirt fronts are rolled, not folded inside band.

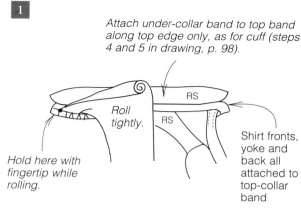

1

Attach under-collar band to top band along top edge only, as for cuff (steps 4 and 5 in drawing, p. 98).

RS

RS

Roll tightly.

Hold here with fingertip while rolling.

Shirt fronts, yoke and back all attached to top-collar band

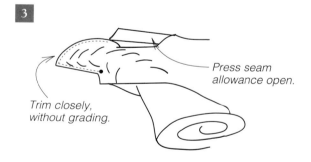

2

WS

Arrange and sew band, one end at a time.

Carefully align all edges, then sew with tiny stitches.

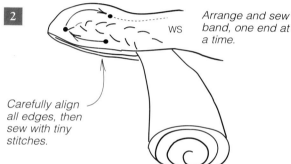

3

Press seam allowance open.

Trim closely, without grading.

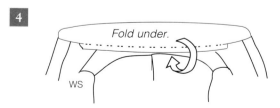

4

Fold under.

WS

When raw edge is folded under, glue-baste and iron in place, then edgestitch collar band all around.

sleeve, all of which makes getting one inside the other a little trickier than with a sleeve and cuff. Instead of folding the fronts up, you'll need to roll them out of the way, as shown in the drawing on p. 99. You may also want to eliminate the interfacing to reduce bulk in the band if you're making a detachable collar. If you want to use interfacing, cut it to match the band. Even with interfacing, you can still stretch shape into the band the same way you practiced with an eased seam.

When making a collar band, you'll also need to clip the curves of the neckline seam on the shirt to the staystitching so that it pulls it out straight to match the band. For more information on this, see the discussion of curved seams on pp. 84-85.

Collar-stand construction

The collar stand for a shirt with an attached collar is joined to the shirt much like a cuff, except that the top edge is left open. The finished collar will be attached to this open top edge — just the opposite of the usual procedure outlined in most pattern instructions. This approach will allow us to try on the shirt with just the stand attached and establish the *exact*, centered points at which the ends of the collar will join the stand. The standard procedure (in which you attach the collar to the stand, then the stand to the shirt) can often leave you with a completed collar you wish could just be shifted over a bit to center it, but it's too late. (You may be wondering why we're not first looking at making the collar itself. This is probably the most difficult part of shirtmaking, and for this reason I decided to save the discussion until last. The irrepressibly curious can skip immediately to p. 106.)

After cutting out the collar stand, also cut a matching layer of interfacing for the top-collar stand, and glue-baste it in place, particularly across the lower edge. Then attach the top-collar stand to the clipped neckline as usual (steps 1 and 2 in the drawing on the facing page). The under-collar stand could be attached at the same time, but it should be stretched in relation to the top stand at least ⅛ in. on each side. You may find this easier to do as a separate step, after you've finished all the pinning and shaping of the neckline to match the stand. In either case, for both top and under stand, start at the center back and sew outwards toward the ends, but don't stitch beyond the edges of the fronts. When you attach the under-collar stand, position it as the bottom layer so you can follow the top-stand stitching line from the previous step. After a stitch or two at the center back, slide the top stand back ⅛ in. from the end of the under stand and stretch all layers until the bubble you've just made in the top stand lays flat. Sew just to the end of the previous stitching line, return to the center of the stand and repeat the procedure for the other side.

Once both parts of the stand are attached, you're ready to roll the fronts out of the way, as described above, only this time you'll find it much easier to do because you're already set up with the shirt between the collar stands. You will need to have already made the collar for this step (see the collar-making directions on pp. 106-109), and you can now measure its length at the point it folds over. Center this length as much as possible along the stands, marking the ends of the opening you'll need to attach it (Step 3). Reinforce the top-side ends of the stand with another row of small stitches, and roll the shirt front up until you can bring the unsewn front edges of the collar stand together around the roll (Step 4).

Now, with tiny stitches, sew the shape you want around the ends of the stand, stopping at the points just marked for the centered position of the collar. You may want to use a template to trace the shape you want on each end in order to get them identical. Don't backstitch in case you want to make small changes when positioning the collar. Trim the seam allowances, as shown, then turn the stand right side out (Step 5).

Have your model try the shirt on, pinning the front and the stand closed just where it feels right (Step 6). I hope you'll find that any pattern on the fronts still matches when the fronts and stand are closed comfortably. The patterns shouldn't be far off, if at all, but it's more important that the collar close comfortably than that the patterns be exactly vertically aligned at the neck button (they'll presumably be covered by a tie anyway when the collar is buttoned). In any case, you can match them vertically again at the second button.

Attaching a collar stand

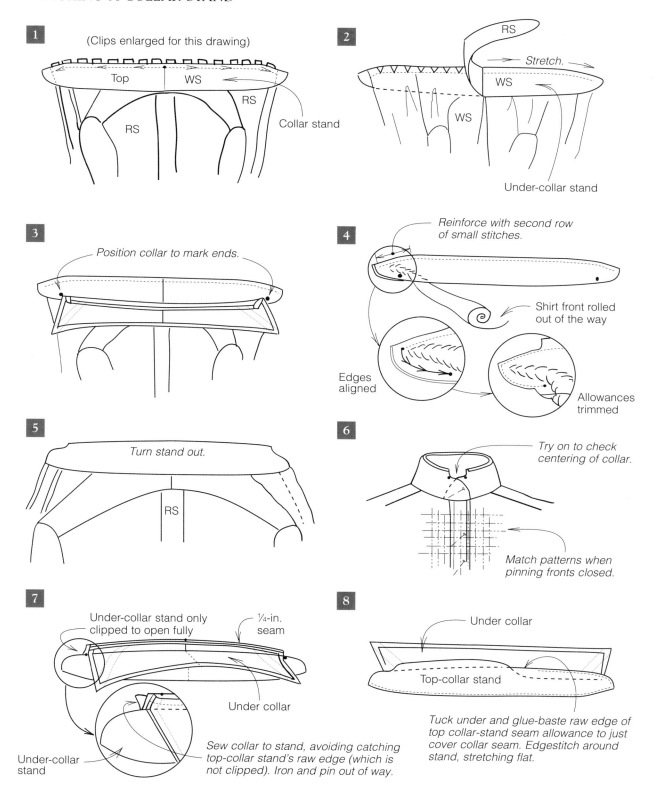

1 (Clips enlarged for this drawing)

Top — WS

RS — RS

Collar stand

2 RS

Stretch.

WS

WS

Under-collar stand

3 *Position collar to mark ends.*

4 *Reinforce with second row of small stitches.*

Shirt front rolled out of the way

Edges aligned

Allowances trimmed

5 *Turn stand out.*

RS

6 *Try on to check centering of collar.*

Match patterns when pinning fronts closed.

7 Under-collar stand only clipped to open fully

¼-in. seam

Under collar

Under-collar stand

Sew collar to stand, avoiding catching top-collar stand's raw edge (which is not clipped). Iron and pin out of way.

8 Under collar

Top-collar stand

Tuck under and glue-baste raw edge of top collar-stand seam allowance to just cover collar seam. Edgestitch around stand, stretching flat.

Now, with chalk or a washable marker, mark exactly where the collar should go. You can hold it up to see how it looks and assure yourself that it's as long as you want before going on. Alternatively, you could wait until this point to make the collar after seeing the length you need. Since you didn't backstitch, the seams at the fronts of the stand can be opened up, if necessary.

When you've got the collar positioned where you want it, clip the seam allowance ¼ in. at the marks on the under-collar piece only, to allow it to stand up (Step 7). Place the collar against the stand, with right side of collar to right side of under-collar stand, and attach the collar carefully with a ¼-in. seam so that it aligns with the marks. Don't catch the top-collar stand. This raw edge gets ironed under, and glue-basted if necessary, and the whole collar stand is edgestitched (Step 8). You'll have to stretch it flat as you stitch, like the collar, to take up the loose upper stand. This will be a collar you can be proud of.

For a separate collar-and-stand combo, the stand is made the same way as above, minus the hassle of attaching the shirt to it. When you're ready to seam the stand together along the bottom edge, sew around the fronts to the collar opening, stretching the inner stand of course to curve it inward, and then edgestitch the entire stand after you've attached the collar. Before attaching the collar, though, have your model try on the shirt and pin the stand on, centering it and marking the position of the buttons on the collar and the buttonholes on the collar band. Then check the position of the collar.

PLACKET CONSTRUCTION

For some reason, plackets have a reputation for being difficult to make, even though there's no stretching, easing or gathering involved, and every seam or folding line is perfectly straight. Perhaps the reputation arises from the fact that there's a lot of folding to do, and the first time you try making a placket, it can seem rather mysterious. I hope I can banish the mystery with a few drawings and suggestions. I find the placket a piece of instant gratification in the midst of more arduous tasks.

First, note that the placket lies on the grainline of the sleeve. On striped cloth, particularly, it's easy to get the placket and sleeve lined up properly. Hence, I confine my marking on the sleeve to one little notch at the slash line of the opening. On the placket, I also notch the two stitching lines on either side of the slash line, plus the two seam allowances, as shown in the drawing on the facing page. If you're working with solid-color cloth and can't see the grainline clearly by following threads, remember that no one else will either. So just get the grainline as straight as possible and don't bother marking the positions any further.

Next, remember that both sleeves and plackets have a right and a left side, so label the parts accordingly. The placket opening comes at the back part of each sleeve so that, right side up, looking from the cuff end, the slash is on the left of the right sleeve, and on the right of the left sleeve. When right side up, the right-hand placket looks like a house with a tower on the right and the left-hand placket like a house with a tower on the left. When matched, either side up, the appropriate placket's tower is toward the center of the sleeve.

If you want to try a placket on a scrap of material, you might want to use the other end of the "sleeve and cuff" sample you just completed. Cut out the placket with a ¼-in. seam all around. With the right side face down, start at the tower and fold the long outside edge in to the wrong side, as shown in Step 1 of the drawing on the facing page. Then fold in the tower's long inside edge, which brings the whole tower over to the wrong side of the placket, aligning the first fold with the notch for the right side of the stitching box. Next fold the two "roof" edges of the tower, making sure to fold over equal amounts and to touch the outside edge of the tower with each fold. (There's a detail of this fold on p. 63.) This will produce a perfectly symmetrical triangular roof (Step 2). Use a little basting glue if necessary to hold the roof or seam-allowance folds in place (don't glue-baste the second fold).

Next, fold the seam allowance on the "non-tower" end of the placket. Then align this fold with the notch for the left side of the stitching box, crease a fold and unfold it. (Step 3). On solid-color material,

MAKING AND ATTACHING A SLEEVE PLACKET

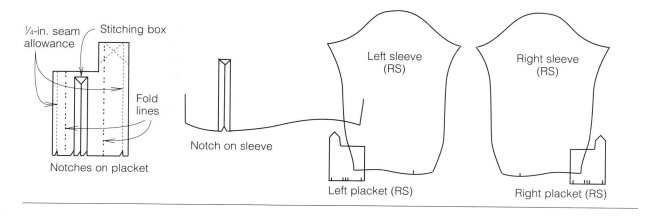

¼-in. seam allowance

Stitching box

Fold lines

Notches on placket

Notch on sleeve

Left sleeve (RS)

Right sleeve (RS)

Left placket (RS)

Right placket (RS)

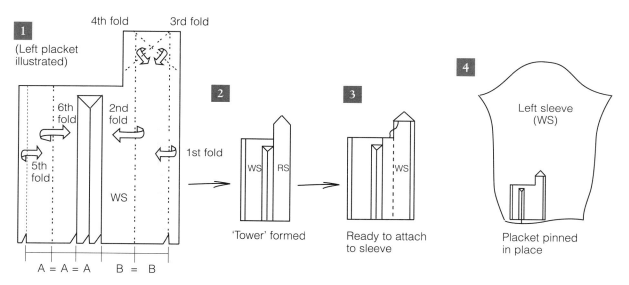

1

(Left placket illustrated)

4th fold

3rd fold

6th fold

2nd fold

1st fold

5th fold

WS

A = A = A   B = B

2

WS   RS

'Tower' formed

3

WS

Ready to attach to sleeve

4

Left sleeve (WS)

Placket pinned in place

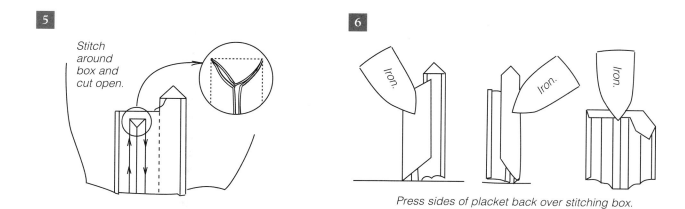

5

Stitch around box and cut open.

6

Press sides of placket back over stitching box.

Iron.   Iron.   Iron.

(continued from page 103)

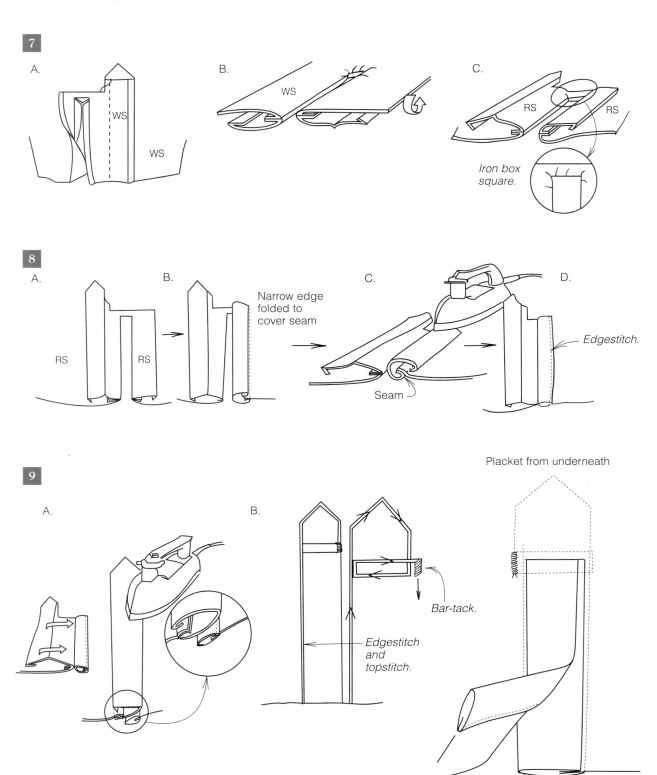

7

A.

WS

WS

WS

B.

WS

C.

RS

RS

Iron box square.

8

A.

RS

RS

B.

Narrow edge folded to cover seam

C.

Seam

D.

Edgestitch.

9

A.

B.

Edgestitch and topstitch.

Bar-tack.

Placket from underneath

I suggest you lightly draw in the stitching box right onto the placket's wrong side. With striped fabric, of course, you just follow a stripe or sew parallel to it.

Lay each sleeve face down and position each placket face down on it, with the tower toward the middle of the sleeve and the slash-line notches aligned (Step 4). Pin the placket in place so the pin will not interfere with the stitching box. Now, carefully sew around the box, keeping the seams as straight as possible. Then cut right up the middle of both layers, and stop between ½ in. and ¼ in. away from the end of the box. Clip right to each corner of the box, and leave a little triangular flap (Step 5).

Before turning the placket to the other side, fold each of the three sides of the placket back over the stitching box, one side at a time, and iron the folds (Step 6). This will help the turn. Now turn the placket to the other side and press the box end square (Step 7). From now on, whenever you're arranging this construction, first lay the sleeve out flat and undistorted. Then adjust the placket as required.

Now, take the non-tower edge and arrange it, as shown, so that the folded-under ¼-in. allowance covers the long stitching line of the box (steps 8a and 8b). Iron the box flat, keeping the tower out of the way (Step 8c). Edgestitch this fold from the cuff edge (Step 8d). Clip the threads and go back to the ironing board. The tower part should now fold over the shorter part you just stitched in place, concealing both lines of stitching (Step 9).

Glue-baste the top of the tower in place against the sleeve, then feel through the tower to find the top edge of the stitching box. Make marks on either side of it ¼ in. apart with your fingernail, chalk or a washable marker. Then edgestitch the tower on the edge opposite the opening. Carefully sew from the cuff end up to and around the points and down to the lower of your marks, then across square to the other side, up again ¼ in. and back parallel.

At this point, I like to finish up with a run of very narrow satin stitches as a kind of bar tack, as shown in Step 9b. (Be careful on very thin, tightly woven fabrics, though, because bar tacks can chew right through the fabric. Test a scrap.) Pull the threads to the back of the work, however you finish, and tie them off or lockstitch with a couple of stitches at a zero stitch length. You're done!

A note on machine stitching: When turning a corner, as in edgestitching the placket points, if it looks as if you'll overshoot, you can adjust the stitch length, with the machine stopped and needle up, until the needle just hits the point you want. Since you're using very short stitches anyway, this should not be a problem if you take it slow.

TURNING COLLAR POINTS

Before we sail into making collars, let's discuss turning out perfect — or at least unembarrassing — collar points. I suppose there are dozens of methods for turning points, and if you've got a workable one, by all means, stick with it. I've got two methods, both of which require some finesse to produce good results. Practice certainly helps, so I suggest you cut some scraps of fabric and interfacing and try out both methods a half dozen times to see which one gives you the best points.

The first method is a home sewer's approach, which you'll probably recognize. You stitch almost right up to the point, then take one or two tiny stitches *across* the point before starting up the other side. Then you trim the seam allowances almost away right at the point, press the seams open, and turn the collar with a point turner. This method can work well, but the point turner can be easily pushed right through the collar point if you're not careful since there's so little fabric left after trimming. Hence the tendency is not to push hard enough and to have to be satisfied with blunt points.

I thought professional shirtmakers probably had a great machine to turn points perfectly every time. Manufacturers no doubt do, but the custom shirtmakers I've talked to all say that for the best results, you have to turn the collars by hand. Here's how Adriana Lucas, a master shirtmaker in New York City, does her points: First, she *never* stitches across the point. She stitches right up to it, turns once, and heads up the other side. She says that's the only way to get a really sharp point — stitch it that way to begin with — which makes sense.

The reason for stitching across the point is to create room for what's left of the seam allowances, but Adriana Lucas doesn't even trim the allowances off. She trims away the interfacing to the stitching but carefully folds the layers of shirt-fabric seam allowance to one side (the under-collar side over the interfacing) to match the shape of the point, as shown in the drawing below, and finger-presses the fold for a few seconds. She's got no time to be reaching for an iron, so she finger-presses the entire collar seam open too.

Next, she folds the last ¼ in. or so of the point over on top of the folded seam allowances and pinches all the layers between her thumb on the outside and her forefinger, which is inside between the top and under-collar layers. Gripping the point firmly, she turns the collar over her forefinger, pushing the point out as far as she can with her fingertip. To get the last ⅛ in. turned, she digs into the collar seam from the outside with a thick, sharp needle and pushes the point out fully. Ideally, the folded layers are all still in place, which causes a little bulk, but it's the same bulk you'll see on most professionally made shirts. If the point is sharp, the bulk is unimportant, I suppose, and her points are like knives.

I find the last step of digging into the collar point with a needle the hardest part of this method, but practice makes perfect. When I choose this method (I pick whichever one I feel more optimistic about at the time), I prefer, instead of folding the last ¼ in. over on to itself, to pinch a flat point-turner between my fingers and the layers, with its point directly in line with the collar point and against the interfacing. This way I can turn the collar over the turner and into a point all at once, but even this takes some practice.

The narrower the point, the harder it is to turn well, so I'm glad I prefer spread collars to long, pointy ones. If perfect curves were easier, I suppose I'd prefer them.

MAKING THE COLLAR

Making the collar is probably the hardest part of shirtmaking, which is why I've saved it for last. Before looking at how to make a collar, let me first restate some terminology to make sure we're all talking about the same thing: When a tie is worn with a shirt, the *collar* is the visible part of the shirt above the neckline. The collar is attached to a *collar stand*, which is usually invisible when a tie is worn. A *collar band* is found only on a shirt with a separate, unattached collar, which also has a stand. The steps involved in making a collar, which correspond to the steps in the drawing on pp. 108-109, are as follows:

STEP 1   Cut out interfacing to the exact pattern shape, adding a ⅝-in. seam on the top edge and no other seam allowances. Fold the interfacing in half and trim the ends off together for exact symmetry. If you want two layers of interfacing, spray-starch one layer before laying down a second piece on top. Iron them together and cut out the interfacing as one. Starching all the interfacing is not a bad idea, because it makes it easier to handle and also prevents raveling.

ADRIANA LUCAS'S METHOD
FOR TURNING COLLAR POINTS

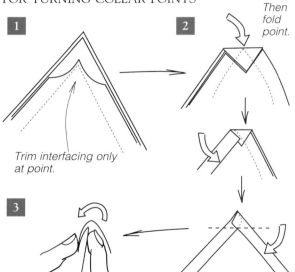

Then fold point.

1

2

Trim interfacing only at point.

3

Fold tip over interfacing and pinch. Then pull under collar over thumb.

STEP 2 Cut out two layers of shirting fabric, using the collar pattern and allowing for about ¼-in. seam allowance all around, except at the top where you'll need to provide a ⅝-in. allowance. Notch the midpoints top and bottom.

STEP 3 Lay the interfacing on top of the wrong side of the top collar. Exactly position the interfacing with regard to stripes or patterns so that both sides are the same. Lightly glue-baste the points and front edge of the interfacing.

STEP 4 To allow for stretching the under collar, trim ¼ in. (or whatever measurement you've determined) from the front ends.

STEP 5 Make slots for collar stays if required in the under collar (the drawing shows two different methods of making stay slots). Note that the slots bisect the angle of the collar point. And also note that stays are not required on rounded, button-down or pinned collars, or those that you always have heavily starched by a professional laundry.

STEP 6 With right sides together and the interfacing on top, match the under collar to the top collar at the midpoint notches and along the bottom edge.

STEP 7 Starting at the middle back notches, edgestitch the interfacing for about ½ in. Pick up both the front ends, which should be offset, align them and, holding the layers behind the needle with one hand and those in front with the other, pull them taut so that the shorter bottom collar stretches to match the top collar. Edgestitch carefully to one point of the collar. Refer to the collar-point discussion on pp. 105-106 and stitch around the point with the method you prefer. Then edgestitch the interfacing up the front edge of the collar until 1½ in. remains. Stop with the needle down. Pull the under collar beyond the top collar about ⅛ in., hold both layers firmly down on the bed, pull from behind and edgestitch, following the edge of the interfacing exactly. Stitch the other side the same way, trying to duplicate any slight errors you may have made.

STEP 8 Trim the point and nearby seam allowances, exactly the same way on each side. Press and stretch the bottom edge flat. Press the seam on a point presser and turn, shaping the point cautiously until it's exactly the same, or as close as possible, to the other point.

STEP 9 With an iron and a sleeveboard, carefully shape the collar, positioning the seams just under the collar's edges. Start at the center back, with top collar face down on the sleeveboard. Then iron the points by placing them on the edge of the sleeveboard, with the collar hanging off, smoothing out any little wrinkles, then rolling the collar around the board to press in a bit of a curve.

STEP 10 When you're perfectly satisfied with the position of the edge seams and all the wrinkles are gone, start topstitching the collar. Start at one end at the raw edge and carefully follow the edge at a ¼-in. distance, sewing down to the point ¼ in. from each side of the collar point. Stop, with the needle down, turn the corner and stitch ½ in. or so. Then pick up the points of the collar and stretch them taut so that the top collar is flat against the under collar. Slowly and smoothly stitch to the opposite point, relaxing the stretch on the fabric at about ½ in. from the point. Then negotiate the corner again and sew up off the other raw end. This method preserves the

MAKING A COLLAR

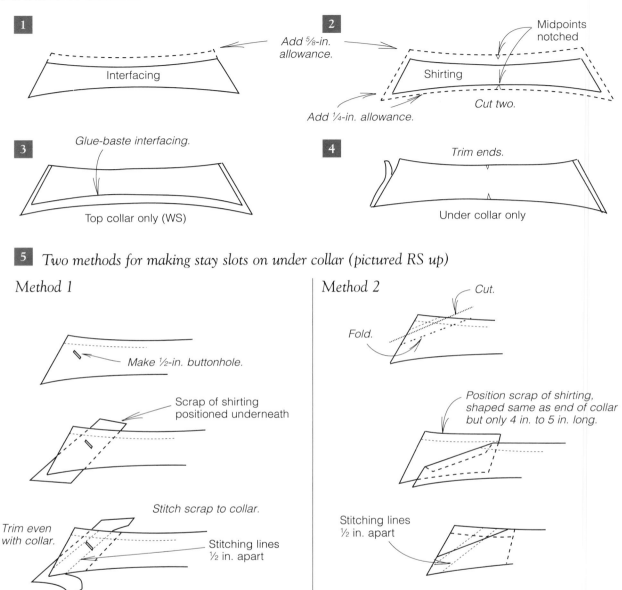

1 Interfacing — Add ⅝-in. allowance.

2 Shirting — Add ¼-in. allowance. Cut two. Midpoints notched

3 Glue-baste interfacing. Top collar only (WS)

4 Trim ends. Under collar only

5 *Two methods for making stay slots on under collar (pictured RS up)*

Method 1

Make ½-in. buttonhole.

Scrap of shirting positioned underneath

Stitch scrap to collar.

Trim even with collar.

Stitching lines ½ in. apart

Method requires no change in interfacing when completing collar.

Method 2

Cut.

Fold.

Position scrap of shirting, shaped same as end of collar but only 4 in. to 5 in. long.

Stitching lines ½ in. apart

Consider using only one layer of interfacing when completing collar.

curve in the collar, eliminates puckering at the topstitching and is easier and cleaner than starting at midback and going off toward the ends.

STEP 11 Now fold under the still-raw ⅝-in. seam allowance toward the under collar, making sure that the under collar is not buckling up under the fold. The under collar and interfacing inside should stick out farther than the top collar as it turns. Iron this edge flat and hard once you're satisfied that enough of the under collar has been taken up. You can use a tailor's ham for shaping and checking the collar. Make sure that the collar points are exactly the same length from fold to point and that the fold hits any pattern or stripe at the same point on both sides — it will if the points are the same.

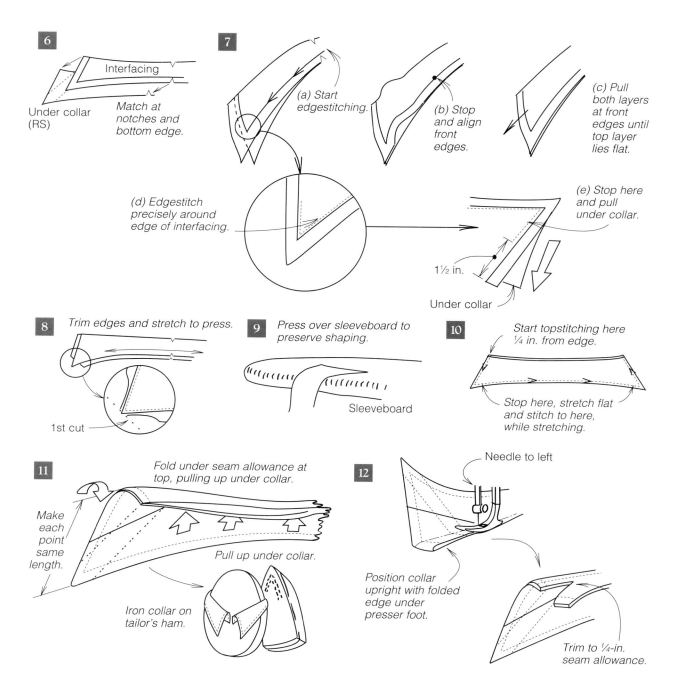

6

Interfacing

Under collar (RS)

Match at notches and bottom edge.

7

(a) Start edgestitching.

(b) Stop and align front edges.

(c) Pull both layers at front edges until top layer lies flat.

(d) Edgestitch precisely around edge of interfacing.

(e) Stop here and pull under collar.

1½ in.

Under collar

8

Trim edges and stretch to press.

1st cut

9

Press over sleeveboard to preserve shaping.

Sleeveboard

10

Start topstitching here ¼ in. from edge.

Stop here, stretch flat and stitch to here, while stretching.

11

Fold under seam allowance at top, pulling up under collar.

Make each point same length.

Pull up under collar.

Iron collar on tailor's ham.

12

Needle to left

Position collar upright with folded edge under presser foot.

Trim to ¼-in. seam allowance.

STEP 12 When you're satisfied with the length of the collar points and the shape of the collar, hold the collar under the presser foot with the needle at far left (or use the zipper foot), and machine-baste the seam allowances together so that the fold is held in place. Trim off seam allowances even and at ¼ in. from the fold. Your machine basting should be at about ⅛ in. from the fold if possible, not directly on it. The collar is now ready to be attached to the collar stand (see pp. 100-102), which is either already sewn to the shirt or completed if the collar is to be a separate one.

CHAPTER EIGHT

SEWING IT ALL TOGETHER

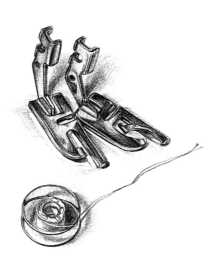

Sewing a shirt together presumes, of course, that you've laid out your pattern on the shirting fabric and carefully cut it out, so let's look at these preliminary steps first since there are some things to keep in mind.

Before you actually lay out a shirt pattern, consider the seam allowances. Most commercial patterns use ⅝-in. seam allowances, whereas most professional patterns have different seam allowances in different parts of the pattern based on the construction technique to be used in each area. Commercial pattern companies appear to believe that no matter how sophisticated the sewer or the pattern instructions, all will be confusion if anything other than ⅝-in. seam allowances are used.

Commercial patterns go so far as to advise cutting out with a ⅝-in. seam allowance and then trimming to another width if a narrower allowance is what's really needed. This seems silly to me. I think I can manage to cut a ¼-in. seam allowance right from the start without getting confused, particularly since this initial cut will be more accurate than a second, trimmed one.

Since a shirt requires a number of seaming techniques and consequently different seam allowances, we're going to cut the allowances to the appropriate widths at the outset. The following seam allowances, which are also shown in the drawing at right, are those needed for typical dress-shirt-weight fabrics:

YOKE   neckline seam, ¼ in.; front and back, ⅝ in.; shoulders, ⅜ in. (flat-felled seams); ¼ in. at each center back if using split yoke.

FRONTS AND BACK   top edge/yoke seam, ⅝ in.; armholes, ⅜ in.; side seams, ⅛ in. on back and ¼ in. on front (flat-felled seams); bottom edge, ¼ in. (rolled hem).

FRONT BAND   ½ in. from fold line, ¼ in. at ends.

SLEEVES   top armhole edge, ⅞ in. (flat-felled armscye seams); underarm seams, ⅛ in. on back and ¼ in. on front (flat-felled seams); bottom edge/cuff, ⅝ in.

PLACKETS   ¼ in. all around.

CUFF   ¼ in. at outer edges, ⅝ in. at sleeve seam.

COLLAR BAND OR STAND   ¼ in. all around.

COLLARS   ⅝ in. on collar-stand end, all others ¼ in.

On the fronts only, add ¾ in. to each center-front line for the button overlap and 1¾ in. for the seam allowance and finishing, that is, 2½ in. in all. See the drawing on p. 117 for cutting and folding lines for the front closings.

I cut out my own master patterns to include the various seam allowances and write a reminder at each seam of the particular allowance needed. This way I

REQUIRED SEAM ALLOWANCES AND MARKINGS

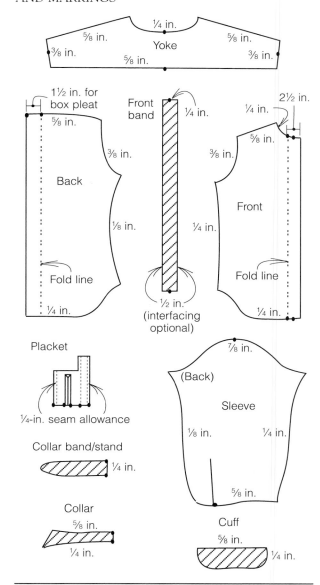

Key

▨ = interfacing

● = center point, match point or fold-line marking

know how much to change any of the allowances if I need to. For instance, if I'm using heavy fabrics, I'll need bigger side seams (¼ in. and ½ in.) in order to feed them successfully through a ¼-in. flat-felling foot.

MARKING MATCH POINTS

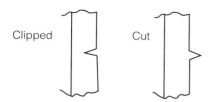

It's faster and easier to clip rather than cut out match-point notches given in commercial patterns.

I suggest marking a pattern with these seam allowances somewhat differently than is done in commercial patterns. There's no need to take the time to cut around the little triangular markers on commercial patterns, which are intended as match points. Instead, just carefully clip about ⅛ in. into the seam allowance at any marking points you need (as shown in the drawing above). You will not need nearly as many match points as the patterns actually call for.

For the shirt you'll make, you'll need only the following markings: small match-point clips at the center front and fold lines on the shirt fronts, top and bottom; match-point clips at the center-back points, top and bottom, of the yoke, neckline, collar band, or collar and collar stand; match-point clips on the yoke and sleeve shoulder seams; center-point and fold-line clips on the front bands; one match-point clip on each sleeve at the placket slash; and clips at the cutting, stitching and fold lines on the placket. Side and sleeve seams are matched at the ends after making sure they're the same length on the pattern.

WORKING WITH STRIPED FABRICS

I think that using striped (or woven checked or plaid) fabric, rather than solid-color fabric, simplifies shirtmaking a little because the woven stripes clearly indicate the grainline. And simply following the stripes resolves any question of where to topstitch or establish fold lines for details like plackets and front bands. What's important when working with striped

ARRANGING ASYMMETRICAL STRIPES ON SHIRT DETAILS

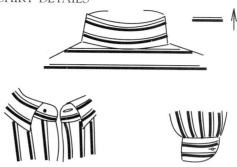

Decide which stripes will be up and which down, and be consistent when cutting all horizontal details (collar, stand, band, yoke and cuffs).

fabric is to be scrupulous in following the lines the stripes mark (whether you're working on top of or just parallel to them). In other words, cuffs and bands should be exactly folded and/or stitched parallel to stripes, each cuff should end at the same place on the same stripe, and so on. You must also be consistent and symmetrical in how you cut out woven patterns. Stripes and checks need to match at the front band and across the shirt fronts and pockets. Sleeve plackets usually aren't matched to the sleeve fabric, although it's a nice touch and no particular care is needed to do it if you follow my directions in the placket-making discussion on pp. 102-105.

When you're using vertically striped (lengthwise-grain) fabric in the shirt body, the collar, yoke and cuffs will all have stripes running horizontally since they're all usually cut on grain. Try to lay out the collar, yoke and cuff patterns so that the stripes are positioned symmetrically on the paired collar points, front yokes and cuffs. This is not a problem unless the stripe is widely spaced or asymmetrical. If the stripe does have a different right and left side, then decide which side will be up and which down on the horizontal details, and cut all of these pieces consistently (see the drawing above).

Checks are usually small enough not to be a problem. If you're working with large checks or plaids, try to lay out the collar so that each point is the same. Then find the center back of the collar and pick that line as the center back of the yoke.

On the fronts, you can assume that any patterns, whether symmetrical or not, will run in the same direction if you cut the material folded in half as it comes off the bolt, using the selvages as the front edges of the pieces. This arrangement may not be possible if the stripe is wide because you normally want to position a prominent pattern repeat exactly on the center-front line. The part you pick may be too far in from the selvage for the layout suggested above to work, but try it first anyway. For economy of fabric, I suggest using the selvages in this way whether there's a pattern or not.

Symmetrical backs are always cut out on a fold at center, so refold the material if necessary to center a stripe or line in the pattern, which need not necessarily be the same as that used at center front. Small details can be cut out one at a time, positioned over similar pattern areas and traced around. Remember, though, for symmetry on cuffs and plackets (particularly when you're working with directional patterns), to position these pairs of details with the right sides of the fabric together. The traditionally tame patterns of dress shirting should raise few, if any, of these layout problems, but you'll need to think about them for sportshirts.

Pattern layout

I've illustrated my typical, very stingy layout in the drawing on the facing page. Note that I've allowed for two detachable collars and two stands but not a collar band. I fold all fabric scraps and cut out cuffs and yokes and so on on the fold, doubling them if possible. Don't be afraid to have the cutting lines on two dissimilar pieces coincide. You don't need to leave any space between them.

The variables in layout, of course, are the widths of the pattern and cloth. The two usual widths for good shirting are 45 in. and 36 in. Infuriatingly, the more expensive materials usually run 36 in. wide. The big question is, can you get the sleeves out of the leftover width after cutting out the back and fronts? If you can, you'll be able to reduce your yardage considerably. If you can also squeeze the collar stand, yoke, plackets and cuffs out of the scraps, the length you need is only a little more than twice the length of the body. In the worst case, when the sleeves are wider than half the fabric's width and cannot be cut side by side on the folded (and then refolded) fabric, each sleeve, the fronts and back must be placed one below the other on the length of fabric, adding two sleeve lengths to the amount of fabric needed. The best case is when, for small garments or on 54-in. or 60-in. cloth, both the fronts and back come from one length. Although fine shirting has no nap, woven patterns may be asymmetrical, and it's best to allow enough yardage for cutting out all in one direction.

I can get a fitted, woman's size 8 shirt from 2 yd. of 45-in. material. And, with my layout for my own altered size 15 shirt, I need at least 2½ yd. at 45 in. and 3¼ yd. at 36 in., unless I want (or can afford) extra collars, for which I would add ½ yd. to either width.

You can save fabric or deal with a too-small piece by using a different material for the inner yoke and making a split, two-piece outer yoke. You can also eliminate the front band, in which case you could possibly get two more collar stands in your layout. And you could make the under collar, under cuff, inner collar stand and collar band of different material (for instance, plain white fabric makes sense on a white striped shirt) or, of course, make a contrasting collar and cuffs. Another trick is to curve the shirttails in a bit more so that the scraps left over are big enough, for example, for a sleeve placket. Plackets can also be cut in two parts, divided at the cutting line at the center of the stitching box, without affecting their construction. I've started doing this as a matter of course, finding that I can almost always get the parts out of scraps without specifically allowing for them.

With narrow fabric, the most significant way to save fabric is to piece the back part of the sleeves, as shown in the drawing on p. 132. Trimming off an inch or more in the sleeve back and then seaming it back on from a scrap may allow you to change a worst-case layout into a best-case one. Many of the superb, old custom shirts I've examined resort to this expedient. (See also pp. 130-132 for more discussion of fabric-saving ideas.)

Shirt layout (on 45-in. fabric)

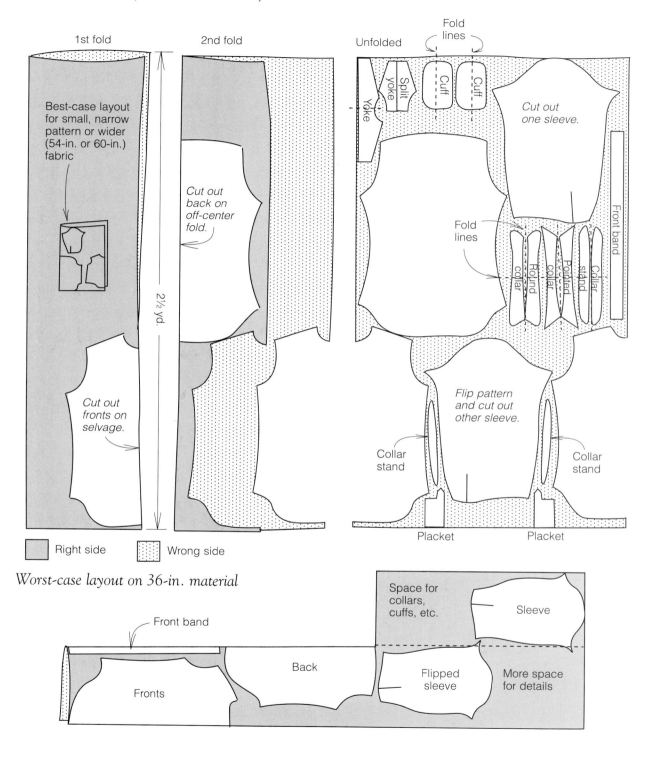

1st fold

Best-case layout for small, narrow pattern or wider (54-in. or 60-in.) fabric

2½ yd.

Cut out fronts on selvage.

2nd fold

Cut out back on off-center fold.

Unfolded

Fold lines

Yoke

Split yoke

Cuff

Cuff

Cut out one sleeve.

Front band

Fold lines

Round collar

Pointed collar

Collar stand

Flip pattern and cut out other sleeve.

Collar stand

Collar stand

Placket

Placket

Right side

Wrong side

Worst-case layout on 36-in. material

Front band

Fronts

Back

Space for collars, cuffs, etc.

Sleeve

Flipped sleeve

More space for details

PUTTING THE
SHIRT TOGETHER

Now that you've read about and, I hope, tried all the techniques I use to make a shirt and you've arrived at a great personal pattern, there's nothing between you and the real thing. All that remains for me to do is to outline the steps. The skills are yours, the problems understood, the materials at hand. Go to it!

STEP 1   Cut out all the pattern pieces, and staystitch the inner yoke fronts and the shirt-front shoulder seams.

STEP 2   Make pleats or gathers on the back and seam the yoke pieces if a two-piece yoke is being used. Machine-embroider the inner yoke if you want a monogram, emblem or another design.

STEP 3   Attach both yokes to the back with a single seam. Grade the seams, keeping the allowance closest to the outer yoke the widest, and press everything toward the yoke. Fold the inner yoke back toward the body so that it's not caught in the edgestitching. Then edgestitch the outer yoke and all the seam allowances.

STEP 4   Construct the fronts, as shown in the drawing on the facing page, attaching the bands or pockets if desired.

STEP 5   Attach the fronts to the inner yoke, with wrong sides together and with the graded seams pressed toward the yoke. Fold over the top yoke edges to conceal the seams and, making sure that yokes are smooth, edgestitch the top yoke to match the edgestitching on the back-yoke seam.

STEP 6   Staystitch around the neckline.

STEP 7   Attach the collar band or collar stand.

STEP 8   If you're using a collar stand, try on the shirt (or try it on your model) and pin the front and collar stand at the center front. Then mark where you want

the ends of the collar to be at the top edge of the stand, centering them carefully. You can then attach the collar stand or delay this step, if you like, until you've completed the sleeve and side seams.

STEP 9   Make the sleeve plackets.

STEP 10   Prepare the sleeve caps for flat-felling and attach the sleeves. Topstitch to complete the flat-felled shoulder seams.

STEP 11   Flat-fell the side and underarm seams together, matching the seams at the hem edge.

STEP 12   Measure the cuffs and sleeve ends to remind yourself how much you've allowed for pleats or gathers. Make the pleats or gathers at the sleeve ends and attach the cuffs. Then complete the collar if you delayed making it.

STEP 13   Make a rolled hem along the shirt's bottom edge.

STEP 14   Try on the shirt and position the buttonholes (see below).

STEP 15   Make the buttonholes and attach the buttons.

On buttons and buttonholes

A commercial buttonhole machine sews the edges of the hole and cuts it out exactly. The buttonhole settings on a domestic machine leave a bigger gap between the edges to make it easier to get in between these edges with scissors or a knife with reduced risk of cutting the satin stitches. For this reason, we home sewers are going to have a bigger problem with the ends of the cut threads inside the buttonhole, despite the fact that we can make a nicer satin stitch than the commercial machine does. To reduce fraying and stiffen the buttonhole a little when I'm ready to cut it out, I sometimes carefully soak the uncut hole with a seam sealer like Fraycheck within the satin stitches. This way I can just cut between the two lines of stitching without bothering to trim close to the stitches or at the ends.

FRONT CONSTRUCTION

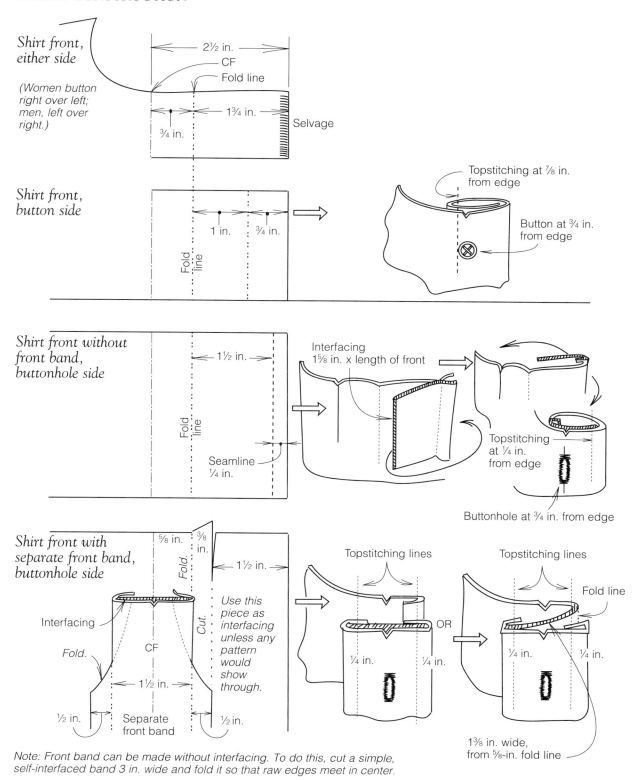

Shirt front, either side

2½ in.

CF

Fold line

(Women button right over left; men, left over right.)

1¾ in.

¾ in.

Selvage

Shirt front, button side

1 in.

¾ in.

Fold line

Topstitching at ⅞ in. from edge

Button at ¾ in. from edge

Shirt front without front band, buttonhole side

1½ in.

Fold line

Seamline ¼ in.

Interfacing 1⅝ in. x length of front

Topstitching at ¼ in. from edge

Buttonhole at ¾ in. from edge

Shirt front with separate front band, buttonhole side

⅝ in.

⅜ in.

Fold.

1½ in.

Interfacing

Fold.

CF

Cut.

Use this piece as interfacing unless any pattern would show through.

1½ in.

½ in.

Separate front band

½ in.

Topstitching lines

¼ in.

¼ in.

OR

Topstitching lines

Fold line

¼ in.

¼ in.

1⅜ in. wide, from ⅝-in. fold line

Note: Front band can be made without interfacing. To do this, cut a simple, self-interfaced band 3 in. wide and fold it so that raw edges meet in center.

I've discovered that I can make a better—that is, narrower—buttonhole on my machine (a Pfaff 1229) by skipping the automatic sequence and just arranging a pair of satin-stitched lines close together, with another pair of perpendicular lines to close off the ends (see the drawing below). If you can make fine adjustments to the needle position on your machine, you may find this approach more effective too.

I've also decided that it's faster and stronger to sew buttons on by hand than by machine, at least on my machine. Believe it or not, I recommend using unwaxed dental floss (for white buttons, of course)

because it's very strong. It's so thick that only one or two stitches are required through each pair of holes before tying off. Waxed dental floss is okay too, but iron off some of the extra wax onto a paper towel if you choose to use this. In either case, if you're brave, you can even burn-seal the knot because dental floss is nylon and melts. Of course, you could simply search out a heavy nylon thread, or, alternatively, use a double or triple length of strong machine thread, all threaded through the single hole of one needle so you can also put the button on with only a few stitches.

The placement of buttons is critical. To determine where they should go, put on the otherwise finished shirt and pin the two fronts together at the widest point of the chest, and where the fronts blouse over the trouser tops or skirt band and tend to pull apart. These two positions are your first two buttonholes. Of course, you also need a button (or pair of holes if you're using studs) at the collar. The other buttons should be arranged evenly between these fixed positions and should include a button somewhere beneath the waistline.

How often you wear your shirts open at the neck determines how close to the neck you want the next button down from the collar. The traditional Brooks Brothers shirt that I remember left an unevenly large gap at this point, assuming, I suppose, that the shirt would not be worn open, sportshirt-fashion. If you choose otherwise, you can position the button at any

MANUALLY CONTROLLED, MACHINE-MADE BUTTONHOLES

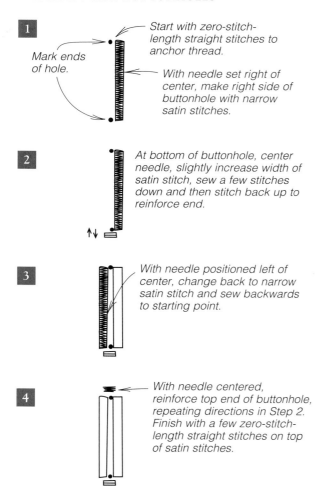

1 Mark ends of hole.

Start with zero-stitch-length straight stitches to anchor thread.

With needle set right of center, make right side of buttonhole with narrow satin stitches.

2 At bottom of buttonhole, center needle, slightly increase width of satin stitch, sew a few stitches down and then stitch back up to reinforce end.

3 With needle positioned left of center, change back to narrow satin stitch and sew backwards to starting point.

4 With needle centered, reinforce top end of buttonhole, repeating directions in Step 2. Finish with a few zero-stitch-length straight stitches on top of satin stitches.

BUTTON PLACEMENT

This distance can be different from others if necessary or desired.

Position first.

Position second.

Not centered

Centered

point below the collar button that suits your taste. All in all, the usual choice is a six- or seven-button front for a man's shirt. If a woman's shirt is much shorter, it would obviously not need as many buttons. Be careful as you establish button placement to preserve the carefully matched patterns you've maintained across the fronts.

Cuffs can button at the midpoint of the edge or a little above or below that point. I like small buttons but I've learned that the smaller the button, the harder it is to keep it buttoned when it's under any tension. Cuff buttons can be larger than the other buttons on the shirt or even different altogether, suggesting cufflinks.

Button placement on button-down collar points requires careful adjustment. To make it as easy as possible to position the holes identically, make them before attaching the collar to the stand. Then, when the shirt is completed, bend a large glass-headed pin, as shown in the drawing at right, and use it to simulate a button, moving the buttonhole around slightly until you find a position that rolls the collar the way you want. When you sew the button on, back it with a folded circle of shirt fabric (the circle helps prevent raveling, and the fold provides thickness). Button-down collar buttons are $5/16$ in. in diameter, what the buttonmaker calls 14L, or line 14. Standard front buttons are $3/8$ in. (16L or 18L). Cuff buttons can be 20L, which equals $1/2$ in.

Finding great buttons is something of a sport for me—although I haven't put nearly the energy into it that I have hunting for fabric. Real pearl buttons are, of course, the standard, but they aren't cheap. Nonetheless, I certainly recommend stockpiling buttons you like when you find them. Buttons seem to go out of style about as fast as fabrics, so I grab them up whenever I can. I've listed a mail-order source in the Sources of Supply on pp. 164-167, though I've never ordered from them. I have had fabric shops order a minimum order from their suppliers of a style I like, however.

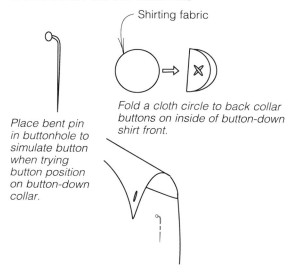

Shirting fabric

Fold a cloth circle to back collar buttons on inside of button-down shirt front.

Place bent pin in buttonhole to simulate button when trying button position on button-down collar.

If you're having no luck trying to match buttons to a particular shade of fabric, try dyeing real pearl buttons, which are said to take dye nicely. (For a flyer on "Tinting Small Plastic Vinyl Items"—ignore the title—send a self-addressed, stamped envelope to Rit Consumer Service, P.O. Box 21070, Indianapolis, Ind. 46221.) Finally, try looking for buttons in thrift shops. A 50-cent shirt you don't much care for may have wonderful old buttons on it. For that matter, you may find just the buttons you need on an old shirt in your own closet.

Ironing the shirt

I think the most sensible sequence for ironing begins with the back of the shirt, which is the least visible part, and proceeds to the front, the most visible, with the yoke, sleeves, cuffs and collar done in that order in between. A little spray starch is really helpful when ironing the fronts and, of course, the collars and cuffs. Since you've made these last two parts and understand their shaping, you should be pretty good at ironing them. I suggest for the back and fronts, that you try ironing on the square end of the ironing board since it's shaped more like the yoke than the pointed end. If you're using the back pleats as darts, iron them like darts, that is, tapering out to a point.

VARIATIONS ON A CLASSIC THEME

fter all this talk about the classic dress shirt, you're no doubt itching to get into some variations of this shirt. You probably started long ago to ask yourself, what if I changed this detail…or that one? And perhaps you've wondered, as I often have, where a particular shirt design fits into the history of shirts and shirtlike garments, and what these related garments are like.

Since I'm attracted to clothing that's functional and grounded in tradition — or is at least aware of it — I also often wonder what other types of shirts people have needed in the past besides dress shirts, and what kind of details and features these shirts had. These sorts of questions are good ways to begin the design process, but they're only some of the many approaches you could take (what, for example, is designer Issey Miyake asking himself during the design process? Or the folks at Patagonia?).

In this chapter I'm going to range freely amidst what I've learned about shirts in the past. My point is not to try to present an exhaustive history of shirts but simply to show the kinds of ideas some historic shirts can spark when you're thinking of designing a new shirt. I hope that the rest of this book will serve as a sort of catalog of details and starting points that you can dip into whenever you want, then set aside as soon as you've got something exciting to work with in your own sewing, and, whenever necessary, return to again with a fresh eye. In other words, I'm more interested in design ideas than in scholarship. I certainly hope that any costume scholars in the audience will indulge me!

For design purposes, I think of shirts in two ways: I consider the overall shape and fit of the major pattern pieces, and then I think of the details, specifically their function and their visual impact on the garment. With few exceptions, body and sleeve shapes can be treated with details of any sort.

Shirts started out—as did most garments in the days before easy access to scissors—as big rectangles of fabric. The shirtmaker simply cut a hole for the head in the center, attached rectangles on each side for the arms (folding them in half along the shoulders) and stitched the sides together. Even into the 20th century, some shirts were still made this way for the sophisticated wearer, and folk garments in many parts of the world still are.

The rectangular theme was often adhered to with great consistency, with little rectangles forming every detail—cuffs, collars, shoulder reinforcements, gussets at neck and underarms, and even decorative ruffles. The shirt in the top drawing at right is a good example of this type of garment and about as far back into shirt history as I'll go. If you want more information on rectangular garments, take a look at Dorothy Burnham's book *Cut My Cote*, or for more on ethnic garments, try Max Tilke's *Costume Patterns and Designs* (see the Bibliography on pp. 168-169).

RECTANGULAR SHIRTS

Classic rectangular shirt

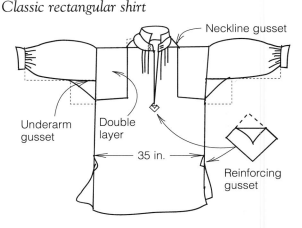

Neckline gusset

Underarm gusset

Double layer

35 in.

Reinforcing gusset

Variations

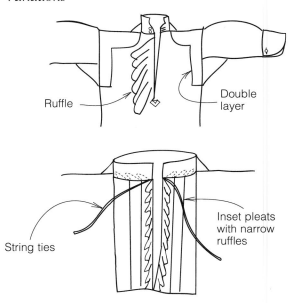

Ruffle

Double layer

String ties

Inset pleats with narrow ruffles

The next logical step beyond the rectangle was to reflect the shape of the body inside by adding to the shirt components a few curves and angles other than 90°. Seams were introduced at the shoulder line to match the shoulders' natural slope, and armholes were cut out to allow the sleeves to start at the shoulder joint, not just at the top of the side seam.

DRAFTS OF EARLY SHAPED SHIRTS

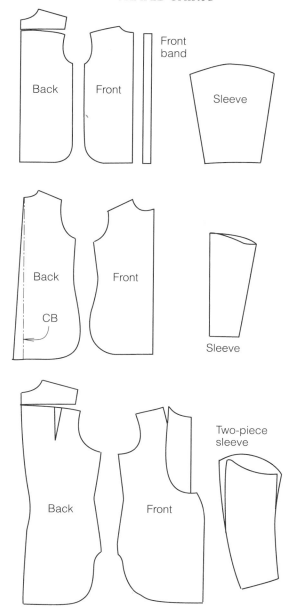

The side seams themselves began to be shaped to follow the waist, and the top of the sleeve was contoured to allow the sleeve to fall closer to the body. (See Chapter 4 for detailed information on fitting. Here we're more concerned with design.) In terms of the shape of the parts and thus the look (and fit) of the whole, these are the extremes of the shirt spectrum: from the no-fit rectangle to the subtly

shaped and fitted dress shirt whose every seam is curved. In our day, these extremes are represented by the body-hugging cowboy shirt and the loose, oversized "big shirt."

Somewhere between the mid- to late 1800s, the shaped shirt became common and started its development toward the classic shirt presented in the previous chapters. This classic essentially came into being in the early days of the 20th century. The drawings at left show a few shapes taken from shirts, shirt drafts and patterns from those transitional days. But before we leave the rectangular shirt, let's look at a few of its details that have left their mark on modern shirts and that might be worth trying out on your own shirt design.

A CLOSER LOOK AT THE RECTANGULAR SHIRT

The rectangular shirt's side seams were usually simply the selvages of the fabric. These selvages were butted together and hand-stitched with a seam that was supposed to be virtually invisible, giving the illusion of no seam at all. If the side seam was made with seam allowances, the sewing standards of the day required that the seams be made precisely in the gap left by a pulled thread at each seamline, again making the seam as thin and invisible as possible. Seams this fine were also rather fragile and so needed side-seam reinforcements. It was standard practice to add a little reinforcing gusset, like the one shown in the drawing on the facing page, to take any strain before the seam ripped.

This reinforcing gusset was such a hallmark of careful sewing that it remained after the flat-felled, shaped side seam appeared. It is still there on the contemporary Charvet shirt on p. 134, and I've seen variants (often clumsily made and falling off) on much more humble, manufactured shirts from the 1950s and 1960s, even though the flat-felled seam is strong enough by itself to withstand the worst stresses most seams will ever see. The gusset is a classic example of vestigial detailing that's very common on shirts, perhaps because shirts are such timeless garments whose traditions fade and change slowly. We'll see other examples as we move through this chapter.

All the rectangular shirts that I've seen had nonlapping pleated or gathered fronts, with simple slit openings 8 in. to 10 in. long and delicate, rolled edges. They usually had gathers at the throat or panels of pleats set into the shirt front on either side, as shown in the drawing on p. 122, often with simple ruffles of gathered self-fabric attached to both sides of the slit. The throat was closed by tying thin cords attached at the neckline, or by buttoning a simple collar band, causing the slit to overlap a little at the top. These are simple details, but, as anyone who's seen a costume drama knows, their effect can be extremely dashing, whether the neckline is allowed to drape open or is held decorously closed.

The stock collar is another intriguing detail of many a rectangular shirt, with lots of unexplored potential for modern garments. Typically this collar is designed with two separate parts—the collar and

the tie—but these can be combined, as shown at top left in the drawing below, and on the garment shown in the photos on p. 145. In either case, the collar buttons in the center to the shirt-front neckline and wraps around to close at the back, with the tie(s) wrapping back to the front for a decorative knot. The shape of the collar and its stiffness or drape depend entirely on the whim of the designer, but the typical effect suggests that this collar was the precursor of the wing collar.

THE BIB SHIRT AND SHIRT-WAIST

In the transitional period for shirts around the turn of the century, a few interesting styles flourished: the bib, or false-front, shirt for men; and the shirt-waist for women. The practice of providing a bib shirt with a chest piece different from the body of the shirt presumably evolved from the pleated and ruffled inset at the front of the rectangular shirt. This detail developed because the front is all that's visible of a shirt when worn with a coat. So, why not put the best, most decorative fabric and details on the front, where they'll be seen? And why bother dressing up the rest of the shirt? A double layer of fabric at the chest also provides extra warmth when the coat is open.

The tuxedo shirt is the obvious heir to the bib style, and the classic "full dress" shirt from that period, from which the tuxedo shirt evolved, is full of interesting details. Perhaps the most intriguing is the shirt's opening in back instead of in front, allowing the front to be one uninterrupted piece. This arrangement is easier to make as well as iron and starch to perfection, and the front is in no danger of gaping open.

The drawing on the facing page of an antique tuxedo shirt in my collection is an interesting example of this type of shirt. Among other notable details, it features a collar band for separate collars, a continuous hem and opening, a pieced sleeve and single-fold cufflink cuffs. We'll see the continuous hem and pieced sleeve later in this chapter and

STOCK COLLARS

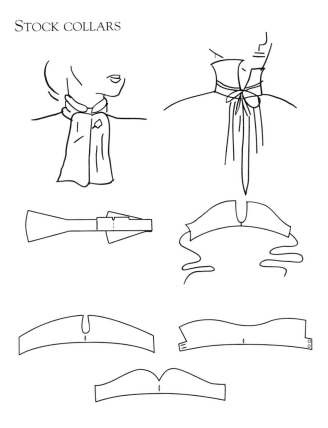

BIB-FRONT TUXEDO SHIRT

Back

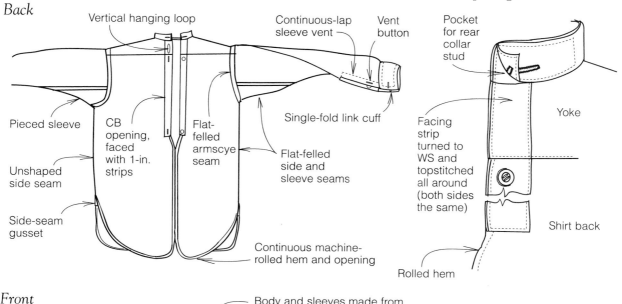

Vertical hanging loop

Continuous-lap sleeve vent

Vent button

Pieced sleeve

CB opening, faced with 1-in. strips

Flat-felled armscye seam

Single-fold link cuff

Flat-felled side and sleeve seams

Unshaped side seam

Side-seam gusset

Continuous machine-rolled hem and opening

Back-opening detail

Pocket for rear collar stud

Yoke

Facing strip turned to WS and topstitched all around (both sides the same)

Shirt back

Rolled hem

Front

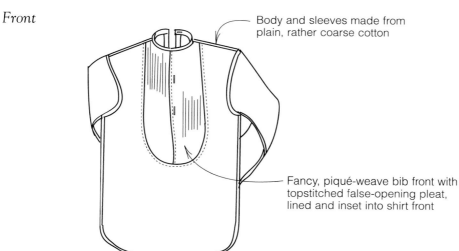

Body and sleeves made from plain, rather coarse cotton

Fancy, piqué-weave bib front with topstitched false-opening pleat, lined and inset into shirt front

discuss them in relation to more modern shirts, but let's pause for a moment over the single-fold cufflink cuff.

I've never liked the bulk of double-fold French cuffs. They seem showy, catch on coat-sleeve hems and feel clunky to me; but cufflinks are nonetheless entertaining. The single-fold cuff offers the best of both worlds: sleek, elegant, linked and

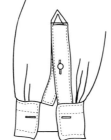

restrained. Why not try them on a dressy shirt? The drawing at left shows an interesting variation of this detail from the 1920s.

The bottom drawing on p. 123 is of a shirt draft from the 1920s showing a very sophisticated full-dress shirt, this time with a center-front opening. But notice that the center back is shaped and seamed, not merely folded, and that the front below the bib is shaped to increase the overlap of the opening beyond the mere inch of modern shirts (shirts with openings from neck to hem are called "coat-style" or "cardigan").

Most intriguing is the two-piece sleeve, cut like a suit coat, with a shallower cap. This is definitely a custom-garment refinement. It's hard to see what advantage it would actually offer to offset restricted movement, but the intent is clearly to fit the shape of the arm better and to reduce to a minimum the bulk at the armpit. Perhaps it's worth a try.

These days, the bib style suggests an earlier era, but it could certainly be updated with a modern touch to introduce either an extra seamline and/or a contrasting fabric. The seam would allow for some shaping in the chest, since a dart could be easily concealed in it, or for an angled style line suggesting broad shoulders and a narrow waist (see the drawing below).

USING SEAMLINES FOR SHAPING

Darts in seam

Visual shaping

My modern version of the bib-front shirt, shown in the photo on the facing page and made from striped silk, demonstrates an early 20th-century practice: pleating a striped fabric in the bib to create a coordinated but contrasting material. I used a more complex stripe than was typical of that period. On the shirts I've seen, only the ratio of stripe to background was changed, which is still a nice idea.

The pattern I used for this shirt was for a man's dress shirt, draped on a woman and adjusted to fit her in sleeve length and neckline. As you can see from the detail photos on the facing page, I've added a Charvet-type reinforcing side-seam gusset (see the Charvet shirt's gusset on p. 134) and an unusual one-piece, detachable collar that reverses (look at the drawing on p. 60 to see how I evolved this collar).

Avery Lucas, a young custom shirtmaker in Manhattan, is reviving the practice of making classic tucked-bib formal shirts out of unusual fabrics. I've seen a white-collared shirt with a tartan plaid body and bib, and a striking white shirt with a navy polka-dotted white piqué bib and cuffs. He also adds an interesting touch to many of his shirts: His French cuffs have a button and buttonhole hidden under the top cuff layer between the link and the sleeve to hold the cuff perfectly in place.

In the late 1800s, the term "shirt-waist" — often abbreviated to "waist" — referred to a lady's blouse worn with a long skirt. Waists came with a great variety of details, from lacy to severe, but all were similar in silhouette, tapering from a wide, puffed-sleeve shoulder and "pigeon-breasted" chest to a nipped waist. The drawing at right from a catalog of the period, reveals that one of the looks favored in waists incorporated details from the man's shirt of the day: high, stiff collars; shoulder yokes; cuffed and placketed sleeves; and concealed-button plackets at center front. Crisp  pleats or soft gathers provided bust room in these shirtlike waists. The whole effect is one of masculine, business-like neatness and restraint, transformed into sheer femininity.

This design confirms my contention that any detail from the Catalog of Design Ideas starting on p. 148 could be (and probably has been) appropriated for womenswear and used in garments that need not otherwise be shirtlike at all. The garments in the photos and accompanying drawings on p. 128 show my modern version of waist styling, which I copied from a designer blouse that seemed an obviously updated period garment.

A classic bib shirt, cut for a woman from a man's pattern. The pleated bib was created by folding out all but one color from the multi-striped silk fabric. The white cotton collar is one of several collar options.

Another collar option that pins and overlaps at center front creates a mock bow (left). At center back of the collar, the chevroning stripes match those on the two-piece yoke, cut so that the stripes are parallel to the yoke front instead of the back (middle). The little gusset at the side seam reinforces the seam at a potential source of stress and also covers the shift from a flat-felled seam to two rolled-hem edges (right).

MODERN VERSION OF SHIRT-WAIST

Back

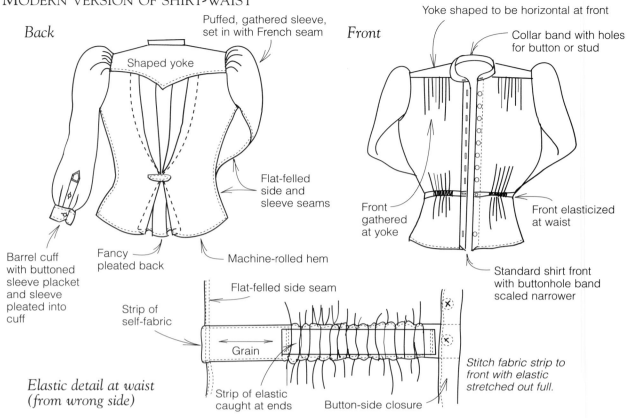

Puffed, gathered sleeve, set in with French seam

Shaped yoke

Flat-felled side and sleeve seams

Barrel cuff with buttoned sleeve placket and sleeve pleated into cuff

Fancy pleated back

Machine-rolled hem

Yoke shaped to be horizontal at front

Front

Collar band with holes for button or stud

Front gathered at yoke

Front elasticized at waist

Standard shirt front with buttonhole band scaled narrower

Elastic detail at waist (from wrong side)

Strip of self-fabric

Grain

Flat-felled side seam

Strip of elastic caught at ends

Button-side closure

Stitch fabric strip to front with elastic stretched out full.

Shirts? Or blouses? Whatever these two (cut from the same pattern) are called, their side seams, cuffs, plackets and yokes, and the plaid shirt's detachable collar (attached with an antique porcelain button) were all made exactly as described in the shirt-construction techniques in Chapter 7.

THE SHIRT IN THE EARLY 20TH CENTURY

The basic shirt of the early 1900s seems to have been a simplified version of what I've been calling the classic man's shirt. The body and sleeve shapes were a little squarer and less fitted, but not by much. Collars were certainly different and more varied, since they were, for the most part, detachable. I've included several patterns for detachable collars in Chapter 6 (see pp. 64-71), but these are mostly styles that are still current in England. The drawing at right shows some of the most intriguing period collars I've seen. Apparently cuffs were detachable, too, but that seems a refinement we can be glad has disappeared.

From the sewer's point of view, the most interesting thing about shirts of this period is the wide variety of center-front finishes and closures that

EARLY 20TH-CENTURY COLLARS

Hole for necktie

Curved ends of wing fold back.

V-opening on band and collar

Complex wings

shirtmakers experimented with. I've illustrated three center-front closures in the drawing below. Some of these designs seem as much concerned with economy of material and ease of application as with anything else, but these issues are certainly worth pausing over. If, in the bargain, you like the looks of these closures, so much the better.

CENTER-FRONT CLOSURES

Outside band

This section rolls outward.

CF bands appliquéd and topstitched over rolled edge

Side seam

This section rolls inward.

RS

Continuous rolled hem

Inside band

Cross section of front

Band

Shirt Stitching

Band stops at waist, held only by rolled hem and buttonholes or buttons.

RS

Continuous rolled hem

Selvage closure

1-layer muslin strip

Selvage

WS

Fronts cut on selvage for ultra-thin effect

Raw edge

Rolled hem

Shirt

Strip

Cross section

One of the basic fabric-saving ideas with shirts is to cut the fronts with as little excess material beyond the button overlap as possible, while still allowing the shirt to open like a coat. Try out these rolled-hem closures, especially on shirts that will always be worn buttoned to the neck. That way the inside of the openings will not be seen, and it will not matter if you've had to finish it with a fabric scrap whose pattern doesn't match or even with a different fabric altogether. Similar finishes on other modern shirts are shown in the photos on the facing page and the drawing at right on p. 132.

The formal shirt in the photo on the facing page has several interesting features besides the rolled hem that continues up the front, among them the square bib finished at the bottom edge with strips of self-fabric. The collar is also fascinating. It's a full-fledged

collar-and-stand combo, but the stand tapers to nothing at the center front (see the collar-detail photo on the facing page). To attach the stand/collar assembly, the shirtmaker used a thin strip of self-fabric, cut on grain, to conceal the raw edges of the stand/neckline seam. The point of all this? To provide the fit and smooth fold of a two-piece collar, along with a very low closure, for people who don't want a turtleneck-like collar stand and who like the point of the collar to lie against the chest rather than around the neck. Ronald Reagan's shirts exemplify this look — perhaps they're made this way.

Tunic shirts were very popular in the early days of this century. But the tunic closures I've seen (such as the one shown in the drawing at left) were definitely not concerned with saving material, since none of them has the simple placket opening that's just an upside-down version of a sleeve placket (the placket allows the center front to be cut on a fold and needs no extra fabric for the closure). These older tunics seem determined to allow the shirt plenty of excess material from the bottom of the opening down to the hem. This is reflected in the way the side seams move outward below the waist in many old shirt patterns, like the one in the middle drawing on p. 123, which suggests incorrectly that these were patterns for the corpulent.

This same penchant for excess crops up in many coat-front shirt patterns of the day, in which the overlaps swing out up to 3 in. beyond the center fronts, starting just below the lowest button, about mid-tummy, as shown in the bottom drawing on p. 123. I can only imagine that this was to ensure that the fronts would not gape open. It probably works fairly well, but I've never tried it myself. Anyway, in whatever form, all this excess material below the waist obviously didn't survive into the modern shirt. Perhaps if you try it in one of your shirts, you'll discover something the rest of us are missing. Let us know.

By contrast, a very useful fabric-saving idea often seen in these early shirts (both custom and ready-to-wear) is the pieced sleeve. The idea couldn't be simpler: Often a sleeve pattern is too wide to be cut from a folded width of fabric, especially a 36-in. wide fabric. But if you cut off a little of the width in the back of the sleeve pattern with an on-grain straight

TUNIC-SHIRT CLOSURE

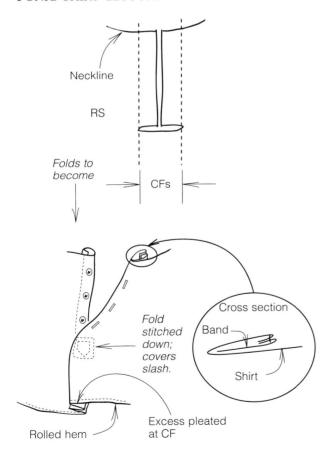

Neckline

RS

Folds to become

CFs

Fold stitched down; covers slash.

Cross section

Band

Shirt

Rolled hem

Excess pleated at CF

A vintage ready-to-wear, bib-front evening shirt with many interesting details. At left is a detail of the collar with its disappearing stand, for those who want a dress collar that buttons low on the neck. In the detail above, note the way the bib is attached and how the little buttonhole strip below it is caught in the rolled-hem front and finished with a simple diagonal fold.

PIECING SLEEVES TO SAVE FABRIC

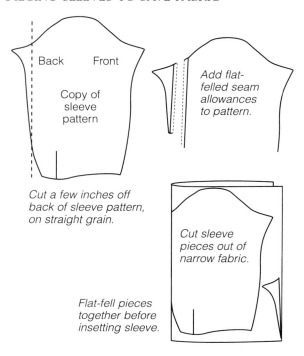

Back   Front

Copy of
sleeve
pattern

Add flat-
felled seam
allowances
to pattern.

Cut a few inches off
back of sleeve pattern,
on straight grain.

Cut sleeve
pieces out of
narrow fabric.

Flat-fell pieces
together before
insetting sleeve.

TRIPPLER SHIRT CENTER-FRONT FINISH

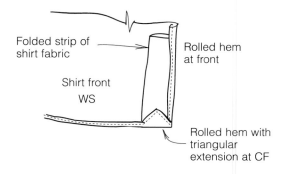

Folded strip of
shirt fabric

Rolled hem
at front

Shirt front
WS

Rolled hem with
triangular
extension at CF

line about 2 in. to 4 in. from the end of the cap seam, as shown in the drawing above (see also the drawing on p. 125), and add seam allowances so you can sew the pieces together again, you'll be able to cut the main pattern piece out of a much smaller piece of fabric. The remaining piece can then come out of scraps. The seam should, of course, be flat-felled so it's very strong and needs only tiny seam allowances. You could even line up the seam with the sleeve-placket slash if you wanted to use one of the various closures there that requires a seam, but then the smaller piece would be too big to cut from scraps.

THE MODERN SHIRT

Now I want to describe a few interesting features that I've found in top-quality dress shirts made since about 1950 or 1960. I want to focus on the attention to details in these shirts—details that you might get when you buy the best and which you might find worth trying on your own custom-made shirt. Up to

this point, of course, this book has focused on most of the features you'll get on a first-rate shirt. Here, I want to throw in a few unessential, but possibly intriguing details. I also want to take a close look at several shirts by famous manufacturers, so we can compare their work with the somewhat arbitrary standard I used in Chapter 3 of the classic man's Brooks Brothers shirt.

One minor but sure hallmark of a carefully made shirt (provided it's well executed) is found at the bottom of the front opening on the buttonhole side, especially if the shirt has a band. A first-class shirt will often have a short extension of the band that's been folded back underneath and topstitched down in that time-honored shirtmaker's shape, the isosceles right triangle—the same triangle that perches at the end of a typical placket and which I described how to make on pp. 102-105. Its purpose is to clean up the finishing of the band at the hem, and it couldn't be easier to make. It simply involves cutting the band about 1½ in. longer than the front, and pressing it into shape after you've finished the rolled hem. You would start or end the hem just inside the edge that will get covered by folding the extension over, as shown in the top drawing on the facing page, which is actually less trouble than rolling all that bulk to match the hem. A lovely shirt that I own from F. Trippler has this detail (shown in the drawing above) even though it doesn't have a band—sure proof of the maker's pride. Notice in the drawing that the underlayer is a separate piece of fabric, as in several of the finishes described in the previous section.

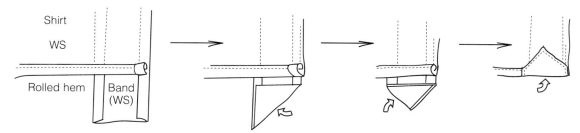

Another classy touch for an unbanded front is to stitch the facing to the front below the last button (and the waistband level) all the way to the hem. Above this point, it's held by the buttonhole stitching alone (along with the topstitching at the edge). This detail even has a minor practical justification: The section below the last buttonhole becomes easier to iron since it's not flapping free.

An equally unnecessary but appealing touch is a quilted stand. This is a stand that's been sewn in some decorative pattern, like that shown in the drawing below, whose edgestitching zigzags from top to bottom edge between the ends of the yoke (see also the quilted stand in the photo on p. 140). (The decorative quilting could just as easily be sewn within, but not connected to, the traditional edgestitching around the stand.) Presumably quilting stiffens the stand a little, but it's primarily a hidden decorative touch, visible only when you raise the outer collar or look at the inner stand.

Conceivably more useful (but not enough to have tempted me yet) is the practice of folding one edge of the under collar or the top stand out of the way of the collar/stand seam before that's made. The folded edge is stitched to the interfacing that does go into the seam, as shown in the drawing below. This reduces a little bulk from the crease at the top edge of the collar (if you folded out the under collar) or from the stand (if you folded that out). Handling the collar in this way makes sense to me, but many fine shirts don't suffer at all from the lack of this detail, so I ignore it. Try it if you like.

Now let's look more closely at two examples of the work of probably the most highly regarded shirtmakers in the world today: Turnbull & Asser of London, shirtmakers to Prince Charles, and Charvet of Paris. I bought from each an off-the-rack woman's size 10 dress shirt, expressly to make the following comparison. Each shirt, shown in the photos on p. 134, cost well over $100 in 1989 (the Charvet was nearly $200) and, I was assured, was made much the same way a custom-fitted version would have been, had similar details and fabrics been specified. You can see some of the details of the two shirts in the three small photos on p. 134, and you can compare a few significant dimensions in the drawing at left on p. 135. It's interesting to me how essentially

QUILTED STAND

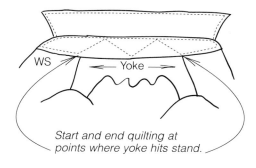

Start and end quilting at points where yoke hits stand.

EXPOSED INTERFACING

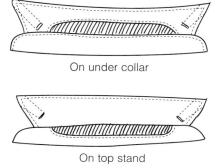

On under collar

On top stand

Extremely precise and well-planned topstitching and edgestitching are benchmarks of well-made shirts. Here are two standards worth aspiring to.

Charvet's signature side-seam gusset is a tiny challenge for the home sewer to duplicate. Turnbull & Asser avoids the issue with a very clean square shirttail.

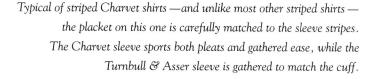

Modern ready-to-wear classics: day shirts for women from Turnbull & Asser in London (beige shirt) and Charvet in Paris.

Typical of striped Charvet shirts —and unlike most other striped shirts — the placket on this one is carefully matched to the sleeve stripes. The Charvet sleeve sports both pleats and gathered ease, while the Turnbull & Asser sleeve is gathered to match the cuff.

the same yet subtly different these shirts are — especially the Turnbull & Asser's flamboyant, oversize details compared to the Charvet's discreet, "feminine" petiteness.

Perhaps the ultimate "modern classic" men's dress shirts I've seen were a group in the Costume Collection at the Fashion Institute of Technology (F.I.T.) in New York City. They were apparently all made for the same customer over a period of years by the firm Doucet Jeune in Paris. Unfortunately, I was unable to photograph these shirts, but I did sketch some of their details (shown in the drawing at right).

The most unusual of these details were the extended collar stand and the little straps under the collar at each end. The stand extension mimics the shaping of many detached collars, which are longer on the overlap end and curved to tuck neatly up

DOUCET JEUNE SHIRT DETAILS

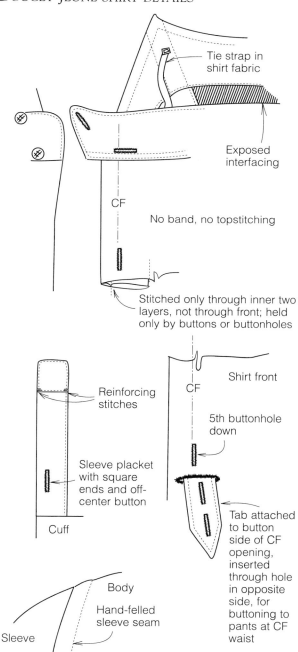

CHARVET (C) AND TURNBULL & ASSER (T/A) DETAILS

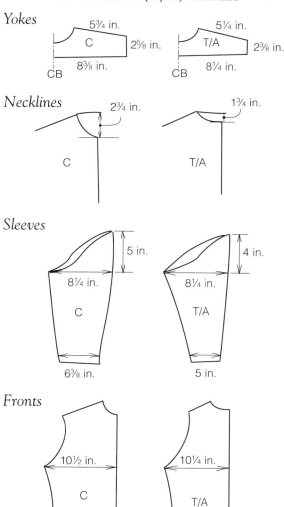

Yokes

Necklines

Sleeves

Fronts

toward the collar/stand seamline under the opposite collar, holding the collar in exactly the position it was designed for. The second button at the tip of the stand makes it impossible for the position to shift.

I'm not sure of the purpose for the straps. Obviously the ends of a necktie were supposed to be slipped into them, but they're too long to hold a tie snugly against the top of the stand. I think they were most likely there in place of buttons, holding the collar down against the stand when a tie was worn. If you want to try straps, you can make them from a turned tube of shirt fabric, or from a strip of twill tape. Attach one end to the under collar only, then catch the other end in the collar/stand seam when the collar is complete.

Another little security device on one of these shirts was located below the fifth center-front button, counting down from the top. Emerging through a wide horizontal buttonhole on the overlap was a short tab with two vertical buttonholes, meant for attaching to an inside-facing button on the trousers at center front. This was often a feature on older shirts with bib fronts. Remember the silent film gag of a starched false front popping loose and rolling up into the wearer's face? The button tab prevents that kind of thing, but its real purpose was simply to hold the shirt front from pulling out at the waistband.

SHIRT WITH ATTACHED ASCOT

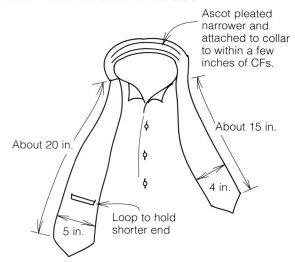

Ascot pleated narrower and attached to collar to within a few inches of CFs.

About 15 in.

About 20 in.

4 in.

Loop to hold shorter end

5 in.

These shirts obviously came from a very precise and fussy society, one that didn't need to get dressed in a hurry!

The really impressive thing about the shirts in the F.I.T. collection was the number of hand-stitched details. Every buttonhole was made by hand, and each hem was hand rolled. Also, the seam allowances at the side and armscye seams were hand-felled to the garment. On some of the shirts, the entire armscye was sewn by hand, both seam and felling. The inside-collar-stand-to-shirt seam was closed by hand, but most of the collar construction and all the topstitching were done by machine.

Also in the F.I.T collection was a Neiman-Marcus shirt with an ascot stitched to the neckline instead of a collar. The ascot, which is shown in the drawing below, was made of the same fabric as the body of this otherwise completely unremarkable French-cuffed shirt. It seems a little extravagant to attach the ascot when you could make an identical one that buttons on and leaves open lots of other collar options for that shirt. An idea related to the self-fabric ascot is one seen in the 1930s and '40s, and occasionally in military uniforms: wearing a necktie made of the same fabric as the shirt.

THE OUTDOOR, UTILITY AND OVERSHIRT

I feel compelled to admit that on an average day I'm more likely to pull on a knit shirt, even for work, than I am to wear a dress shirt. Hence, most of my shirtmaking plans have lately revolved around outerwear shirts, shirts that are more like jackets and which I can wear over other things (like knit shirts and turtlenecks), indoors or out. These shirts can be made from a wide variety of fabrics because they don't need to be washed or cleaned as often as a cotton dress shirt does, and they're a wonderful way to expand the usefulness of your basic shirt patterns and construction techniques. Best of all, there's a host of intriguing details that make sense on these shirts, which can, of course, be freely incorporated

A sportsman's collarless pullover, made from ultrasoft moleskin cotton, with knit-fabric sleeves for maximum mobility, which were cut without alteration from the shirt's sleeve pattern.

into any shirt for any purpose. Outer shirts can also be nothing more than basic dress shirts made from heavier fabrics.

For shirts like these, however, I use a different pattern from my dress-shirt pattern. It's only about a total of 1 in. fuller around the body, but the armholes are about 2 in. deeper, and the sleeve cap height is about 1 in. shallower. By the time the sleeve pattern gets to the elbow, it's the same width as my dress-shirt pattern, but that could be easily adjusted. The yoke is much longer front to back (about 1 in. more in front and 2 in. in back), and it extends beyond my dress-shirt yoke about ½ in. on each side. This is plenty of extra room for wearing over turtlenecks and light sweaters, but for wear over heavy sweaters I'd want to make the pattern at least one size bigger.

My overshirt pattern is a commercial pattern that I happened to have tried and liked. I've also draped it and made a few changes over the years. You could, of course, copy a shirt you have that fits well over what you want to wear under it, and drape that if you think the shoulder slope could be improved. A shirt you'll wear over a few thin layers is worth fitting more precisely than one you'll wear as a jacket over thick layers of sweaters since these layers will take up a lot of slack.

For improved freedom of movement, you might want to find a pattern quite different from the dress-shirt standard I've been discussing up to now. Look for looser sleeves with much shallower caps and squarer bodies with flatter armscyes, like the "big shirt" discussed in the draping chapter on pp. 48-49.

A bigger yoke is appropriate, so that the double layer can provide its strength over more of the shoulder area. Outer shirts are likely to have tails designed to hang outside instead of tuck in, but these can be easily created on any shirt pattern.

Backs

A good way to increase the room to move your arms in a shirt without changing its basic shape is to add expansion panels on the back near the armscye. A pleat at center back can add nearly as much extra room, but it's not as appropriate in heavy fabrics. It also usually adds width down the entire length of the shirt (unless it's been stitched down, as in the blue corduroy shirt in the photo below), whereas

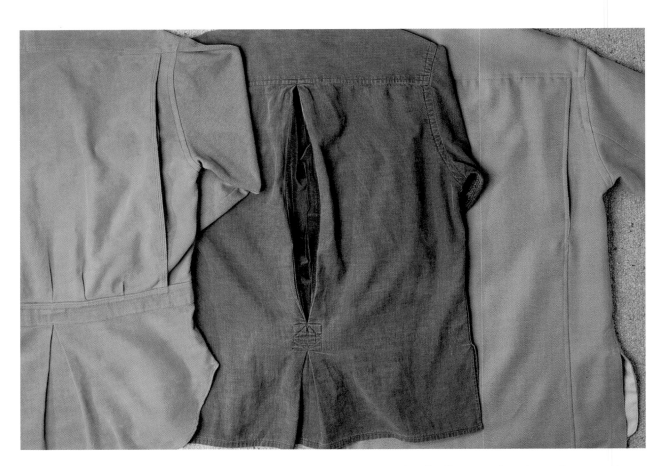

Strategies for providing back room. All these shirts—the moleskin at left, the wool-twill pullover at right and a much-worn corduroy cardigan shirt in the center—were cut from the same basic overshirt pattern. I redrafted the back of each to provide shoulder room with two kinds of bi-swing backs and an inverted center-back pleat.

expansion panels do not. In addition, these panels are a nifty option, definitely not found on ordinary shirts, which makes them worth adding to your one-of-a-kind masterwork.

A back with expansion panels is commonly referred to as a "bi-swing back," a tailor's term for the same feature on a sportcoat. The panels are actually complex pleats, which can be arranged in two basic ways: You can fit a panel into a vertical seam from yoke to hem, or add a waistline seam (usually covered with a beltlike strip) and insert the panel only above the waist. The photo on the facing page shows examples of these options, and the drawings on pp. 152-153 show how the back pattern can be modified to add them to your shirts.

With either approach, you've got the option to shape the back if you like, but the seamed and belted waist makes this unnecessary. Typically it holds in the back at the waist, allowing it to blouse out above the waist but hang smoothly over the rear and hips. You can pleat or gather the section of the back between the yoke and waist as well as add expansion panels. And, as shown on the corduroy shirt in the photo, you could inset a contrasting fabric in an inverted pleat, stitching the pleat down at the waist and then allowing it to spread open again below the waist — this time showing the original fabric. The seam at the bottom of the contrast fabric is concealed under the box stitching at the waist.

Fronts

I'm fond of asymmetrical closures on outer shirts, especially when set into tunic fronts, like the one in the photo on p. 140. The parts I needed for my wool-twill shirt front are shown in the drawing below, and you'll find a variety of other options for asymmetrical fronts in the Catalog of Design Ideas on pp. 150-151. I collect photos from catalogs and fashion magazines as an idea bank for shirt variations, so if I want to use one of these I have to invent a pattern and the construction sequence to go with it. Designing details and making the patterns to go with them has become one of the chief pleasures for me of sewing my own clothes. I'll scan the pattern catalogs for a similar detail and check out the method of construction, but the more of this you do, the easier it is to do without help.

The steps are simple. First, I spend a lot of time picturing how I want the new detail to look and deciding how I'm going to achieve it, mentally scanning the construction options I'm already familiar with that might be adaptable to my purpose. (Could this detail, for instance, be a variation of a placket or pocket or opening that I already have a pattern for?) Sometimes I'll make a small sample to test the idea. When I settle on something, I trace the section of the pattern I'm going to redesign, then sketch on it the finished shape of the refinement I want to add. It's often helpful at this stage to cut out a paper version of part or all of the new detail, and hold it up to myself in front of a mirror, so I can

PATTERN FOR WOOL-TWILL SHIRT FRONT

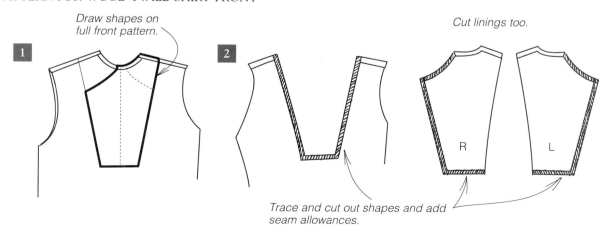

Draw shapes on full front pattern.

Cut linings too.

R   L

Trace and cut out shapes and add seam allowances.

The bib front recut as an asymmetrical, overlapping closure. This wool-twill pullover has a faced hem (middle detail); elbow patches cut in one with the sleeve placket (left) and attached to silk-lined, two-piece sleeves; and a quilted collar stand (right). At the last minute, I decided buttons would ruin the design, so I finished the closure with hooks and eyes.

evaluate the proportions and position. When I'm sure of the detail and its pattern, I draw in the precise outlines with a ruler and dressmaker's curve.

Finally, referring to my sample if necessary, I trace off any parts of the pattern that need to be cut separately, and add seam allowances to each edge that will be sewn to another. This is the most likely step for mistakes, so I check over everything again to make sure I'm not leaving out any seam allowances, before I cut the pattern out in fabric.

Patches and padding

Elbow patches are a sensible idea for a shirt that will be worn as the outer layer, especially if the patch is made from a more durable, wear-resistant substance than the sleeve (leather, for example). If you make the patch out of the same fabric as the shirt, though, the elbow will still be stronger than without it, but you're likely to have to patch the patch or replace it at some point, which isn't the most practical idea. And if you've made the patch an extension of the sleeve placket, as I did on the wool-twill tunic shirt (see the detail photo at left on the facing page and the pattern for this patch-and-placket combo on p. 73), you'll need to replace the entire assembly. So, as you work out your design, you'll just have to decide between practicality and fun. You can see what I chose.

Patches and padding to protect an outer garment (and wearer) from the wear and tear of a particular activity are classic and useful additions to any shirt. Hunters, for example, often have extra layers at the

shoulder to bear the butt of a rifle. Similarly, epaulets that button (like the one in the drawing below) are designed to provide an extra layer against wear as well as to hold straps for gear in place on the shoulder. You might put in a reinforcing layer wherever your garments have worn out before. Like specialized pockets, all these extras are great if used, but can be silly if they're added just for effect.

Linings

Shirts are easy to line, and an appropriate lining can greatly improve the pleasure of wearing a shirt. Usually it's best to cut the shirt and lining fabric for each lined part in two duplicate layers and treat the layers as one throughout the construction, which, I suppose, is technically called underlining. But consider each edge separately; you may want to handle each one differently.

For example, in order to make my wool-twill tunic shirt easier to pull on over other garments, I lined the sleeves with a lightweight silk, which works like a charm and feels great. I simply pinned the layers together around the placket area and treated them as one to make the placket, then worked with two raw edges at each seam, which was often awkward. I realized too late that it would have been smarter to arrange the layers with right sides together first and stitch around all the edges except at the cuff, then trim the seams and turn the sleeve right side out, before making the placket. That way the layers would have been securely held at every point and the underarm and armscye seam allowances would have been already finished. I wouldn't have had to try to flat-fell the underarm seam, which was a real challenge. A plain seam would have worked fine. Nor would I have had to fold under the two loose allowances at the armscye seam since they would already have been folded, ready to topstitch from the outside. Next time, I'll cut different seam allowances (¼ in. at the underarms and ¾ in. at the armscye), and this shirt will be a pleasure to make as well as wear.

For years, L.L. Bean has sold a rugged canvas shirt fully lined with a plaid cotton flannel. Since the collar, stand, cuffs and yoke are all double layers, the inside layer is simply cut out of lining fabric and

EPAULETS

Epaulet attached on top and at front of yoke

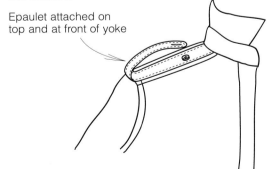

L.L. Bean lined shirt front

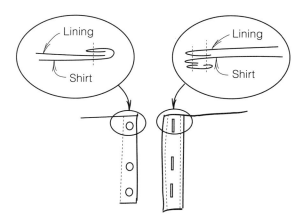

Made from the same basic overshirt pattern as the pullover shirt on p. 140, this shirt/jacket with machine-knitted sleeves differs only in the cut of the center-front overlap, which I redrafted to resemble a suit coat. I lined and faced the jacket but didn't use any shaping, tailor's padstitching or canvas interfacing. When folded over, the simple collar band resembles lapels.

constructed as usual. The double-layer sleeves and body sections are flat-felled together at the side, underarm and armscye seams, and rolled together at the hem, so it *can* be done. The drawing above shows how the layers are stitched at the center front.

I recently saw another attractive treatment of a lined shirt. It was the same as the L.L. Bean shirt, except that both layers were silk, each a different color (the inside soft white, the outside a glossy blue), with the top collar made from the lining fabric, so the shirt looked reversible. It probably wasn't, but it was an interesting effect to see the inside color peeking out wherever the shirt folded over to reveal it.

Knitted sleeves

I've made two shirts with knitted sleeves, and I love them both. Knitted sleeves are easier to put in than woven sleeves (no seams to finish), and they're wonderfully comfortable. I used knitted yardage for the sleeves on the moleskin shirt (see the photo on p. 137), but the classy way to go is with hand- or machine-knitted sleeves that are shaped, rather than cut, to your pattern. This way you can have the cuffs knitted in one with the sleeve, instead of sewn on. For the shirt in the photo at right, I gave machine-knitwear designer Karen Morris my sleeve pattern to translate into knitting. Then, after I finished the side and underarm seams, I stitched the sleeves into the finished armscyes by hand.

For the moleskin shirt sleeves, I used a cotton fleece fabric. I stitched the underarm seam with a stretch/overcast stitch on my regular machine and attached the sleeve with a straight stitch. I topstitched the raw edge from the top to mimic flat-felling. The best thing on this shirt is probably the cuffs. Los Angeles designer Linda Wakefield gave me the idea of using sock tops for a totally seamless cuff.

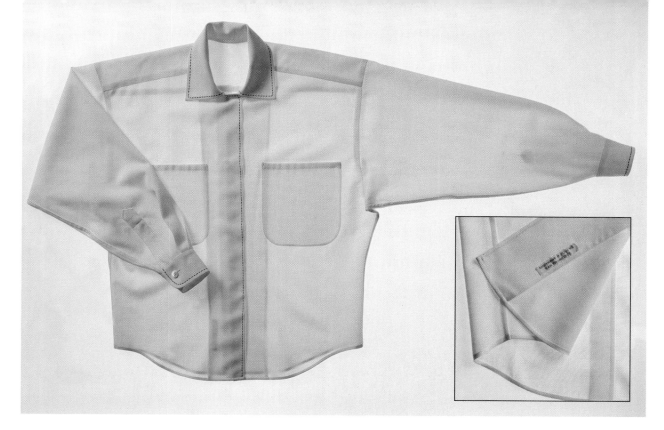

A classic rectangular 'big' shirt by designer Shermane Fouché. Note the shallow armscye, almost complete lack of sleeve cap and the resulting sleeve angle: 90° to center front. A bias-bound hem, especially in silk, is an elegant solution for bulky materials.

I think it would even make sense to buy a pair of matching socks expressly for cuffs. You can fold the socks double or use them as long, single-layer cuffs. Try it.

The whole idea of using different fabrics in a single shirt is full of possibilities, and not just when you're short of fabric. Contrasting sleeves is the most obvious choice, but you could match the yoke and collar to the sleeves, or just make the fronts in a contrasting fabric. Using different fabrics has nothing to do with utility, but it could. Orvis, a famous outfitter of hunters and sportsmen, puts a lightweight, airy fabric on the back of a rugged-fabric shirt for summer shooting. In the Bibliography on pp. 168-169, I've listed Orvis and a few other sources of mail-order catalogs whose garments have interesting details you'll find inspiring for shirtmaking.

THE MODERN NON-DRESS SHIRT

What happens when you leave the classic dress shirt completely behind, but still want to make shirts? Absolutely anything you want. This section presents what I've found to be the most interesting shirt ideas from modern designers. I've got a few actual garments to show you, but the rest is a Catalog of Design Ideas (see pp. 148-157), culled from the photos I've collected over the past five years. It's a grab bag, to sift through at leisure.

The white wool gabardine shirt by San Francisco designer Shermane Fouché shown in the photo above is my token camp shirt. In other words, it has a fold-over collar without a stand or a band, which is caught from the yoke forward in the one-piece faced fronts instead of being stitched down to cover the

Copied from a ready-to-wear blouse, this silk shirt has no yoke, but the seams, hem, cuffs and plackets are all derived from shirt-construction techniques.

entire neckline. It represents a vast category of garments, indubitably shirts, that has been left out and unmentioned until now simply because I don't know enough about their collars to say anything useful about making them. But I couldn't pass this shirt by because of its extremely elegant hem finish. It's a double-folded bias band of silk, machine-stitched to the front, then pressed over and hand-tacked to the wrong side.

Shermane Fouché's shirt's clean, square shape is also a perfect example of how the boxy, rectangular heritage of the earliest shirts is being revived today. Both this shirt, and the black silk one in the photo above, could almost have been cut from a single piece of fabric from center front or center back to cuff, had the fabric been wide enough. There's almost no shaping in the armscye or sleeve cap, and, in the

case of the black shirt, no excess fabric to form a "gusset." The sleeve on the black shirt is technically a kimono sleeve, but if you put an armscye seam through it, it can be constructed just like a shirt sleeve, complete with flat-felling, or it can be serged, as Shermane has done. (See the Sources of Supply on pp. 164-167 for information on where to get Shermane's pattern, to which you could add a collar stand or band if you wanted to.)

The black silk shirt in the photos on this page and the facing page hasn't even got a yoke, but the cuffs, placket and collar band are pure, classic shirt, as is the machine-made, flat-felled, continuous side/underarm seam. Flat felling was a perfect way to stitch and finish the sharply curved seam. The hem is also machine rolled. I used French seams at the shoulder to finish them. The button-on collar

There are three versatile collar options for this black silk shirt: a reversible plain collar and band, cut in one (left); a one-piece stock collar and tie (middle and right); and a plain white cotton collar (shown in the drawing below).

variations include a stock (see p. 124), a reversible collar and a white cotton collar that I designed to be worn with the shirt collar open at the neckline (see the drawing at right). You can see the evolution of the design for the stock collar in the drawing on p. 60 and find a full-size pattern for this collar on p. 71. You'll find a pattern for the reversible collar on p. 69.

The black silk shirt is also the first shirt described in this book that has a concealed-button placket. It's simply a faced front cut wide and folded to cover the buttonholes. Other ways to achieve this effect are shown in the drawing on p. 146.

I had been planning to show you how knit fabrics could be sewn into shirts with tunic openings and woven shirt collars, complete with stands, without any need for a supporting placket, because of the nonraveling, stretchy structure of the knit fabric. Then I met up with a friend and was surprised to see her wearing the blue broadcloth shirt shown in the photo on p. 147. Its simple tunic opening seems to do the impossible: slit the woven fabric down to a point, then stop, yet not ravel. Both sides of the slit are seamed to additional fabric, but where does the seam allowance at the end of the slash come from? And where does it go along the sides of the opening, which appear to fit together seamlessly?

DETACHABLE COLLAR

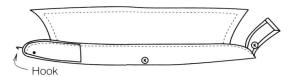

Hook

Add two strips of interfaced collar fabric to ends of inner stand, catching them in seam or topstitching along top edge only. Sew buttons to inside of strips only, matching buttonholes at ends of band. To close collar, sew hook and eye on either end of stand.

The fold-back cuff overlaps and buttons like a plain cuff.

COVERED-BUTTON PLACKETS

All folds in these seven different plackets are caught in the collar stand. The first three plackets are made from a single piece of fabric; the others use additional fabric strips.

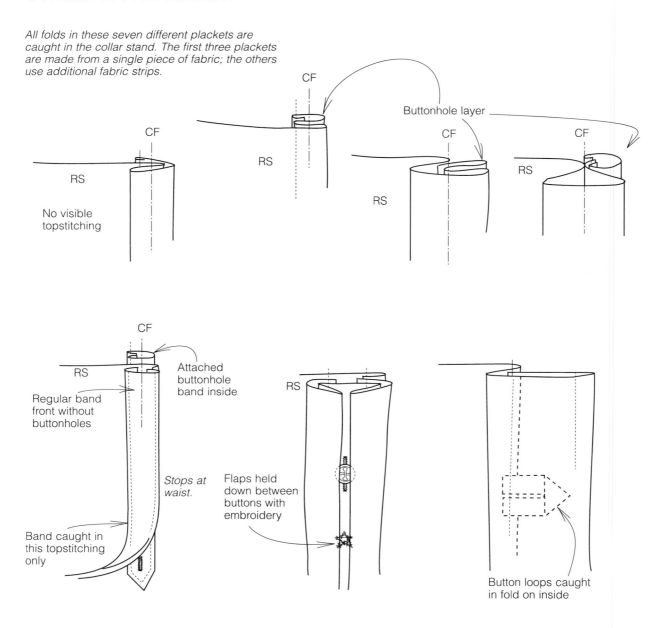

I borrowed the shirt and examined it carefully. The reason it works is that the fabric is plain, so you can't see the slight shift in the grain as it pulls in toward the slit. It's a minor, but fascinating triumph; not very strong, but very clean. The directions for this detail are shown in the drawing on the facing page. They're a slight variant of the opening on the rugby shirt in the photo.

A rugby shirt is a knit shirt with a woven-fabric collar and internal placket. The point of making one yourself, apart from fit, is to make it in unusual fabrics (like wool jersey, as shown at right in the photo on the facing page) and colors, and with a collar of your choice. Off-the-rack rugby shirts usually have a one-piece collar of heavy white twill. In the most exclusive English stores for outfitting

PLACKETLESS SLIT-FRONT OPENING

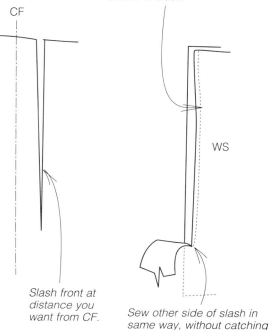

CF

With RSs together, stitch facing strip to one side with ⅛-in. to ¼-in. seam, tapering to point at end of slash.

WS

Slash front at distance you want from CF.

Sew other side of slash in same way, without catching front facing. End stitching at same point.

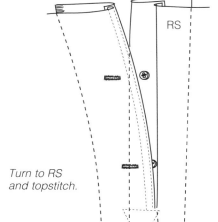

RS

Turn to RS and topstitch.

A rugby-shirt front opening is a clean, simple detail for both woven and knit fabrics. Why not add a woven shirt collar and band to a knit shirt? The one on my knit shirt (right) detaches, but it could have been sewn permanently in place. The design of the blue broadcloth shirt's placketless slit-front opening is shown in the drawing at left.

equestrians you can buy exquisite knit "rugby" shirts like this, with plackets and collar bands instead of collars, woven of the finest cotton and intended for supporting riding stocks and detachable collars, and to be worn under those bright red, nipped-waist riding coats called "pinks." You can pick up a few in Sea Island cotton for summer, and some more in silk or cashmere for chilly fall mornings. Or you can make your own, perhaps from a purple cashmere jersey, with a collar of creamy silk….

A CATALOG OF DESIGN IDEAS

BODIES/FRONTS

No buttons — fronts stitched together in this section only

Flat-felled princess seams

Deep, inverted pleats

Inverted pleats stitched down below waist

Deep, loose pleats from yoke to hem

Mega-gathers front and back and at sleeve

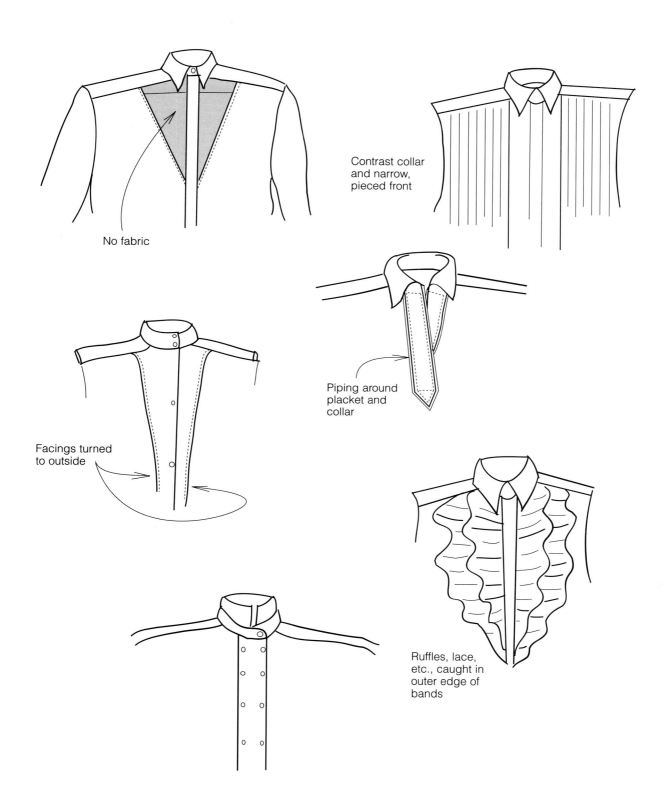

No fabric

Contrast collar and narrow, pieced front

Piping around placket and collar

Facings turned to outside

Ruffles, lace, etc., caught in outer edge of bands

ASYMMETRICAL OPENINGS

All can open right or left.

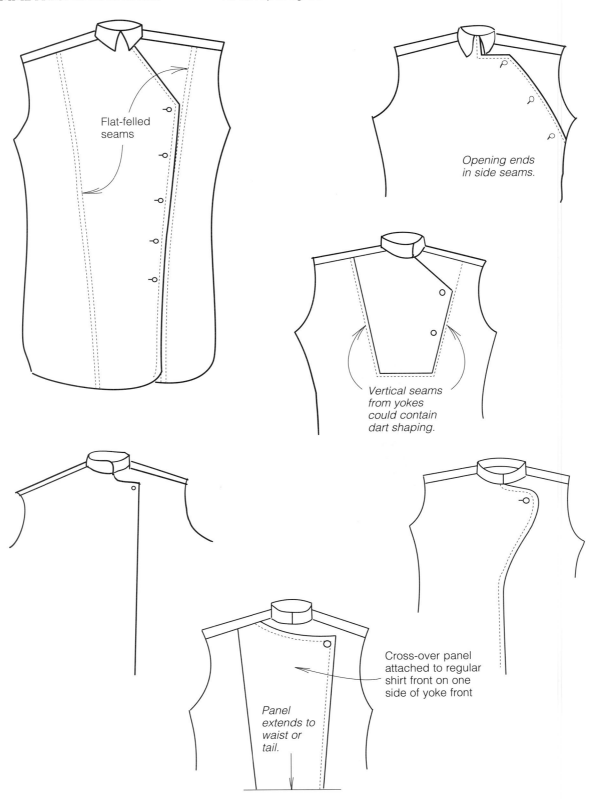

Flat-felled seams

Opening ends
in side seams.

Vertical seams
from yokes
could contain
dart shaping.

Cross-over panel
attached to regular
shirt front on one
side of yoke front

Panel
extends to
waist or
tail.

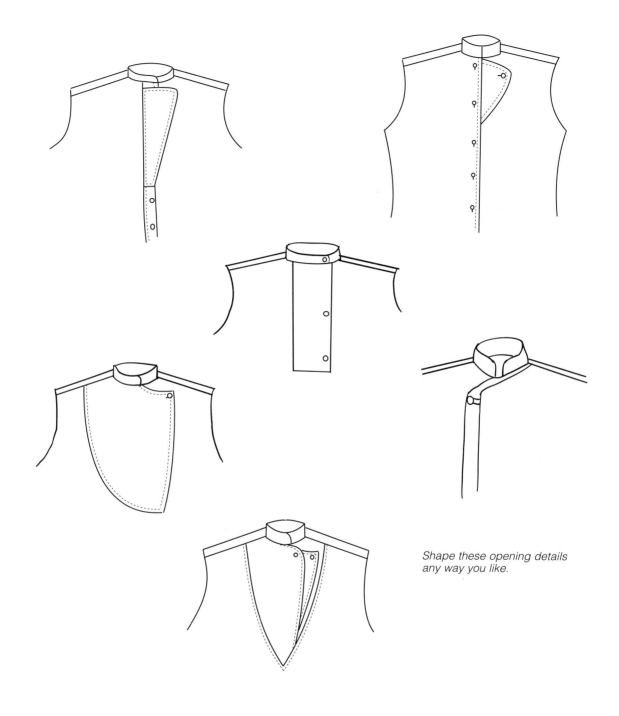

*Shape these opening details
any way you like.*

DESIGNING BI-SWING BACKS WITH BELT

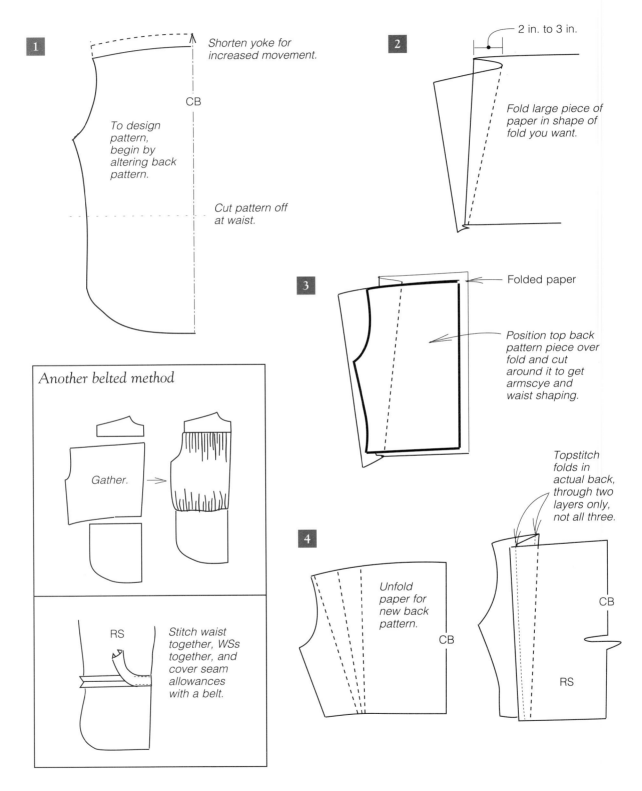

1 Shorten yoke for increased movement.

CB

To design pattern, begin by altering back pattern.

Cut pattern off at waist.

2 2 in. to 3 in.

Fold large piece of paper in shape of fold you want.

3 Folded paper

Position top back pattern piece over fold and cut around it to get armscye and waist shaping.

Topstitch folds in actual back, through two layers only, not all three.

4 Unfold paper for new back pattern.

CB

CB

RS

Another belted method

Gather.

RS

Stitch waist together, WSs together, and cover seam allowances with a belt.

Designing bi-swing backs without belt

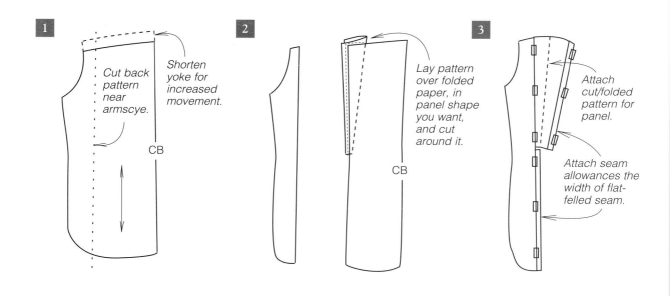

1 Cut back pattern near armscye.

Shorten yoke for increased movement.

CB

2 Lay pattern over folded paper, in panel shape you want, and cut around it.

CB

3 Attach cut/folded pattern for panel.

Attach seam allowances the width of flat-felled seam.

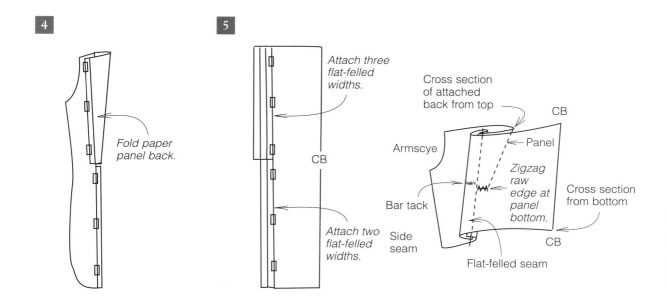

4 Fold paper panel back.

5 Attach three flat-felled widths.

CB

Attach two flat-felled widths.

Cross section of attached back from top

CB

Armscye

Panel

Zigzag raw edge at panel bottom.

Cross section from bottom

Bar tack

Side seam

CB

Flat-felled seam

COLLAR AND NECKLINE TREATMENTS

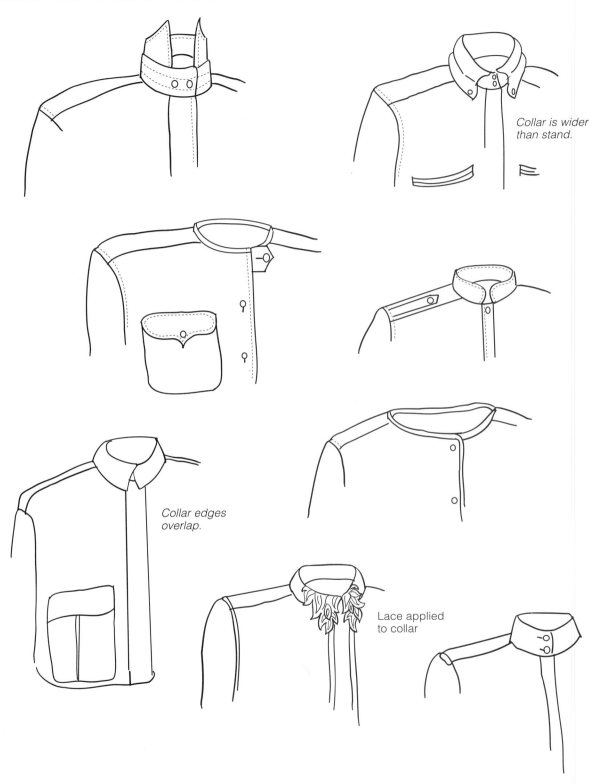

Collar is wider
than stand.

Collar edges
overlap.

Lace applied
to collar

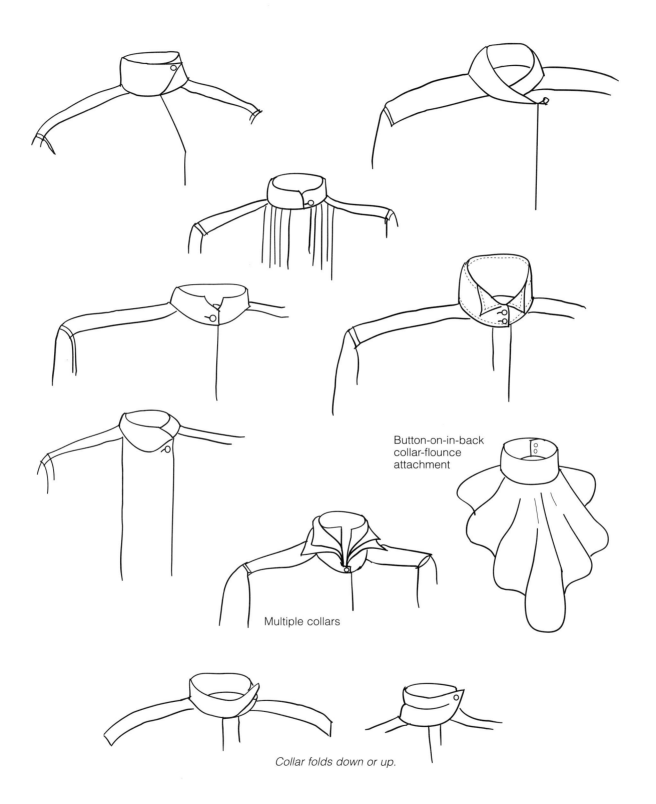

Button-on-in-back
collar-flounce
attachment

Multiple collars

Collar folds down or up.

POCKETS

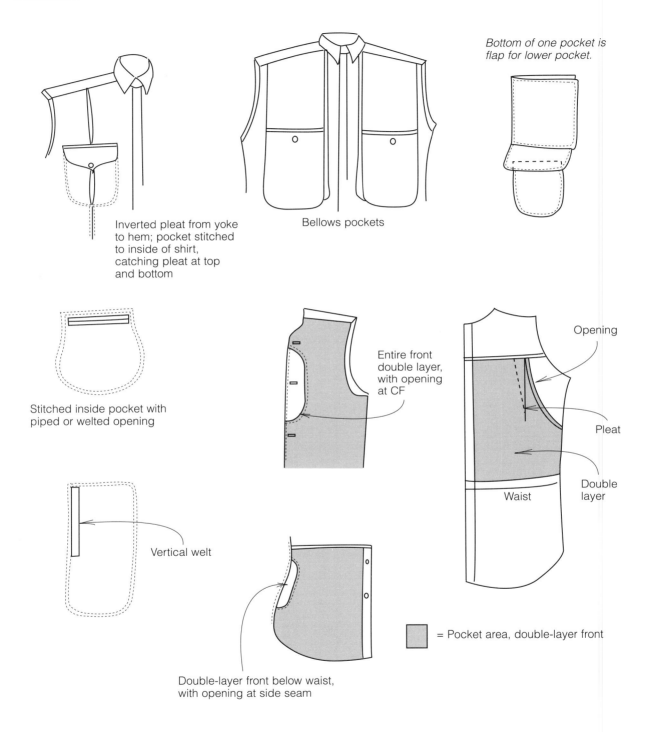

Inverted pleat from yoke to hem; pocket stitched to inside of shirt, catching pleat at top and bottom

Bellows pockets

Bottom of one pocket is flap for lower pocket.

Stitched inside pocket with piped or welted opening

Entire front double layer, with opening at CF

Opening

Pleat

Double layer

Waist

Vertical welt

Double-layer front below waist, with opening at side seam

☐ = Pocket area, double-layer front

SLEEVES

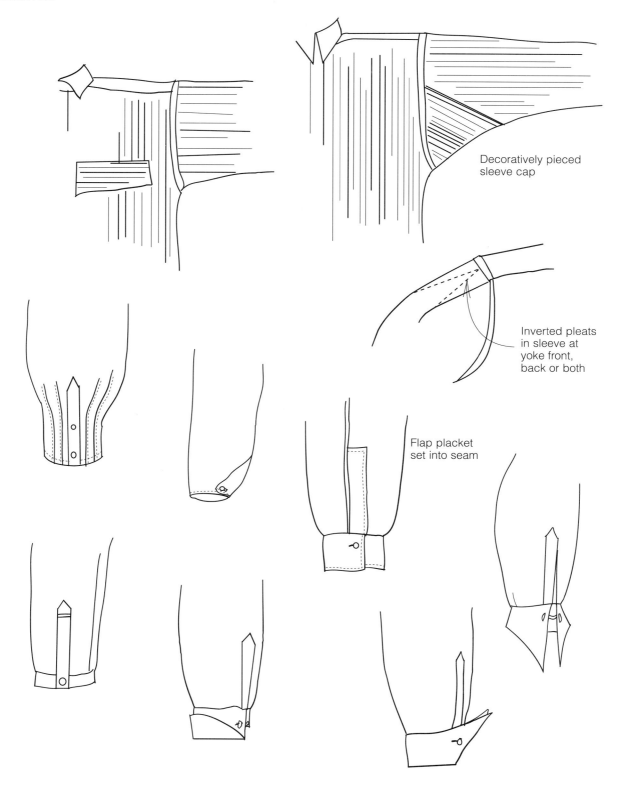

Decoratively pieced
sleeve cap

Inverted pleats
in sleeve at
yoke front,
back or both

Flap placket
set into seam

Addendum: Monogramming Shirts

Monograms are a common addition to custom-made shirts. I can't really see why you'd want to wear your initials on your chest — and on your cuff or collar really seems too much — but I can understand the impulse to mark your own creation as yours in some way, or to mark a gift as coming from you and to customize it for the recipient.

Designers identify their clothes with little embroidered emblems like alligators or polo players, and manufacturers, of course, always put in labels. I like to label or mark the shirts I make in a similar way, especially since it's easy to do and doesn't slow down the making too much. I make my monograms with free-motion machine embroidery, which you can do on any zigzag machine that allows you to drop or cover the feed dogs. With the exception of the Prince Ferrari label shown in the photo below, which got me started on monograms, the examples on these pages are my own efforts.

As with most skills involving dexterity, it's easy to get serviceable results with free-motion embroidery but it takes time and discipline to develop real finesse. I'm short of both, so I limit my projects to those in which serviceable results will do. First, I never embroider on large garment pieces, only on small pieces like the inside yoke, a pocket or a scrap I can cut a separate label from. If the embroidery doesn't work out, I can easily toss the fabric involved and try again without jeopardizing the whole shirt.

Second, I always work with a design that I'm sure I can execute well, with a little luck. That means working simply, and incorporating the irregular and asymmetrical into the design. For example, I can usually make each letter in a monogram or word look reasonably good, but to expect them all to be exactly the same height is too much. So I draw the letters different heights to begin with, hoping that the looseness will look personal and pleasing, not just sloppy. My monograms in the photos on the facing page exemplify designs like this, and you can get lots of ideas from books on lettering. If you want to embellish your work and can accept serviceable results, or if you've got the will to develop real control, I think you'll find the technique fascinating.

The machine-embroidered label on this shirt intrigued me when I came across it in a vintage clothing store and eventually got me started doing my own machine embroidery.

Free-motion embroidery is an easy, entertaining way to personalize shirts (and other home-sewn creations). Options range from simply adding the name or initials of the owner (or maker) to elaborate monograms and personal logos, like the harp (for a musician) and the integral sign (for a mathematician), and brief messages.

Machine embroidery

Besides a zigzag machine with feed dogs you can deactivate, you need only a small spring-type embroidery hoop, like the one in the drawing below, and a water-soluble marker. I use the same cotton machine-embroidery thread that I use for constructing shirts (see p. 12), but you'll probably want some colors for embroidery that you wouldn't normally sew with, like red or gold. Rayon thread doesn't make as smooth a satin stitch for me, and it gets a little stiff when it's ironed, so I wouldn't want it next to my skin. Cotton stays nice and soft.

MACHINE-EMBROIDERY HOOP

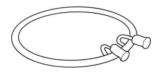

The idea is to set your machine to make a very narrow zigzag stitch, the width of the letters or shapes you want. Next draw the shapes you want on the fabric with the pen, and then cover the shapes you've drawn with narrow zigzag stitching. You move the fabric under the moving needle yourself, without the aid of the machine's guiding mechanisms, the feed dogs and presser foot. You keep the fabric taut in the embroidery hoop and hold it against the needle plate as you move it with your fingers instead of with the foot, which would both keep you from seeing what you were doing and restrict the motion of the fabric. With the presser foot and feed dogs out of the way, you can move the fabric in any direction, not just forward and backwards. That's why it's called free-motion embroidery.

To give it a try, draw a few vertical lines, then some circles, loops and letters on a scrap of shirting, keeping them between ¼ in. and ½ in. tall. Center your drawings over the hoop with the spring removed. The spring goes on top of the fabric, and slips down inside the hoop, stretching and holding the fabric like a drumhead when it's released.

On your machine, drop or cover the feed dogs and remove the presser foot. Load a bobbin with white machine-embroidery cotton, and thread a bright color through the needle, which should be a size 70/10 or 75/11. Loosen the top tension a little. You want the top thread to pull to the underside, and the white bobbin thread never to be seen. You might get better results by slightly tightening the bobbin tension as well, but remember to loosen it again before going back to construction. Go to your narrowest zigzag, or if you can continuously control the width, set your dial near the low end. Position the hoop under the needle, and lower the presser-foot lever.

Even though the foot is removed, you must lower the lever, otherwise the top tension will not be engaged, and you'll get a mess on the bottom of your work. Forgetting to lower the lever is the most common mistake in machine embroidery, and not just for beginners, because, without the foot to show you, you can't tell at a glance whether the lever is down or not. Learn to check it, and be prepared to forget a few times.

When all's in place, pull the top and bottom threads to the left and hold them, with your hands positioned as shown in the drawing below. It's not necessary to pull the bobbin thread up

GETTING READY TO EMBROIDER

Grasp hoop with your fingers about 2 in. apart on either side of needle.

through the fabric. Just hold it for the first stitch or two so it doesn't show on the right side. After that, the stitches will keep it in place.

The trick now is to run the machine fast enough so that a clear, solid satin stitch forms, while you move the fabric smoothly in the appropriate direction to cover the lines you've drawn. Start with the vertical lines, working from top to bottom. Your instinct will probably be to run the machine fairly slowly and to move the fabric too quickly, so that you see a zigzag instead of a satin stitch. Try running the machine at full speed, and see how slowly you can move the fabric before the thread starts to build up into a lump. You should see the thread forming a glossy line that almost stands up from the fabric like a tiny bead of icing. You'll come to recognize the sound the machine makes when it's running at a good speed for you.

When I come to the end of each line, I bring the needle and take-up lever to their highest position, so I can slide the fabric without the threads catching. This way I can leave the presser foot lever down all the time. I don't snip any of the little

connecting threads until I'm finished with the whole embroidery, so I need to hold the threads only at the beginning (see the photo below). I don't clip the threads on the back at all, since they won't be seen. That way they can't slip to the front. I pull on them a little to bring the snipped ends on the front to the back when I'm done. I've never had any trouble with embroidery unraveling; the stitches are too tiny and dense.

Now try some curves, and notice what happens when you move the fabric sideways: It's hard to make a smooth line, because the zigzag is going in the same direction as you are. I've found that I have to move the fabric more quickly in the horizontal

parts of curves, and slow down in the vertical parts. Working this way keeps the lines thin when I'm going sideways and thick and shiny when I'm going forward or back, which turns out to be an advantage with letter shapes, because many letters are thick and thin in just this way, as you can see in the drawing below. I think of the line of satin stitch as the same shape I would make with a pen with a wide nib: It's

THICK/THIN LETTER SHAPES

Practice making simple shapes first, stitching over patterns and lines drawn on the fabric, and moving from one to the next without cutting the thread.

thick when I'm pulling or pushing it, and thin when I'm sliding side to side. If I move at the same speed through all parts of a letter when I'm stitching, my line tends to stay a uniform thickness, which is fine for simple block letters but looks a little unsophisticated.

After you get comfortable with making curves and loops, try writing your name in script. Write it out with the pen first, then follow the continuous line with the satin stitch.

Refinements

If you tend to get little spots of white thread at the start and end of lines, use the same color thread in the bobbin and needle, especially for embroidery on the outside of garments. Try going over lines that need smoothing a second time, maybe with the stitch width set a tiny bit wider. For more dramatic thicks and thins, make your shapes first in straight stitch, then cover the thick parts with zigzag, starting and ending in the horizontal sections so the satin stitch flattens out to meet the straight stitch, which should be all you see in the thinnest sections.

Also try experimenting with any automatic stitches your machine can make. I've gotten interesting results making large letters with my machine set to make a wide satin stitch that tapers at each end. I can adjust the length of the motif, so I set it to about 1½ in. and try to match the tapering to those parts of the letters that I want to taper. It takes some fiddling, but it's worth a try.

I don't much like the built-in letters on computer machines, which I find too mechanical and thin. But if you have them on your machine, try covering thick sections with free-motion satin stitching, for a glossier, richer letter. If you've got a continuous stitch-width adjustment, try changing the width as you stitch. You'll have to control the hoop with one hand, which is tricky, but it can be done. That's how I made the tapering body of the little harp motif in the photo below.

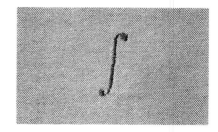

Working on clothes

After I've cut out the shirt, I make sure that there's enough fabric to make another pocket or yoke, or whatever I'm going to work on, in case I make a mistake. If it's the inner yoke and the shirt's for me, I'll go ahead even if fabric's short. I can always cover a botched monogram with a label, or live with it. I don't cut the neckline out of the yoke (see the drawing below) so that there's plenty of fabric to hold in the hoop, but otherwise I work on

Leave yoke neckline uncut until monogram is finished in order to have enough fabric to hold onto.

completely cut-out pattern pieces so I'm careful to position the embroidery just where I want it. I draw in the shapes on the fabric with the water-soluble marker, then center the drawing in the ring of the hoop. When I'm done, and all the threads are clipped and the hoop is removed, I liberally spray the work with water to wash out the blue marks. Then I iron it dry. Occasionally the marks come back under the heat of the iron, but a little more water and another ironing finally get rid of them.

After you've practiced stitching simple lines and shapes, try words, numbers and even short phrases.

Sources of Supply

Shirting fabrics

There are three general sources to investigate when searching out shirting: local fabric stores, mail-order fabric sources and custom shirtmakers, both local and worldwide. The first two sources are great for some things but not for a wide selection of dress-shirting materials, which is simply too specialized an area. For a terrific selection of shirting—too great, really, if you're a "fabricoholic" like me—go to the professionals. Below is an annotated list of what I've found in each category.

LOCAL FABRIC STORES

Look for the classiest, natural-fiber-oriented shops, but don't overlook big bargain fabric stores, especially for cottons you can use as interfacing.

MAIL-ORDER FABRIC SOURCES

Although none of these mail-order companies offers a really wide selection of dress shirting, I've found that some are better than others and that some have unique finds.

Britex Fabrics
146 Geary St.
San Francisco, CA 94108
(415) 392-2910
Has a huge inventory and will respond to very specific inquiries about their stock and what you want.

The Fabric Carr
P.O. Box 32120
San Jose, CA 95152
(408) 929-1651
An interesting source of notions and unusual interfacings. I use their Silk-weight fusible cotton on the bias for silk collars and cuffs.

G Street Fabrics
11854 Rockville Pike
Rockville, MD 20852
(301) 231-8998
Like Britex, G Street has an enormous inventory and handles specific inquiries about their stock and your needs.

Gohn Brothers
Box 111
Middlebury, IN 46540-0111
(219) 825-2400
A wonderful source of treasures from another era, this shop serves the Amish and Mennonite communities. In the fabric realm, they sell real 100% cotton workshirt chambray for a few dollars a yard. It's heavy and beautiful. They're also a good source for bleached muslin and heavy flannel in basic colors. Their catalog (no pictures, of course) is a wonderful read.

Mini-Magic
3675 Reed Rd.
Columbus, OH 43220
(614) 457-3687
Specializes in top-quality fabrics with patterns small enough to be suitable for doll clothes and usually has many fine cotton shirtings, as well as lots of other fabrics suitable for shirts and blouses, such as tissue-weight wools.

The Rainshed
707 N.W. 11th St.
Corvallis, OR 97330
(503) 753-8900
Carries chamois cloth and lighter-weight cotton flannel in many colors. (Also a great source for outerwear fabrics and activewear patterns.)

Southern Fabrics
5015 Westheimer Rd., #1210
Houston, TX 77056
(713) 626-5511
Usually has a good selection of top-quality shirtings.

CUSTOM SHIRTMAKERS

For the real thing, be prepared to go international. *Anytime* you run across someone advertising custom dress shirts, ask if they'll sell yardage. For some reason, the largest custom-shirtmaking enterprise in the United States, the Custom Shirt Shop, does not sell yardage. This is a shame since they've got some great fabric, but I think it's their loss. So, on to others.

In the United States, it's just a matter of opening the Yellow Pages of the phone book, both at home and when you're visiting a city; looking under "Shirts — custom made"; and making inquiries. Sometimes it's helpful to go to the shop in person and make friends with someone there. I think they may need reassurance that you're not a competitor. The prices could be high, but if they stock fabric you may be able to find a bargain. (Remember, too, if you do find a local shirtmaker, to ask which shirt laundry is the best in town.)

American Sember Trading Corp.
114 East 32nd St.
New York, NY 10016
(212) 889-6188
Sells shirting fabric and all-cotton collar and cuff interfacing to shirtmakers. Used to have a 10-yd. minimum order but recently changed that to a 10% cutting charge for any orders under 10 yd. They still prefer to deal with businesses rather than individuals, but they're not concerned with the size of your business or how long it's been in existence. Their shirtings are beautiful and their interfacings unique. I use their #380A collar lining for firm dress-shirt collars.

Ripley Shirt Co.
P.O. Box 4157
Dallas, TX 75208
(214) 941-0311
Provides tailors all over America with swatch books from which their customers can select. Ripley makes the shirts; the tailor makes a commission. They do sell yardage. To find a tailor in your area who deals with them, write or call Ripley directly. They have a good selection of basics and sport shirtings as well as lots of (heaven forbid) poly/cottons. They'll send you a shop-at-home sample set.

Joseph Rudee & Son
170 Sutter St.
San Francisco, CA 94104
(415) 781-8989
An example of an individual shirtmaker who will sell yardage, but probably only locally. Typically shops like this one don't have a catalog or send swatches since they're not in the yardage business, but try them by mail or phone if you really know what you want or for basics like white oxford cloth.

Now for the real treasures. If you're willing to wait for overseas mail, you can have access to a mind-boggling selection of the world's most exclusive and beautiful shirtings. I've ordered from only one of these sources, Turnbull & Asser, but the others are equally willing, and all are apparently quite used to dealing with customers who want yardage and will send huge swatch selections — usually free. Upon request, Turnbull & Asser will also send incredible shirting and pajama silks as well as sportshirt materials, including lots of solid and check Viyellas. (You'll see many of my Turnbull & Asser swatches in the first photo following the Introduction and in the examples of poplin broadcloth on p. 4.) I've even called these people directly for swatches, which is rather thrilling and only costs a few dollars for three to five minutes (ask your long-distance operator about time differences).

The prices will be given in pounds sterling (call a bank for the current exchange rate), and the cost may be high. When this book went to press, for example, poplin ran almost £12 to £15, or about $21 to $26 per 36-in. wide meter. The best way to buy from these sources is with a credit card (Visa and MasterCard are international, of course). That way, you can let them figure out the exchange rate on the day the sale is made.

Below is a list of places with pedigrees as long as your sleeve and priceless reputations, which I know sell by the yard. I'm sure there are many others throughout the world, but these will keep you very happy!

Harvie and Hudson
77 Jermyn St.
London SW1 Y6JD
(71) 930-3949

Hilditch and Key
73 Jermyn St.
London SW1 Y6NP
(71) 930-5336

Turnbull & Asser, Ltd.
71-72 Jermyn St.
London SW1 Y6PF
(71) 930-0502
As you can see, these three are all neighbors, on the most famous address for men's furnishings in the world —Jermyn Street, the Saville Row of the shirt.

Ascot Chang
41 Man Yue St., 2/F Block D
Hung Hom, Kowloon
Hong Kong
(3) 644384
Another world-famous shirtmaker, and a source of wonderful shirtings. Don't bother to try their U.S. location, which does not sell yardage.

Notions

For basic notions, try the following sources:

Clotilde, Inc.
1909 S.W. First Ave.
Fort Lauderdale, FL 33315-2100
(800) 772-2891

Nancy's Notions
P.O. Box 683
Beaver Dam, WI 53916-0683
(800) 833-0690

Sew/Fit Company
P.O. Box 397
Bedford Park, IL 60499
(708) 458-5600
Offers a good deal on really big cutting mats for use with the rotary cutter.

FOR FELLING AND HEMMING FEET, FIRST TRY YOUR LOCAL MACHINE DEALER AND THEN TRY:

The Sewing Emporium
P.O. Box 5049
1079 Third Ave.
Chula Vista, CA 92012
(619) 420-3490
Also sells large, inexpensive cutting mats; will customize sewing feet.

The Yardage Shop
421 Main St.
Ridgefield, CT 06877
(203) 438-6100

FOR COTTON MACHINE-EMBROIDERY THREAD:

G Street Fabrics
11854 Rockville Pike
Rockville, MD 20852
(301) 231-8998

TreadleArt
25834 Narbonne Ave.
Lomita, CA 90717
(310) 534-5122
Will match color swatches.

FOR SHIRT PATTERNS:

Folkwear
The Taunton Press
63 S. Main St.
P.O. Box 5506
Newtown, CT 06470-5506
(800) 888-8286
Has vintage and ethnic shirt patterns.

Kwik Sew Pattern Co., Inc.
3000 Washington Ave. North
Minneapolis, MN 55411
Carries very large men's shirt patterns.

Shermane Fouché Patterns
P.O. Box 410273
San Francisco, CA 94141
(800) 642-6208
Offers a variety of patterns of Shermane Fouché's own design, including the shirt on p. 143, which make up what Fouché calls "The Core Wardrobe."

FOR PATTERN PAPER:

Better Pak
675 Dell Rd.
Carlstadt, NJ 07072
(201) 804-0202
*Will ship a 600-ft. roll of 45-in.
wide gridded pattern paper, the kind
used in the garment industry,
anywhere in the country for $39
plus shipping (usually about $7);
CODs accepted. It sounds like a lot
of paper, but if you make your own
patterns or copy garments, you'll be
glad to have it around —or split a
roll with a sewing friend.*

FOR CUSTOMIZED BODY FORMS:

Carol Stith Zahn
1288 W. 11th St., Suite 200
Tracy, CA 95376
(209) 832-4324
*If you want to drape shirts or any
garments on yourself, the best way
to do it is on a personalized body
form. I've got a poured-foam cast of
my torso, called My-Twin Dress
Form, that Carol Zahn, the inventor
of this form, made for me and which
has changed forever the way I fit
clothes. I think it's the only way to
go if you sew for yourself. You can
order a kit (for about $70) or get
five other sewers together and have
Zahn come to your town and make
the forms for your —either way it's
a bargain.*

FOR INTERESTING BUTTONS:

C.M. Almy & Son, Inc.
10 Glenville St., Box 2628
Greenwich, CT 06836-2628
(203) 531-7600
*Almy supplies the clergy and stocks
a few different collar buttons —and
clerical collars.*

Renaissance Buttons
826 W. Armitage
Chicago, IL 60614
(312) 883-9508

*FOR STARCH, IF YOU CAN'T FIND
LINIT LIQUID STARCH LOCALLY:*

First Preference Products
P.O. Box 630C
Lakeville, CT 06039
(203) 435-0881

Mail-order book sources
FOR BOOKS IN PRINT:

The Unicorn, Books for
Craftsmen, Inc.
1338 Ross St.
Petaluma, CA 94954-6502
(800) 289-9276

FOR OUT-OF-PRINT BOOKS:

Hard-to-Find Needlework Books
96 Roundwood Rd.
Newton, MA 02164
(617) 969-0942

Wooden Porch Books
Rte. 1, Box 262
Middlebourne, WV 26149
(304) 386-4434
*Send $3 for three issues of
their catalog.*

Bibliography

Some of the books listed below are out of print but they are valuable resources, which you may be able to find in your local library (be sure also to check the interlibrary loan service) or through a book dealer who specializes in out-of-print titles. I've listed a couple of sources for hard-to-find books on the previous page.

On general sewing

Hellyer, Barbara. *Sewing Magic.* La Grange, Ill.: Sew/Fit Company, 1982 (out of print).

Focusing primarily on speedy sewing methods and knit sportswear, this book is full of clever and, to my knowledge, unique construction ideas.

McCunn, Donald. *How to Make Sewing Patterns.* San Francisco: Design Enterprises of San Francisco, 1977.

A detailed fitting method based on a fitted shell from which other shapes are derived. Really good discussion of basic fitting ideas totally geared to the home sewer working alone.

Mansfield, Evelyn. *Clothing Construction.* Boston: Houghton Mifflin Co., 1953 (out of print).

A really wonderful book with dozens of ideas for women's clothing details, including a placket with no visible stitches, shoulder darts hidden in pockets, cowboy-style shaped pocket openings —all based on custom dressmaking techniques and styles from the 1930s and '40s. Not at all the typical out-of-date sewing book.

Parker, Julie. *All about Cotton: A Fabric Dictionary and Swatchbook.* Seattle, Wash.: Rain City Publishing, 1992.

The second volume in a wonderful series (the first is All about Silk) *in which detailed descriptions of the various fabrics are accompanied by actual swatches. No top-quality shirting swatches but lots of pertinent information, expanding on the information I presented in Chapter 1.*

Shaeffer, Claire. *Claire Shaeffer's Fabric Sewing Guide.* Radnor, Penn.: Chilton Book Co., 1989.

Should be on every sewer's shelf. A great reference for whenever you want to try a new fabric.

On pattern drafts

Kogos, Fred, ed. *Designing and Drafting Shirts for Men and Boys.* New York: Kogos International, 1962 (out of print).

I looked high and low for this book and was disappointed when I found it. It's quite old and aimed at manufacturers but is definitely of interest to the devoted shirtmaker. The shirt drafts are very basic, but it has a draft for a classic formal shirt. As in most drafts, there are no construction guides. Full of strange ads for shirtmaking machinery circa 1950 and probably still in use today.

Poulin, Clarence. *Tailoring Suits the Professional Way.* Peoria, Ill.: Charles A. Bennet Company, 1973 (out of print).

A good source for more information on using drafts and, incidentally, a great book for anyone interested in tailoring suits for men or women.

Roberts, Edmund, and Gary Onishenko. *Fundamentals of Men's Fashion Design: A Guide to Casual Clothes.* 2nd edition. New York: Fairchild Publications, 1985 (out of print).

The best single book for anyone who wants to make original shirt patterns using industry techniques. Also includes pants, sweaters and jackets.

On clothing

Burnham, Dorothy. *Cut My Cote*. Toronto: The Royal Ontario Musuem, 1973. (Distributed by the University of Toronto Press. Call (416) 667-7794 to order and give the book's ISBN number: 0-88854-046-9.)

Tilke, Max. *Costume Patterns and Designs*. New York: Rizzoli International Publications, Inc., 1980 (out of print).

These two books are indispensable for anyone interested in traditional, historical and folk garments, including shirts and their ancestors.

Flusser, Alan. *Making the Man: The Insider's Guide to Buying and Wearing Men's Clothes*. New York: Simon & Schuster, 1981 (out of print).

Not only an interesting (and opinionated) guide to traditional style, this book also has a detailed guide to great clothing stores in the United States and abroad, including many custom shirtmakers and their wares. A good introduction to "deluxe" clothing.

Catalogs

Clothing catalogs are full of ideas and a wonderful resource for the home sewer. I've found the following to be inspiring, especially for men's shirts. Obviously, there are dozens more catalogs in which to find inspiration.

Bullock & Jones
340 Post St.
San Francisco, CA 94108
(800) 227-3050

Top-quality menswear only.

Cattle Kate
P.O. Box 572
Wilson, WY 83014
(800) 332-5283

Contemporary clothing with the look and feel of the Old West. Catalog $3.

Orvis
1711 Blue Hills Drive
P.O. Box 12000
Roanoke, VA 24022-8001
(800) 541-3541

Request their hunting and fishing catalogs for specialized clothing of superior quality for men and women.

Paul Stuart
Madison Ave. at 45th St.
New York, NY 10017
(212) 682-0320

Exquisite-quality men's and women's clothing. The best-looking clothing catalog I've ever seen.

The J. Peterman Company
2444 Palumbo Drive
Lexington, KY 40509
(800) 231-7341

Always has some interesting shirts, for men and women, among their timeless and quirky high-end selections.

Wathne Corp.
1095 Cranbury S. River Rd.
Suite 8
Jamesburg, NJ 08831
(800) 942-1166

A beautiful catalog (well worth the $5 they charge for it) of top-quality sport and formal wear for men and women —like a British Hermès.

Index

EDITOR: *Christine Timmons*

DESIGNER/LAYOUT ARTIST: *Jodie Delohery*

COPY/PRODUCTION EDITOR: *Peter Chapman*

ILLUSTRATOR: *original drawings by David Page Coffin, computer-rendered by Jodie Delohery*

PHOTOGRAPHER: *Susan Kahn*

ART ASSISTANT: *Iliana Koehler*

TYPEFACE: *Goudy*
PAPER: *Mountie Matte, 70 lb., neutral pH*
PRINTER: *Ringier America, New Berlin, Wisconsin*